COST, CHOICE AND POLITICAL
ECONOMY

FOR JEANNE

Cost, Choice and Political Economy

Jack Wiseman
Emeritus Professor of Economics
University of York

EDWARD ELGAR

Published by
Edward Elgar Publishing Limited
Gower House
Croft Road
Aldershot
Hants GU11 3HR
England

Gower Publishing Company
Old Post Road
Brookfield
Vermont 05036
USA

British Library Cataloguing in Publication Data

Wiseman, Jack, *1919–*
  Cost, choice and political economy
  1. Economics
  I. Title
  330

ISBN 1 85278 165 3

Printed on FSC approved paper
Printed and bound in Great Britain by Marston Book Services Ltd, Oxfordshire

Contents

Acknowledgements

There is no adequate or sensible way to acknowledge all those who have contributed to an intellectual development extending over at least forty years. The autobiographical essay identifies the early stimulation I received from my evening class teacher, my later debt to the people I still think of as 'my' professor, Lionel (Lord) Robbins, and 'my' tutor, Ronald Coase, and the many colleagues who provided help, inspiration and support, most notably at LSE, York and Virginia. My thanks to all of you, not least for the undeserved tolerance with which you have borne my interruptions and verbosity over the years. I hope only that, if you read this volume, you will decide that your virtue has brought some reward.

I am grateful to Jim Buchanan, Tony Culyer, Edward Elgar, Stephen Littlechild, Alan Peacock, and in particular Susan Wiseman and Tim Armstrong, for valuable comments on the autobiographical material. I must also thank Mrs Penny Page and the Centre for Health Economics, University of York, and staff at the Center for the Study of Public Choice, George Mason University, for help in the preparation of the manuscript for publication, and my wife Moira for her patience and support.

My late wife Jeanne lived with the evolution of the ideas in this volume. Its dedication to her is a small acknowledgement of one of my many debts to her.

Preface

The essays reprinted here span my career as an academic economist. The volume begins with the first paper I wrote on economic theory, published in 1953. Some of the later papers await publication as I write (1988). The final chapter was written for this volume: it attempts to encapsulate my present thinking about the subject and its future. The papers were chosen for inclusion from a larger and intellectually more diverse output. This Preface explains why and how – that is, it sets out the purpose of the collection, and what I hope the reader may get from it.

The biographical essay (Chapter 1) was included at the instigation of my publisher, Edward Elgar. I accepted with some reluctance his argument that my personal history might add interest to the development of my ideas. I am glad I agreed. Not only do I think he was right, but I so enjoyed the writing that I have to believe that the result will give at least some readers a little pleasure.

I have always been suspicious of, and tried to avoid, undue specialization within economics. As Chapter 1 explains, I early became uncomfortable with the notion that there existed some special class of human decisions that could be labelled 'economic'. How could I not therefore be dubious about the idea that there were sub-categories of the subject whose study could be compartmentalized? This is not to suggest a belief that it is intrinsically wrong to study 'special subjects' such as firms or labour economics, but only the view that satisfactory examination of such topics needs always to be grounded in a continuing awareness that we are concerned with different aspects of a common problem. The tools we use should all come out of the same intellectual toolbox. Most economists would probably agree with this in principle. But their behaviour is something else. An illustration of major importance, which I discuss at length in the text, is the continuing absence from the subject-matter of economics of a unifying general theory of group-participative behaviour, though the importance of the concept is clear from the regularity with which the elements of such a theory turn up in a variety of specialist contexts.

Accordingly, I have always regarded myself as free to pursue any topic that I found intellectually stimulating, with my interest in theoretical issues periodically aroused by the discovery that there were no satisfactory tools in the box to deal with the problems that challenged me. This in turn, and increasingly through time, directed my attention to the nature of the tools. Did we just need better designed navigation instruments? Or did progress require that we stop designing the instruments on the assumption that the earth is flat? The essays are my search for answers to these questions.

In so far as I have been required to specialize (for example, by teaching commitments), I have been fortunate in the intellectual breadth of the fields (effectively, industry and trade and public finance/public sector studies) of my concern. I have written relatively little in macroeconomics, but that in turn has been at least partly because of distrust of a body of analysis that was initially poorly grounded in individual behaviour (and to some extent still is).

In respect of publication, the result has been that, running as a current through a broader stream of output extending over thirty-six years, there is an evolving system of thought about the nature of my subject. I would like to think that all or most of my output shows some intellectual consistency. But the papers I have chosen for inclusion here are those that best exemplify the development of a common set of ideas.

In retrospect, the dominant emerging themes can be seen to concern, first, the nature of the universe requiring to be explained. (Crucially, the need to recognize that we live in a radical-subjectivist world, in which the future is characterized by unknowability, and people's plans must be expected to have unforeseen consequences.) Second, the fact that scarcity and the consequent need to choose characterize all aspects of the behaviour of individuals in society, and not just market behaviour. As a corollary of this, subjective opportunity-cost becomes the general explanatory tool for the study of a much broader range of human endeavour than is embraced by mainstream economics. Third, recognition of the need for a normative framework more comprehensive and sophisticated than that of Paretian welfare economics. The construct emerging as appropriate is a development and generalization of libertarian public choice. These are the themes I try to pull together in the final chapter, which essentially suggests the outline of a 'new political economy', the writing of which is my next project.

Within the broad development, a number of interrelated topics recur. These are worth identifying, though of course, individual essays take up more than one such topic and hence fit more than one classification. There is a continuing preoccupation with the nature of cost. This began when I was still an undergraduate, and it is a topic to which I have persistently returned. Indeed, it so pervades the collection that it would be pointless to try to identify particular essays: the collection begins with discussion of cost-pricing rules, and concludes with discussion of subjective opportunity-cost as the key explanatory concept of a new political economy. Among other themes, there is critical appraisal, and suggestions for revision, of mainstream economic analysis (Chapters 2, 3, 7, 8, 12, 13). The need for a broader conceptual framework (a distinct and larger issue than that of internal revision) is also a recurrent theme (Chapters 4, 5, 9, 11, 12). Applications of the evolving ideas to policy issues are developed in Chapters 4, 6, 9, and 10.

In conclusion, Chapter 14 attempts to bring the strands of thought together in the form of a specification of the necessary characteristics of a new, public choice-oriented political economy (and as a by-product attempts to throw light on the philosophical problems associated with the nature of coercion and its absence). This last essay is of necessity an inadequate summary. But it is intended to whet the appetite rather than provide the feast.

It points the road; there is always a long way still to travel.

1 'Talks too much . . .'

Family background

Pupils at my grammar school were given a report book in which each of their teachers recorded a termly mark and comment. Some variant of the heading of this chapter appeared on most pages of my book. No doubt the teachers had a propensity to copy one another; the system made heavy demands on their imagination. But the comment was not without substance. It was prescient, in that my subsequent teachers, colleagues and students would surely have endorsed it.

It has been my good fortune to have pursued an academic career in which disputation, whether verbal or written, can be reckoned as virtue as well as vice. I have myself greatly enjoyed all of it; and if my friends have suffered a little, as I am sure they sometimes have, I can hope only that my talking and writing has also occasionally given them something, as theirs has surely given to me. Though I have greatly enjoyed my life as an academic, I was a little surprised at the suggestion that this volume of essays might be enhanced by writing about it. But while my own story is not particularly unusual, there have been influences upon my development that it will give me great pleasure to acknowledge. Beyond that, I can recall how as a student I used to speculate about the personalities behind the names in my reading lists; if there are others like me, they may enjoy my story. (When I was an undergraduate, textbooks by Boulding and Stigler used to sit side by side on my shelf. Stigler was tall and thin; Boulding tall and bulky. When I met them as a budding academic, imagine my delight that they fitted their images!)

I was born in 1919 in the Urban District of Brierfield, one of the necklace of textile-weaving settlements spread along the Pennine valleys by the Leeds and Liverpool Canal; a cradle of the Industrial Revolution (and as I would later discover, of the British Labour Party). I was the youngest of six surviving children, and something of an afterthought; my youngest sister was ten and my eldest sister twenty years older than myself. My father was a foreman at the coalyard of the local Co-operative Society (the offshoot of Owenite socialism). The rest of the family: my four sisters and brothers, and my mother when she was not preoccupied with young children, were weavers. Family affiliations were important. My mother 'asked' for the children as they left school, and

1

they all finished working at the same (family-owned) cotton mill (the term derives from the earlier use of water power in converted flour mills).

There was never a lot of money about as I was growing up. Employment was irregular, and my father was incapacitated from his forties by a 'chronic bronchitis' which I would now suspect was pneumoconiosis. But we did not want, and we were a happy and united family. (We have stayed that way. 'Home' has always been the same Pennine valleys, for our wives and husbands as well as ourselves, and only now is age beginning to break up the 'clan'.) It was perhaps fortunate, at least for me, that we were not richer; it saved me from being over-indulged. My mother adored children, and I was an unexpected bonus. As I also had four older sisters, two still young enough to be a 'proxy mother', I did not lack affection. (It was not a demonstrative affection; I do not recall being kissed by my sisters until I was leaving for the Army at eighteen. At the same time, my mother was arranging to replace me by taking a neighbouring baby for day care!)

The members of such a family are likely to see their parents through different windows. The father my eldest sister tells me about is an active and positive man of whom I have no memory. I myself remember him as a kind, physically strong but silent man. I recall him coming home black from work. But when I was becoming aware he was already incapacitated and spent his time doing odd jobs around the house, or simply sitting (he had poor eyesight, did not wear spectacles, and I seldom saw him read).

The driving force of my youth was my mother. I grew up in what sociologists describe as a working-class family with an aspiring mother. She had little formal education, beginning work in the mill at eleven. But she was literate in an untutored way, and very articulate. Save for father, who perhaps had simply capitulated by the time I was coming along, no one else was short of a word in season. I don't doubt that it was in the family that the love of talk began: my early memories are of being told to stop arguing, stop talking, or stop dragging my clogs. Being so much the youngest gave me advantages. Not only was I indulged, but I could often escape the summary punishment that a younger mother had visited upon my siblings, simply because she was becoming less agile.

Mother's ambition embraced all her children, and she was very conscious of the benefits of education. I was not more intelligent than my sisters and brother, but the structure of the family gave me better opportunities. I owe much to all of them. Little could be done for the older ones. Once they began earning, as part-time weavers from eleven, a little more became possible. My younger sisters went into the mill full-time at fourteen. But in the evening there was music; a weekly lesson, one in violin, one in pianoforte, at two shillings an hour from a teacher up the street. On the other evenings, practise, practise, practise. When I read that the uneducated under-value investment in education, I think of all the two shillings scraped up by my mother and people like her, the prevalence of upright pianos in four-room terrace houses, and of my mother, herself unable to play, listening to those girls to ensure that the weekly 'piece' had been mastered. The number of upright pianos per family with children would have been a very good measure of the considerable frustrated demand for education.

There was plenty of sheet music about, but little reading material. I remember the (union-subsidized) *Daily Herald*, replaced in my adolescence by the more readable *Daily Express*. But little else. I cannot say that I was ever conscious of the handicap this is supposed to produce. I don't remember beginning to read; I seem always to have read everything I could lay my hands on. In so far as I experienced frustration, it came not from access to reading matter, but from my mother's ambivalence. She encouraged me in every way she thought proper, but she was concerned for my health. I was early discovered to be short-sighted, and wore spectacles from the age of seven or eight. I was the only one in the family to do so, though my father should have done. The problem was organic, but mother believed that I 'strained my eyes' by reading in poor conditions and 'too close to the book'. Consequently, I was restricted in my reading by artificial light (gaslight in my early years), and in bed. I tried to circumvent this with the aid of one of my most precious possessions, a torch. In the evening, I would seek an opportunity to stuff my reading material down the top of my pants (less easy than it might seem, as boys wore 'short pants' – above the knees – until 'grown up' at fourteen). I would then go to the outside closet and read there by torchlight. (I still treat the household toilets as libraries, though I read in more comfort now.) When I dared linger no longer, I would return to the house and go straight to bed, there to read by torchlight until my brother joined me. There were risks, of course. Mother was no fool, and the smuggling of paper and torch from outside loo to upstairs bedroom through a living room where the family congregated was always hazardous. In relation to this, finding reading material was no problem.

There were two sources; what we called 'bloods' and the public library. The bloods were weeklies. I think some of them had a few cartoons, but the core consisted of serial stories. My favourites were the *Wizard*, the *Rover*, the *Gem* and the *Magnet*. From the time I could read fluently, I tried to keep up with all of them. The *Wizard* and the *Rover* were my favourites. Their serials were 'adventure stories' (I recall an African character named Clicky Ba, who bashed people with a cricket bat). The other two specialized in schoolboy stories. I enjoyed them, although the English public (that is, residential fee-paying) schools they described were as alien to my experience as latter-day science fiction. Bloods cost twopence, and I had twopence a week I could spend on them. There was an active second-hand market – A knock at the door: 'Has your Jack owt to swap?' – in which I gained my first experience of barter. I might buy the *Wizard* new, read it, and through time transform it into all the others. I learned the importance of lags; the longer I waited, the more favourable the new-for-old price. More, with the exercise of patience, it was possible to read everything by trading only in the second-hand market and so release the twopence for other consumption. One could even pick up worse-for-wear old copies of the *Gem* and *Magnet* free. There was a nice trade-off between a voracious demand for reading and a positive return to waiting. This trading activity had an educational spin-off. I had to carry sets of serial episodes in the memory for the variable time-periods from one acquisition of each of the four bloods to the next – excellent, if completely inadvertent memory-training. It also gave me an interest in literary style. The general standard of this kind of pulp journalism could not be high. I believe that the writers were generally paid by the thousand words, and I have read that one of them could produce 100,000 words a week. But standards varied. For example, Frank Richards, who wrote the Bunter school stories, became something of a cult figure long after his death. One developed a feel for 'good writing'.

The public library was a free lending library funded by the local authority. In the days before paperbacks, books were simply not a possible form of consumption expenditure in a family like my own. As I graduated to the reading of books, I came to depend more and more upon the public library, and my interest in second-hand markets expanded to include books.

Schooldays and after (1926–39)

My first proper school was the local council school. In retrospect, I would guess that many of the teachers themselves had inadequate formal education. It was possible to become a teacher at such a school by 'sitting with Nellie' – staying on after school-leaving age and learning 'on-the-job'. After the First World War, returning servicemen were allowed to qualify in the same fashion. One teacher encouraged the acquisition of skill in 'composition' (the writing of essays) by striking pupils on the head with a jumbo (foot-long) pencil; one stroke per spelling mistake. We had a poor semi-illiterate who got at least fifty strokes every Thursday. I have often wondered what happened to his ability to spell.

The statutory school-leaving age was fourteen, and the school had some 400 pupils aged around seven upward. At eleven, we were allowed to sit a scholarship examination, the successful winning places at a grammar school. There were two kinds of scholarship, funded respectively by the county and town authorities; the former was a little more prestigious. In my year, my school acquired one county scholarship (myself), and two others.

Nelson Grammar School was a very different place. I would not attempt to defend the ruthless surgery that denied access to its facilities to so many. But the school itself was excellent. We were made to feel privileged, not as the fortunate recipients of charity, but in the much more positive sense that we had been chosen for responsibility. We also got a good education. The school was perhaps seven miles from home: two tram rides. We had to wear school uniform, and my mother took as much pride in my appearance as I would let her. There was the possibility that I would still be at school when I could have been earning. These were not trivial costs to a family like ours. But my parents, whose own formal education I had probably outstripped by the age of twelve, and my family, who had been denied similar opportunity, gave me nothing but encouragement. I enjoyed school. My performance was reasonable; I stayed comfortably in the A stream with results that fluctuated with my interest in other things. My teachers thought there were other reasons ('Talks too much', my reports would say, 'Would do better if he talked less and worked more'). I understood their irritation. But in retrospect, I'm sure they got it wrong. For me, talking has always been an integral part of learning; I need someone to bounce my ideas off. I have always enjoyed 'having written' (so that I have something to communicate) much more than 'writing', which is a solitary act. For similar reasons, I am stimulated by collaboration.

Nightly homework was a standard part of our studies, and my mother did her best to ensure that I did it properly. My elder sisters were married and had left home by now, but in my early years at Nelson Grammar there were still a lot of people and competing activities in a 'two-up, two-down' (two main downstairs rooms, two bedrooms) house. My sisters would work toward their examinations – both eventually acquired music teaching qualifications – in the living room. Above, I sat in the bathroom with my back against the hot water boiler, and did my homework on a board resting across the bath. I worked to the strains of music coming through the floor. It was not a distraction; it gave me a lasting if untutored love of the violin. But I was never more than a listener. There had been attempts to integrate me into the family's musical interest, but I had no feel for it and wanted only to get my nose in a book. My youngest sister, a talented violinist, was put to work on me when I was seven. I was irritated by the discovery that, though I imitated her as best I could, the noises never came out the same. That experiment ended when I threatened to stick the bow up her nose. When I was put to the piano, the keys permitted rather more mechanical progress, and I achieved the halting performance of a couple of simple waltzes. But it was clearly hopeless, and that sister was glad to accept the excuse that practice was interfering with my school work. But mother was nothing if not persistent. It was a tradition that males in the extended family sang in the church choir, and I was made to join my brother and an ancient deaf uncle there. I think that lasted about three years. I enjoyed the social aspects of the choir, and for a while became interested in other church matters. I was tolerated out of respect for my family, and because with the encouragement of the choirmaster I developed a talent for mime. But that also could not last; it came to be accepted that I would spend my time reading and talking in a family environment of music.

School work was directed towards two examinations taken around the ages of sixteen and eighteen. The first of these, and for most students the last, was a combined leaving examination (School Certificate) and minimum university entrance qualification (Matriculation). For practical purposes, the two constituted two different levels of job qualification. For the vast majority of students, university was not a part of the possible future. There were few open scholarships, and even fewer that met the subsistence costs that families themselves were in no position to provide. When a senior student did get a university place to study languages, my school regarded the event as so unusual that we were given a half-holiday. University certainly had no place in my own plans. I had little idea what went on there, and no practical incentive to reduce my ignorance. I already thought I was in love with words, but even this took the form only of a general interest in becoming an 'author', which ambition I expected to pursue while bringing money into the family by working at the white-collar 'job' which Matriculation would help me to get.

Economics was not taught at school. My first exposure came from a new history teacher in my last school year. Until then, I had found history a fairly boring subject, dominated by a need to remember dates and things about kings and queens much less interesting than the doings of the same kind of characters in my newly-discovered Shakespeare. Now I was being told that there was a history which was about Brierfield and about the kind of people I saw around me; the cotton mill my family worked in; the canal down the hill which had been dug to bring the cotton to the early mills; the neighbouring enclave of Irish Catholics whose 'navvy' forebears had stayed behind after digging the canals and railways (though many more probably went on to Liverpool and finished in America). These were exciting discoveries, but I was rising fifteen and near to leaving school when I made them.

I completed Matriculation at fifteen, in 1935. My mother wanted to 'ask' for a job for me in the office of the family employer. I was reluctant, though jobs were hard to find. I was suspicious about the industry. The mill was providing irregular employment for my family, and the high unemployment in the area was clearly not unrelated to the depression in textiles. I began applying for other jobs, copying the specimen letter I had learned at school (one advertisement: 'Matriculation essential', turned out to be for a shop assistant at a multiple tailor). Eventually, I found myself a clerical job with a small supplier of dental dressings. I stayed only a short time, but used part of it to teach myself touch typing 'on-the-job', using some ancient Pitman's *Commercial Educators*, picked up for coppers second-hand. This has proved very useful, together with the shorthand acquired at evening classes over the same period.

Just after my sixteenth birthday, I went to work at the local voluntary hospital as registration clerk. The hospital was dependent upon charitable contributions, and in a depressed region was desperately short of funds. I was the junior member of a team of three which constituted the central administration, responsible not only for admissions, all patient records, and general day-to-day administration, but also for all lay and medical committees and fund-raising activities. Before I was eighteen, I had made an investment in administrative and office skills that has had value throughout my working life. I also developed an interest in health care which undoubtedly influenced the subsequent development of my interests within economics. I liked the work, and looked forward to a career in hospital administration. But I was just sixteen, and I was advised that I was a little too young to begin preparing for professional examinations. So I attended evening classes. These were provided in a variety of subjects under the auspices of the local authority. Having done some shorthand and book-keeping at local classes, I opted for a more demanding course in commerce in Burnley, where my hospital was located. The classes were not without interest, but I found them somewhat dull. Our teacher was thorough, and concerned to be sure that we knew what the syllabus required. (I can still write the legal definition of a bill of exchange in Pitman's shorthand without pause for thought.) There was not much concern with analysis, and less with argument. But of necessity we had to learn something about how markets work, and I began to perceive relationships with my earlier snippets of economic history. The next year I signed up for a course in economics.

This was my first formal confrontation with the subject that was to absorb me. In retrospect, it seems to have occurred at a time of adolescent energy, intellectual and physical, that I have never since matched. I was working full-time, and on four nights a week I would go to the church hall for a game of billiards before walking home. I had reading to do for my classes. I also read three library books each week; two fiction, one non-fiction (when I became interested in the hospital pathology laboratory, I borrowed what turned out to be a university microbiology text and read it). I played cricket at weekends, and was secretary of the church cricket club and young men's class. These were joint tasks, for church attendance was a necessary qualification to play in the team. I read Edgar Allan Poe and became interested in the short story. In my spare time I scribbled stories and studied how to market them – but not very efficiently; my literary ambitions were being pushed aside by my growing interest in economics. I ran a mail order club to finance a summer holiday. Wonderful days; there seems to have been time for everything.

My introduction to economics proper came from a Mr Stephenson. He was a fine teacher, who transmitted to me his own love of the subject. He also provided a role model, in that he was the son of a large family of miners who had found his way to Manchester University by extraordinary persistence. He showed what could be done, though I had still no idea that I might emulate him. Remarkably, he introduced me to Keynesian ideas in an evening class in Burnley in 1938. I had been intrigued by my glimpse of economic history; I was captured by the idea that there were cures for the afflictions of unemployment with which I was growing up. This was something more than book learning. My faith in the power of economics and economists has suffered many setbacks since then. What has never changed is my sense that its concern is the practical betterment of the human condition, to which end theoretical abstractions are tools to be judged solely by their utility. More, Mr Stephenson instilled in me an appreciation of the importance of analytical understanding, at a crucial time in my development. The bloods had paid off; I had at this time an extraordinary recall. Without deliberate memorizing, I could 'see' whole pages of my own notes, visualizing even the ink blots on the page (I was never very tidy). It was a practically useful but potentially dangerous facility. My teacher saved me from making it a substitute for thought.

I had not felt particularly challenged by the local examinations, and in the previous year had opted to take the Commerce examination of a national but London-oriented body concerned with post-school students; the Royal Society of Arts (RSA). I now took the same examination in Economics, and was awarded a Distinction and the Society's Silver Medal. More important, I was also the recipient of a scholarship provided by the Leathersellers' Company (a Guild of the City of London) to study for a degree at the London School of Economics; an institution about which I then knew nothing. My immediate and instinctive reaction was rejection, not because I did not want to go, but because the prospect still seemed unreal. My sisters and brother were all by now married, my parents retired, and I saw myself as the – pitifully inadequate – eighteen-year-old breadwinner. Happily, my family was as supportive as ever. I was told to leave such matters to my elders; who did I think I was? But that was not the end of the problems. The award covered only fees for evening study (the School provided facilities for a degree to be completed over five years by students in full-time employment), which was difficult for someone not already settled in London. My teacher, always encouraging, pressed strongly for a bursary from a local trust; it was lost because my home lay outside the trust deed limits. There was nothing for it but to find a job in London. The thought of five continuous years of evening study excited rather than deterred me, for I now knew that I was to become an economist, though with only a very general notion of what that meant. More daunting were the immediate practical problems; I had never lived away from home or cared for myself, and my most daring travel involved a camp holiday in the Isle of Man and two train journeys of less than fifty miles; a day each in Manchester and Birkenhead. But I began writing for jobs, and got an offer of appointment at a small hospital in Hounslow (on the basis of a photograph; the rail fare to London was not an expense lightly incurred by employers at that time). My plan was to begin work in September, and start at LSE in October 1939.

The more I discovered about the School, the more eager I became to get there. But my planning was still less than whole-hearted. We were in the shadow of the Second World War, and I had made my commitment. I had been inclined to pacifism. But when I became persuaded that war was unavoidable, I realized that I could not remain uninvolved. That decided, the impulsiveness of my years took me to the other extreme. A few months before war was declared, I went to the nearest barracks (which happened to be infantry) and enrolled in the Territorial Army, which provided part-time training in peace-time and ensured immediate mobilization in time of war. In fact, I was called to the colours on 1 September 1939, two days before the official declaration of war, and a week before I was due to go to London to begin my new life. I became a soldier reluctantly, but sustained by a deep conviction. I had come too far to be stopped now. To me, the war was simply an unpleasant interlude; something to be endured so that I could get back to my vocation.

The distraction of war

I was poor infantry soldier material anyway. It is one of the most mindless even of military occupations. An interest in promotion might have made it less so; but only at the price of a reduced life-expectancy. I was willing to do my duty; but my ambitions lay elsewhere. I spent five years in the army, mostly in infantry, then in the Army Service Corps and, while awaiting demobilization, as a sergeant in the Army Education Corps, teaching soldiers who thought they already knew how to become civilians. It was a life of boredom interrupted periodically by fear, and I did not enjoy it. But there is room for learning from every experience. The army provided opportunities, mostly unwanted, to measure oneself against others. It provided important training in self-reliance for someone with my sheltered upbringing. It broadened my experience and gave me a taste for travel which I have never lost. Above all, it gave me a proper sense of my own unimportance. The army teaches you humility. Through my army experience, not all those authorized to give me orders were fools or morons. But a fair proportion were; and all were servants of a system which demanded unquestioning obedience. You learned to obey and keep your mouth shut, or you learned to suffer. It may surprise some, but I hope by no means all of my friends to be told that I believe that I learned this lesson well. The army in no way destroyed my love of talking. But it taught me discretion; and it is a lesson I hope I still remember when it matters.

I was demobilized in 1946, in time to realize the goal which had sustained me through the war by entering LSE in October that year. I had become less promising material. The last five years had not been intellectually stretching. I had read little of significance, and had published a couple of immature and sentimental short stories. When obliged to take a course in clerical skills, I had opted for a correspondence course in shorthand teacher training. It provided a few useful insights, but I was posted abroad before completing. Prior to demobilization, I attended a two-week further education course taught by military personnel at the University of Göttingen. I learned something about the nature of university teaching from a geographer who gave me new insight on a subject I had earlier found boring, and acquired a vocabulary of improper but now archaic French from a wonderful linguist. But this was very little; the machinery was certainly rusty.

On the other hand, some things were better. I could become a full-time student, supported by a government grant. This required evidence of acceptance by a university, which was generally decided by a competitive entrance examination. At the time, that would have been a major obstacle. But my RSA scholarship qualified me for entrance. The doors were open; I could become an economist.

London School of Economics (1946–63)

Student days
I spent my first term at the school learning to read again, and my first academic year orienting myself. It was a year of general study, leading to an intermediate screening examination. Teaching was by general lectures supplemented by small-group classes and personal supervision. My class teacher in economics was William Baumol, himself a newly-arrived graduate student and part-time teacher. I doubt whether I made much of an impression. He is I think a little younger than me, exemplifying the strange social structure of the School at that time. The vast majority of the student population was ex-British Services, mostly male, with a scattering of females, younger school leavers of both sexes, and some Americans. In the light of my later experience, they were a very serious lot. They also played hard; I suspect the female minority had a wonderful time. Specialization began in the second year. The BSc (Econ) degree permitted specialization in a range of subjects, from sociology to geography. Of the nine qualifying papers, three were general (in economics and statistics) and three in the special subject area. But within economics, there was a choice between something like ten areas, headed by professors of universal distinction – Robbins and Hayek (Analytical and Descriptive), Meade (International Trade), Sayers (Banking), Paish (Finance), Allen (Statistics), Ashton (Economic History), Phelps Brown (Labour).

It is an implication of this arrangement that the second-year lectures in Principles of Economics are attended by all BSc (Econ) students, and that they have differing degrees of knowledge, interest and commitment. It was a difficult lecture assignment, and the wise tradition was to give it to a senior professor; in my own time, Lionel Robbins. These were the first of his lectures I attended. It was a most skilful performance; how skilful I fully appreciated only after I became a teacher myself. For perhaps forty minutes, the fundamentals of the topic were laid out in a generally accessible fashion. In the last ten minutes, we were taken on a brisk tour of the frontiers of knowledge, so that the budding specialists took away a perception of the things they needed to know more about. An excellent method, though it did cause me to struggle through Hayek's intellectually formidable *Pure Theory of Capital* because I had difficulty with the assigned chapter.

I opted for the 'core' economics special subject: Analytical and Descriptive, over which Robbins presided. Teaching was by lectures on special topics, supplemented for those who wished by 'optional' lectures given by staff with a topic they wanted to talk about. The associated classes changed in form as we became more senior, towards seminars in which the students were expected to play an increasingly active and the tutor a more passive role. It was a system which might have been invented specially for me. But it was and is more than that. This intellectual questioning and openness to difference is in my view the essence of the School's scholarly distinction. There is nothing objectionable in the emergence of schools of thought. But the greatness of the School is that it transcends them; it is our 'broad church'. (The history of the development of positive economics is a good example.) Those seminars were a stretching and an exciting experience. We were somewhat more mature, at least in years, than the usual intake. But we needed encouragement to debate, rather than sit and listen, when faced in a small-group situation with the scholarship and urbane worldliness of Robbins or the incisive pragmatism of Peter Bauer. In my final year, Hayek spent most of a term's classes on the Ricardo Effect, with which he happened to be preoccupied. He also gave a lecture on Mill, so thorough that one imagined him taking notes under the bed while Harriet imposed her prejudices on John. That we did debate on such occasions is a tribute to the skill of our teachers and to the School's traditions. In the same tradition, students were encouraged to take their problems to the staff. You could knock on anyone's door. You might be asked to return at a more convenient time; but you were never rejected. Most problems could be resolved without recourse to this, by reference to the personal tutor responsible for keeping an eye on your progress, setting essay assignments, and discussing your problems. It was this undergraduate experience as much as my later period as a teacher at the School, which created the attitudes I later brought to the making of teaching and research policy.

It was through the tutorial relationship that I came to know Ronald Coase. As in other matters, he had his own perception of the role of a tutor. It might be called demand feeding. He never sent for his students. But if they wanted to see him, he had all the time in the world. I learned later that he was reputed to have written a termly report which read 'I have no recollection of ever having met this student'. I took full advantage of this arrangement, and through it gained some confidence in my own potential, and the enduring interest in cost theory of which this volume is a result. He was at this time making his significant contributions to the theory of public utility pricing, and was later to make further contributions of fundamental importance to our understanding of cost. But it is piquant, in retrospect, that my interest should have been stimulated in this way. He was not much interested in subjectivism, and, despite having been taught by both Robbins and Hayek, my own awareness of the problem was slow to emerge. But Coase's own enthusiasm was infectious, and I learned enough from him to know that I wanted to know more.

By now, my ambitions were becoming focused. The National Health Service had just been created, and an economics graduate with my experience would not lack professional opportunities. But that was at best a fall-back position. If my academic performance so permitted, I would become a university teacher. I had still only a consumer's view of what that implied. But I wanted economics to be something I lived, not a qualification for doing something else.

Before Finals, Lionel Robbins interviewed us all to discuss our plans. I saw no point in dissembling; I told him that I wanted an academic career, and that in preparation I would like to complete a doctorate at a suitable American university. His response surprised me; he asked my age. Told that I would be twenty-nine on graduation, he said that I did not have the time to waste, but should look immediately for a suitable appointment. Asked how, he told me to get a good enough degree, and we would 'see what came up in the summer'.

That was not an easy summer. Almost no posts were advertised, Robbins went off to the USA and I was to marry in the September. When we met in August, Lionel had little to suggest, save that I should apply for the one-year assistant lectureship then being advertised at the School, which post, he emphasized, was neither in his special area nor in his gift. I applied, got married, returned from honeymoon to a traumatic interview with the Director and ten economics subject professors, and was appointed to a one-year post. Albeit shakily, my foot was on the ladder.

Teaching at LSE

My appointment had two important characteristics. Assistant lectureships were probationary and the School commonly appointed for one
year in the first instance, renewable up to four before appointment to
a tenured lectureship. Salary related to post with no allowance for age.
Returned soldiers such as myself started at the same level as graduates
from school, and the starting salary was the same as that then being
advertised for underground train drivers working standard overtime.
The drop-out rate was high in the early years. The situation was less
cruel than the description makes it appear. The School's reputation was
such that those not retained were normally appointed to lectureships
elsewhere. But it was a demanding situation, practically and intellectually. Our position was worse than that of the train driver, particularly
in respect of housing. The market was distorted by rent restriction and
the effective reservation of municipal housing to local citizens. Prices
were consequently driven up in the relatively uncontrolled 'furnished'
sector: the only one available to the footloose such as myself. My wife
was completing her own training and could earn little. Something like
two-thirds of our income went in rent. But while survival demanded
some outside earnings, these carried their own costs. From the very
beginning, it was plain to new staff that they would be judged not just
by their development as teachers, but by the potential they showed as
writers.

The second characteristic concerned my duties. I was appointed to
teach in the sub-discipline of Industry and Trade, and this was a significant reason for my waiting five years for appointment to a tenured
lectureship. The professor responsible for the Industry and Trade sub-
discipline was Arnold Plant. He was unusual among staff at the School,
in his self-esteem and his perception of status. Neither my naturally
loquacious and questioning temperament, nor the encouragement of
intellectual enquiry engendered by Robbins and my other undergraduate teachers, fitted me for the subservience he expected of his juniors.
In consequence, I was never asked by him to contribute directly to
special subject teaching, but was involved only in the kind of class
teaching undertaken by all junior staff.

Teaching skills were acquired by 'learning by doing'; not even the
'sitting with Nellie' provided for my school teachers. It works, as children learn to swim if thrown in the water. But it is questionable whether
it is a good way to produce Olympic champions. One of my first classes
contained Maurice Peston and Roger Alford, both to become respected
colleagues. Given the open forum nature of the School tradition, one
needed to learn fast to keep any kind of control. I remember ceding

the blackboard to them in a discussion of the effects of coupon rationing on the demand curve, and the problem I had in getting it back. I enjoyed every minute of it; I was doing what I wanted. As I had no specialist lecture assignment, and I was still absorbed by cost theory, I offered an optional course of lectures on collectivist economic planning. The obvious interest of the 1930s controversy to me was enhanced by the apparent lack of connection between this debate and the policies of post-war socialist Britain. But it was in no way a fashionable subject; five students attended the first lecture, four continued. But I persisted; it was good training, and I wanted to know the material anyway. (Many years later, I was gratified to be told by one of the students that the lectures had changed his whole perception of the subject. He was by then himself an established academic.)

My one-year temporary appointment was extended for a further three years. I had as yet written nothing of interest, though ideas were developing. My reaction to the pressure to write, which was a more significant career obligation than a doctorate, was a mixed one. I wanted confirmation; but I wanted to publish nothing that did not completely satisfy me. This conflict can create a damaging 'block'; I have gifted friends who have never overcome it. But the intellectual climate of the School was a great help. It was the best academic club I have ever known. There was hardly an economic problem concerning which one could not obtain both enlightenment and a reading list simply by raising the question in the common room at morning coffee. It was a stimulating experience; the 'names' were by now my colleagues, and were becoming people. Although he was by no means alone, I remember Robbins as the great raconteur; I still sing for my supper by repeating his stories about personalities ranging from the Webbs through Pigou to his contemporaries. Hayek left for USA not long after I was appointed; Laski died. But the School was still full of interesting personalities and distinguished colleagues from whom one could learn. Many of them turned up at the weekly Analytical and Descriptive staff seminar (The 'Robbins Seminar'), which was the week's event. Distinguished visitors, often unexpected, were common. I remember Robbins' old graduate student, Abba Lerner, sitting on the floor wearing dirty canvas shoes and talking even more than I ever did. Bill Phillip's water-flow machine model of the Keynesian system was first demonstrated there, having been transported from Streatham on the back of a lorry (a fascinating tale, unhappily too long to tell here). There were other seminars; I learned much about business behaviour from one organized by Ronald Edwards, at which businessmen discussed their own decision processes.

Apart from Robbins, I received help from many other people, and began to make friends. Among the Industry and Trade group, Coase continued to be a source of stimulation, and I was also much influenced by George Thirlby and Basil Yamey. Thirlby was an interesting but personally difficult character who contributed more to economics than has been recognized, and less than he might have done. The most adequate recognition is in the volume which he edited with Jim Buchanan (Buchanan and Thirlby, 1973). At this time, he was preoccupied with the nature of costs and its relevance to an understanding of 'administration' (now more commonly labelled 'organization' or 'institutions'). It was Thirlby who first awakened my interest in subjectivity; that is, in cost-as-decision. He used to claim, not entirely unreasonably, that there were nine posts at LSE with the term 'Administration' in the title, but that he, who had no such title, was the only one who taught the subject. He was an unhappy man. Naturally morose, he found his teaching burdensome. The need to reconcile his concepts of cost with the requirements of a teaching programme preparing students for an unseen examination set at least in part by others was disturbing for him. Thirlby believed many of his views originated with Plant, and since the latter had also been instrumental in bringing him to LSE from South Africa, he tended to be blamed for George's problems. But it must be questioned whether anyone could have tailored a teaching programme to his liking. I liked George personally, and my wife and I tried hard to treat him as a friend. Eventually we failed; his emotional unpredictability alienated us, as it had others. I lost contact after I left LSE. He retired at the earliest possible date, and is now dead. I am sorry that this is the only way that I can fully acknowledge the intellectual debt I owe him.

Basil Yamey, through the vagaries of wartime, was a little my junior in years, but my senior in academic experience and appointment. We became, and remain, fast friends, though we now meet relatively rarely. Outside academic matters, we shared an interest in economic policy, exemplified by our long involvement with the Institute of Economic Affairs, and in gastronomy. This latter had its oddity: Basil is a true gourmet, combining an interest in food and drink with a natural fastidiousness that has kept him trim, while I am a natural glutton, being educated at this time by my dietician wife and already needing to curb my indulgent appetite. Academically, Basil compensated so far as he could for the lack of intellectual stimulation from my sub-departmental heads. He also not only encouraged but helped me to write. A joint paper which we wrote towards the end of this period provided a singular training in draughtsmanship. More generally, he aroused in me a concern with behaviour (how things happen), complementary to the subjectivist insight. (He disliked such phrases as 'It is the purpose of the market . . . ' because of the implication that the market itself is purposive rather than simply an instrument. Lack of concern with what the actors on the economic stage are doing, and why, is a major deficiency of mainstream economics.)

Outside this group, I was also close to Louden Ryan, shortly to return to Trinity College, Dublin and a distinguished career of academic and public service, and Alan Peacock. My interest in public utility pricing led naturally to an interest in the emerging phenomena of the nationalized industries, which in turn aroused an interest in the behaviour of government. There was at this time a common if unarticulated belief that the economist's competence somehow changed when resources came to be used by nationalised industries or for welfare ('social services'). The former was a matter for 'public administration', the latter for 'social administration'. That is, the 'practical' problems concerned the organization of delivery rather than the efficiency of markets or resource use. Since Peacock was teaching Public Finance, it was natural that we should find common interests. But more than that; there was a personal as well as an intellectual empathy which has evolved over the years into a deep and lasting friendship as well as a fruitful and mutually enhancing academic partnership.

Over this early period, my affinities with particular colleagues in the Industry and Trade specialism were close and valuable (I have in mind in particular Yamey, Thirlby and Coase, up to his departure to USA). I was developing other linkages, as I have just described. I had little empathy with the professors in my specialism, or indeed respect for them. At that level, I continued to see Robbins as my mentor. He showed me no special favours, but was unfailingly helpful, and I valued his guidance, advice and leadership. It was the good fortune of people like myself that his influence transcended narrow interests without the need for formal authority. With the possible exception of the Director, his was the major single contribution to the character of the Department and the School over the period that I was part of it. (The Director, Sir Alexander Carr-Saunders, was himself a remarkable man. The School was afloat in outstanding and unusual academic personalities, not only in economics but also in the sister disciplines. Such a group does not make governance simple. But Carr-Saunders ran things with genuine authority but in the same libertarian style that I have described for the Department. In my early years, I was a member primarily of the main general Committees. These seemed to be run by consensus. The voting rights of assistant lecturers were complex, but matters so seldom came to a formal vote that I never bothered fully to understand them. Indeed, the only important matter concerning which I recollect such a vote concerned a (defeated) proposal to change the name of the School. I do not think it is a style that would be possible now, and have often wondered how Carr-Saunders would have coped with the disturbances of the 1960s. I am sure he would have found a competent way. A great source of his strength, from which I hope I learned, was a genuine interest in and store of information about all his colleagues, however insignificant. He knew, for example, that I was a keen cricketer and involved in the sporting activities of the School. A chance encounter at lunch would be brightened by a knowledgeable discussion of current performances. Everyone I knew had some similar experience, and there were a lot of us.)

When I was appointed to a lectureship, it was, not surprisingly, with the support of these colleagues and in the different sub-discipline of Business and Public Finance. I was by now thirty-four years old, and had begun to publish. My interest in collectivist economic planning generated the first paper in this volume. (Writing it was an unique experience. It had been so long in the gestation that it was finally written overnight in first and final draft. That is an experience I have not ever repeated.) I had also published some 'applied economics'.

The change was agreeable, both personally and intellectually. I would be able to work more formally and extensively with Peacock in Public Finance. Our senior colleague was Frank Paish, Professor of Business Finance. At Robbin's suggestion, I had earlier begun to share a course of undergraduate lectures with Frank and had become attached to him. He was my kind of economist: practical, policy-oriented, and concerned with theoretical and technical sophistication only to the extent that the problems he tackled so demanded. He has left behind nothing like the theoretical reputation of Lord Kaldor, but in the running debate that these erstwhile colleagues conducted over the years, it seems to me that Kaldor had the more sophisticated theories, but Paish had the better feel for how the economy actually worked. Paish had few grand designs, but was for example predicting and explaining stagflation, using quite unsophisticated expository tools, when most of us were just beginning to recognize its existence. In personality, he met as closely as anyone I have known the description of a man without enemies. Unfailingly kind and generous, he was also modest to a fault, the fault being a degree of self-effacement that denied him the larger reputation his talents merited. He had two other characteristics, one which I envied, the other I shared. The first was the ability, given to very few academics, to discipline an intellectually creative life to a firm working schedule. He departed very little from a nine-to-six working week, protecting his private life from his work-habits.

The trait we shared was the love of a good anecdote, and so much the better for being a bit near the bone. In his background were public school and the Royal Artillery in the First World War. He swore that he heard nothing during his military service that he had not encountered in recognizably similar form at school. This prompted his thesis that the Romans had probably heard them all: there were no new stories, only variants on a set of original themes. (What a school that must have been: I dare not name it!) He first offered this thesis for my consideration over lunch at a table in the middle of the student refectory, the senior common room being closed. It must have been a memorable occasion for his large but unnoticed student audience at neighbouring (and not-so-neighbouring) tables: for Frank had the reputation of being one of two teachers who found it easy to lecture to an Old Theatre audience without the help of a microphone. (I was the other one.) With myself, Frank was one of a risqué story 'brotherhood', diverse in talent and rich in variety. The other core members were Peacock: Scots and Navy, but eclectic, feeding on a catholic acquaintance and a phenomenal memory; Yamey: drawing on colleagues (a large number of the LSE staff had Jewish backgrounds, almost always unorthodox) for a fund of Jewish stories from the philosophical (the buttered bread) to the earthy (the encounter in the toilets of Minsk) which I have made part of my own collection; and Buchanan: providing a periodic transatlantic leavening. I am not sure how to describe my own contribution: perhaps as what you would expect from a North countryman conditioned by five years of life in the infantry.

The change did require some new investment, in that I must now begin reading in those areas of public finance that were relatively new, but I saw no need to abandon my earlier interests. In particular, I had already begun to perceive the need to extend the theory of public utility price to embrace the broader problems of state productive activity, though it would take me a long time to find satisfying means to do so. Together I suspect with many others, I was also beginning to be increasingly interested in, and uncomfortable about, the glaring inconsistencies between the analysis of individual choice-through-markets and the study (or lack of study) of the government as the instrument of policy implementation. This was a period of broadening interest, then, but also of continued preoccupation with costs and decisions. My concern with marginal cost pricing crystallized in the paper on public utility price, and the broader interest in nationalized industry merged with my evolving interest in the behaviour of government. This development was stimulated and encouraged by my deepening association with Peacock. The son of a professor, Alan was a valuable guide through the professional jungle. Given our evolving personal regard, a mutual love of debate, and a shared propensity for collaboration, it was inevitable (or so it now seems) that we should begin to write together. He has always had great intellectual energy, and an ability to throw up new ideas at a rate that some colleagues have told me they found enervating. I never did; I would pick up the balls I wanted to run with, or throw up a few of my own, and ignore what did not interest me. He did much the same, and since he found the energy simultaneously to work with a host of collaborators, the arrangement suited us both very well. He did not share all my own enthusiasms, and in particular has never had the same interest in subjective cost. Involvement with him greatly added to my productivity, and also affected its structure. Over this middle period of my academic career, a good deal more than half my published work was in collaboration, and much of what I would regard as significant in the rest evolved out of my continuing interest in cost (as the content of this volume illustrates).

Our collaboration was not a tranquil one. We proceeded by draft and disputation, and whatever emerged with both our names on it was truly the fruit of a joint intellectual endeavour. That the arrangement persisted for so long is sufficient evidence of our mutual benefit. In time, as we have come to know each other's minds more intimately, the scope for disputation has reduced. This greatly speeds up the rate at which output emerges. But sadly, it also diminishes the accompanying excitement and sense of innovation. It is this, rather than any loss of friendship or mutual regard, that explains the decline in our joint output in recent years. Then, there was a lot to explore. Specialists in public finance could not be expected to ignore the fact that getting on for a quarter of UK public expenditures was being taken by 'social services', for example. But we had no satisfactory techniques for their study. We began to explore spending for purposes such as education, health, and old age pensions, both as expenditure categories (leading us eventually into cost-benefit appraisal), and as new areas for the application of the logic of individual choice (becoming in time the new specialist field of economics of human resources). This growing diversity never caused me to lose my interest in cost and choice. But I began to see the role of the individual as decision-maker against a broader backcloth, and I needed time for my ideas to settle.

An intriguing result of our collaboration was a book on public expenditures which is probably more cited than anything else written by either of us (Peacock and Wiseman, 1961, 1967). It came about almost accidentally. Peacock had accepted an invitation from the National Bureau of Economic Research to collect historical data on the growth of UK public expenditures. The data bank was growing; but it seemed pointless just to publish the statistics. What to do with them? We began to kick ideas around. We quickly agreed a negative finding; received doctrine was no help. At this time, interest in expenditures was limited to the macroeconomic effects of the budget and some emerging interest in cost-benefit appraisal. Otherwise public finance was concerned essentially with taxation. In so far as there was any attempt at all to explain the size and distribution of public expenditures, it used Pigou's conception of the government as a unitary being, balancing utilities at the margin like any consumer. This fitted poorly with the periodic shifts in the share of government observable in the data. Inspection of the data suggested some alternative 'explanations', though we saw these essentially as speculations. The book has generated ongoing interest and controversy, from which two points deserve mention here. It has been persistently, and correctly, pointed out that the statistical testing of our hypotheses was inadequate. When our ideas were evolving, the new positivism and related econometrics was emerging from a group (Lipsey, Archibald and others) meeting along the corridor. We knew something of what they were up to, but had neither the time nor the inclination to be diverted by trying our ideas on them. What is of interest is that neither our own subsequent work, nor to our knowledge that of anyone else, has produced much by the way of enlightenment that goes beyond our own early speculations. The essential reason for this lies in the second of my two points. The argument of the book, and of the subsequent literature, attempts to explain the time-pattern of expenditures without any adequate (or indeed explicit) behavioural model. I do not think that either of us would be content to write such a book now. Certainly, I would myself see any 'explanation' of historical series of this kind as necessarily grounded in a public choice model that related change to the behaviour of the 'actors' (public sector decision-makers) involved. But that is easier said than done. What is clear in retrospect is that I myself was engaged in a discovery process; I had yet to appreciate the full relevance of my ideas about subjective cost and individual choice in this broader and non-market context.

It might be said that I spent the later 1950s 'learning my trade'. The discovery that there could be so little interest in collectivist economics in socialist Britain was my first lesson in academic fashion. Macroeconomics was the fashionable subject then, to be followed by economic growth and then by positivism. To interest oneself in less popular topics was a dubious strategy for anyone ambitious for academic advancement.

At the same time, I was becoming increasingly aware that subjectivist ideas were potentially destructive of a good deal of neo-classical intellectual capital. I learned that not everyone treated this problem in terms of its intellectual merits: academics welcome skill-obsolescence no more readily than do other people. Not infrequently, the response was to treat the argument as unnecessarily destructive, and therefore properly ignored unless accompanied by positive proposals for an acceptable 'new orthodoxy' (so that, for example, criticism of marginal cost:price 'rules' carried weight only if accompanied by the specification of 'rules' to replace them). It is not an argument with much intellectual merit, and I treated it seriously only in so far as I recognized it as an obstacle to the acceptance of my general position.

These discoveries did not much change my attitudes or interests. I had waited a long time to do what I wanted: if following my own intellectual bent now would slow my material progress, so be it. Nor was I entirely persuaded that it would. If the problems that I had taken for my own were as significant as I believed, then the wheel of fashion must surely turn. If they were not, there was only myself to blame. I would try to convert the sceptics by identifying the positive contributions that emerged from my claimed insights. But I would have done that anyway, for my ultimate concern has always been with practical matters; my criticism of established theory emerges from the conviction that sensible policy is unlikely to be founded in intellectual error. Beyond that, I could wait. The debate is far from over: perhaps it never will be. But my own concerns have certainly moved closer to the centre of general interest. No one now doubts that there is a case to answer (the resurgence of Austrian economics is sufficient evidence of that), or that economics stands in need of a better paradigm. Nor do I myself doubt who is winning. Beyond that, I would be unhappy could I not still find dragons that needed slaying.

In any case, I began to write more freely in this period, and much of my writing was policy-oriented. The publications have a more eclectic look. That is not surprising. I had shifted my teaching interest, my ideas were in flux (as I have just illustrated), and I was keen to become more broadly involved. The topics that interested me may not have been fashionable. But they were intellectually challenging, and were to evolve into recognized specialisms – public choice, human resource economics, cost-benefit appraisal. This is one part of the explanation of the lapse of time that occurs between the papers in this collection. I had not lost interest in cost theory; rather, new and more embracing concepts were evolving. Meanwhile, any relevant writing had a policy orientation; it helped me work through ideas, but did not throw up grand new insights which would now justify reprinting.

I was also broadening my academic acquaintance. The School was a lodestone for visitors, and there was a steady flow of Americans in particular. I made a number of friends, and one, Jim Buchanan, who was of special and lasting importance. He arrived at the School in 1960, and we established a personal and intellectual rapport which persists to this day (I am writing this in the Centre which he founded). I cannot think of any intellectual issue that we have been unable to resolve, which is not of course to say that we agree about everything. But there are two areas which I would identify with hindsight as profoundly significant. Jim had just completed his pathbreaking work with Gordon Tullock, *The Calculus of Consent* (Buchanan and Tullock, 1962). My introduction to the early insights of the logic of public choice was the first step towards the integration of my subjectivist individualism into a coherent specification of choice-in-society. There was a long way to go; but now there was a path to follow. The second insight emerged separately, in the context of discussion of Buchanan's work on public debt (Buchanan, 1958). I thought highly of the book, but saw the argument as an (unarticulated) elaboration of an opportunity-cost formulation of the debt policy problem. Discussion of this stimulated in Jim an interest in subjective cost and in the LSE tradition in cost theory, from which, given his extraordinary intellectual energy, there quickly emerged a book on cost theory and the edited volume with Thirlby to which I have already referred. The two insights are more profoundly complementary than either of us then recognized. The development of a political economy of public choice incorporating the insights of subjectivism and unknowability is the outstanding intellectual task I personally see before me.

The one aspect of our relationship that I find difficult to explain is the fact that Buchanan and I have published nothing in collaboration. We have common intellectual interests, we both have a history of collaborative production, and our ideas have often marched in step. I suspect that the reason lies in our very different work-rates and in the need for physical proximity. I am exaggerating, but not absurdly, when I say that he writes a book while I am composing a letter home. It might have been possible to adapt to this if we had been able to spend extended periods in the same environment. But limited visits left too little time even for stimulating talk, and (probably sensibly) neither of us seems to have seen correspondence as a possible substitute.

Extra-mural activities

My interests and activities were broadening in other ways. Together with Yamey and Peacock, I was an early and active participant in the Institute of Economic Affairs. Our explicit goal was the improvement of general education about the role of the market; our essential method the demonstration of how market arrangements might be used to resolve identified practical problems of policy. It is difficult to communicate at this point in time the antagonism that this seemingly innocuous purpose could generate; and not only among the economically illiterate. A future Governor of the Bank of England once offered me a ride. Told I was going to IEA, he expressed surprise that I was 'one of that Fascist lot'. Less unpleasantly, if little less obscurely, I was labelled a 'right-wing radical reactionary'. Happy days . . .

I attended my first meeting of the International Institute of Public Finance in 1954. The intellectual content of the proceedings was not impressive. But I began to develop a network of overseas colleagues with diverse intellectual backgrounds which has grown in size and value over many years. It was reassurance that when faced with an undergraduate choice between a language and a further course in mathematics, I had not been wrong in my choice. I became interested in France, both professionally and socially. François Perroux's Paris-based Institut de Science Economique Appliquée had a branch office near the Institut Français in Kensington. I became friendly with the Director, Maurice Niveau; we shared a common interest in economics and gastronomy. Eventually, after Maurice had returned to Paris, I took over as temporary part-time director, and was fortunate that it took three years before I was replaced, during which time I had become familiar with Paris, French economists and the French economy, and confirmed in my love of French cuisine.

Literally by accident, I had also become an expert of sorts in fisheries economics. Summarily (the full story is too long to tell here), I became rapporteur for a Food and Agriculture Organization (FAO) Expert Meeting in Rome after wrecking my car following an audience with the Pope. Since I knew what had been happening, I became joint editor of the resultant volume; and an FAO consultant. It is a fascinating subject, in which questions of property rights, which were interesting me more and more in other contexts, were emerging as of fundamental importance. Among other things, the association with FAO was instrumental in making feasible my first visit to North America. In 1961, I participated as consultant at a large FAO conference in Ottawa, travelled across Canada to Vancouver to teach summer school at the University of British Columbia, and managed to visit Toronto and Washington before returning home. It was a broadening experience; my wife and I determined to return as soon as possible.

The opportunity was not long in arriving. I had met and become friendly with Earl Rolph when he spent a sabbatical at the School. At his initiative, I was invited to spend the 1962–63 academic year as Visiting Professor at Berkeley. It was an ideal time. I had just been promoted to Senior Lecturer. Peacock had already been appointed to the Edinburgh Chair (which deprived me of his day-to-day comradeship but not of intellectual stimulation; our collaborative activities continued unabated). Ralph Turvey had become Reader in Public Finance. I shared the teaching with him, but with ample time to initiate teaching of the 'economics of welfare services'; I began to lecture about education and health long before the economics of human resources became a recognized sub-discipline. In one sense, I had reached my career goal. Shortly before we married, I had explained to my future wife that my commitment to an academic career had certain disadvantages from her point of view. Particularly, given my age at graduation, the prospect that I would ever attain a full professorship had to be regarded as remote. A readership was a more realistic career ambition. Although this was the judgement of a pretty ignorant beginner, it was a realistic appraisal of the situation at the time. There was no growth in the system, and promotion was determined by wastage. A late start was a severe handicap in such a situation. All this began to change when the recommendations of the Robbins Committee on Higher Education began to be reflected in the growth of existing universities and the creation of new ones. I was approaching forty, and was in no way unhappy with my lot. I would not have left LSE for anything less than a full Chair in a Department I liked (Peacock had agonized over the move to Edinburgh); but it had become worth looking at possibilities. It was a good time for new experience. In fact, it was to be a turning point.

The Berkeley year produced one immediate change; it forced my wife into a decision about her own career. She enjoyed her work as a caterer-dietician, and we had managed to combine it with the provision of a happy life for our young daughter. She shared my own love of travel, which itself quickly disappears if it entails lengthy separation; I have always resisted solitary trips lasting more than two weeks. So far, she had managed to square the circle by taking unpaid leave. This was impossible for a further period of as long as a year. Her resignation was not all sacrifice, given her love of travel. But sacrifice there was; I was lucky to have a partner who identified so completely with my own ambitions. It was a most enjoyable year. We lived close by Earl and

Peggy Rolph, who did everything to make our stay pleasant. We made lifelong friends of John and Fran Culbertson (John, from the University of Wisconsin, was also a Visiting Professor) and explored the delightful city of San Francisco with them. As always, I was stimulated by the changed intellectual environment. I was blown somewhat off my planned course, allowing myself, for example, to become interested in US tax problems. But it was in every way a productive year. Notably, I was working on a joint monograph applying an extended logic of choice to UK education policy – a clear development of my ideas about cost and choice which could not have a place in the present volume. I was also working on the revised edition of Henry Phelps Brown's *A Course in Applied Economics*, and learning from my co-author about simplicity of style. While I enjoyed the University and the Department, however, I was less enamoured of the general teaching arrangements. After LSE, the system seemed remote and uncaring. The first year of undergraduate study was treated as a 'weeding-out' period in which the dropout rate was very high. Teaching this group was a chore left largely to junior staff, teaching assistants and unwary visitors; seniority was rewarded not only by income but by the relinquishment of such chores. Without general examinations, it is difficult to maintain common standards in such a system. Student unrest was just beginning, and erupted in the year after I left. I am not so naive as to believe that the wave of student unrest which spread around the world can be attributed to such causes. But I have always believed that an unsatisfactory teaching structure was an important contributory cause of what came to be known as 'the troubles at Berkeley'.

Nevertheless, we were sufficiently enamoured of our experience seriously to discuss emigration as a long-term possibility; I had a Fulbright Fellowship, and was obliged to return to UK for at least three years. But there were family commitments which made for difficulty. In any event, news arrived which changed the picture. Peacock had accepted appointment as Head of Department at the newly-created University of York. It was clear that his reasons for doing so could not have been primarily financial, since academic salary structures were so controlled in UK that there was little competitive bidding at the professorial level. But the non-pecuniary inducements would have to be pretty strong. He, and even more his wife, were deeply attached to Edinburgh (they have now retired there), and he had created a sound Department. Simply, York offered the kind of new challenge that Peacock has always found it difficult to resist. York was one of the post-Robbins new universities, and Lord Robbins was himself Chairman of the steering committee responsible for setting it up. It seems not unlikely that he identified Peacock to the newly-appointed Vice-Chancellor as a desirable ally. He was not only the first Professorial appointment, with special responsibility for the development of the social sciences (which were to be a major teaching area) and the personal appointment of Head of the Department of Economics and Related Subjects. He was also to be Deputy Vice-Chancellor (ultimately an elective post, but one he held throughout the early formative years), with a major role in the creation of the new university. Such opportunities have been rare in Britain: York had first petitioned for a university some three hundred years ago. He could not let it go.

From my point of view, the important consequence was that an opportunity arose to implement a 'scenario' which Peacock and I had from time to time discussed as a 'hypothetical contingency' rather than as a firm 'plan' (Chapter 13 gives an example of this kind of 'contingency planning' as practised by Robinson Crusoe). We had both observed, when invited to give seminars at universities with relatively small Departments of Economics, that the tendency to make appointments to teach 'specialisms' produced a degree of intellectual isolation. If I may be forgiven for referring to respected colleagues in such a fashion, the zoos had too few of each species for efficient breeding. We saw the remedy for this in a different approach; start from commitment to a research area, and use this to attract like-minded people willing to undertake the necessary teaching obligations as the price of membership of the specialist group. But it had been little more than idle talk. It would call for a specialism of appropriate technical diversity. But what better than public finance, already becoming ever more embracing? There were manifest practical difficulties in trying to adapt an existing Department. Collaborative research would be crucial and would have to be funded; there was no public sector source of such funds, and no obvious private source. But in the York context, practical possibilities emerged. There were no prior commitments to staff or to research, and there existed local charitable trusts with a strong interest in the new University and a brief to support research in the social sciences. At Peacock's initiative, the Joseph Rowntree Memorial Trust provided a priming grant to fund an Institute of Social and Economic Research (ISER), which was to provide facilities for social science research generally, and which, in the case of economics at least, was intended from the outset to contribute to the creation of an integrated teaching and research facility.

I was appointed as the Institute's first Director. This was a post with professorial status, and with an obligation, consonant with the general philosophy I have described, to carry one-third of a normal teaching

load. I had only one more term at LSE before going to York at the
beginning of 1964. I did not go without some heartsearching. I was
leaving what I regarded as the best economists' club in the world for a
totally new and quite small venture. We were leaving one of the world's
great capitals for what was, despite its history and beauty, by comparison a small northern country town. But it was a new adventure; and I
was embarking upon it with my closest colleague. London was not
impossibly far away. We need not be cut off, either from the School
or from the city. Events were to belie our expectations, which should
have come as no surprise to someone with my kind of views about our
perception of the future. But if there was 'plan failure', it was because
outcomes exceeded expectations.

The University of York (1964–   )

I arrived in York at the beginning of 1964, and remained as Director
of the Institute of Social and Economic Research until I took partial
retirement at the end of 1982 Session, continuing as part-time Professor
of Economics until 1987, when I became Emeritus Professor. It was
my longest academic appointment, and my final one. Life at York was
demanding and stimulating, both intellectually and organizationally.
The organization story is worth the telling. But it is for a rather different
audience, of those interested in the creative problems of teaching and
research organization. Here, I can give only a thumbnail sketch, sufficient to provide the background for the intellectual developments
which are the concern of this volume.

I was immediately involved in the customary problems and excite-
ments of the creation of a new University. The first three hundred
students had been admitted in the October before I arrived. But Peacock and I also had our private vision to realize. Our goal was the
creation, on a small scale and within our limited resources, of the kind
of questing and collaborative intellectual climate that we both saw as
the great strength of the LSE tradition. Formally, Peacock was Head
of the Department of Economics and Related Studies, and I was Director of a Research Institute responsible for the development of research
not just in economics but in all the social science disciplines, which at
that time were all being taught as part of a common first degree. In
terms of the development of economics in particular, the collaboration
was an intimate one, built upon our existing empathy. Peacock had
negotiated the Institute's priming grant, and continued to be actively
involved, both formally and informally, in its governance and development. For my own part, I carried a partial Departmental teaching load.
This was at my own insistence. I enjoyed and continued to be stimulated

by teaching, and was unwilling to be cut off from it (though in fact, some commitment to teaching became a standard condition of research appointments, as it furthered our general objectives). I was able to involve myself fully in other Departmental concerns. Together, we spread the gospel that teaching and research were mutually reinforcing activities in which teachers, research staff and students had a common collaborative involvement as well as a personal one.

Initially, our ideas were greeted with some scepticism by British colleagues. If people were appointed primarily with an eye to their sympathetic research interests, how would we provide an adequate undergraduate teaching input? It was never a practical problem. The plan was attractive to specialist colleagues, and the appointed colleagues had skills enough between them to meet all needs: teaching assignments never involved more than the customary degree of gentle coercion. It was more difficult to get agreement as to who should – or, better, who should not – teach public finance, and the problem of whose Chair should have that title was settled by no one having it! We would stand on the record: the venture succeeded beyond our most optimistic expectations. It created a productive and happy academic staff. When turnover became high, it was because we were producing more young men regarded as ripe for advancement than our rapidly growing Department could absorb. The Institute Research Fellows were integrated with academic staff through both research supervision and part-time graduate registration, and in turn participated with other graduate students in a specialized graduate school which quickly established an international reputation in public sector studies.

It would be foolish to say that I missed nothing of the atmosphere of LSE. The School will always remain for me a unique institution. But I did not miss it enough to need to go back: I was getting quite enough intellectual sustenance without that. Within our special field of interest, we quickly established our own academic network, for the existence of the specialist group was a powerful magnet for other scholars. That would have provided sufficient stimulation had there been no other outside contact at all, which was far from the case. Also, if we were to succeed in spreading our collaborative message, Peacock and I had to provide an example. We were already engaged in collaborative ventures. But I became concerned in the supervision of research staff to a greater extent than ever before. It was yet another rewarding but time-consuming activity, doubly productive in the training of new scholars (almost all our Research Fellows moved on to university teaching or cognate appointments) and in the early 'blooding' of younger academic colleagues.

The priming grant provided funds for the salaries of a director and a secretary for a period of five years, and a commitment to fund two modest research projects. When I resigned from the Directorship in 1983, the full-time research staff was around thirty, and the foundations were firmly laid for a further growth which has since more than doubled that number. When Peacock moved on to become Principal of the University of Buckingham, he left behind a Department with an outstanding reputation.

The broadening of my intellectual interests which had already begun was reinforced by this environment. I was instrumental in the creation of a new degree structure in economics and politics (now a fully-fledged degree programme in Economics, Politics and Public Choice), and taught primarily in the areas of human resources (economics of health and education), social policy and microeconomic problems of public expenditures. My formal research commitments followed a similar pattern. I was less involved than formerly in cost-and-price type problems, either as teacher or formal researcher, but became increasingly concerned to use the same insights in the new areas that now demanded my attention.

The scope of my activities was also broadening for other reasons. There comes a time in most academic careers when, to borrow the phrase used by Sir Patrick Hastings of his life as a barrister, 'you are no longer looking for people: people are looking for you'. Over the period incorporating my move to York, I was becoming part of a widening academic network productive of growing opportunities of involvement in interesting new activities. When I accepted the York appointment, I was already committed to spend some months in Ottawa as a consultant to the Canadian Royal Commission on Taxation (the Carter Commission). This was an interesting experience, though I suspect one that in the event benefited me more than it did the Commission. With the Commission's agreement, I spent most of my time developing a decision structure for the control of taxing and spending in a federation. The paper, completed in 1964, was deemed finally to lie outside the Commission's terms of reference, which precluded discussion of the principles of federal/provincial government relations. The paper remained in informal circulation for some twenty-three years, and was published last year. It appears in the collection in chronological order (Chapter 4), as it marks a step in my thinking towards an intellectual construct embracing group behaviour and non-market decision-making (See Chapter 5). I continued to be active in the affairs of the International Institute of Public Finance, becoming a Vice-President in 1966, and President 1975–8. In 1966, I was one of the founder partners of Economists Advisory Group, which I believe was the first UK economic consultancy to be created and directed by academics. It was a successful venture (the company still exists, though with only one surviving original partner), and one that I found intellectually rewarding through exposure to the realities of the market place and the exigencies of firm deadlines. But it was demanding of time, particularly in the early years. Since there could be no conflict with academic obligations, the weekends disappeared.

It was also in this period that I began to work with Stephen Littlechild. He was then Professor at the University of Aston, and we first met at a seminar he conducted in York. The topic was public utility (telephone) pricing, on which he was already an authority and I could be called an established cynic. But although highly qualified technically, Stephen had himself begun to be doubtful about the intellectual underpinnings of neo-classical economics. We quickly established a rapport, and began, and have since continued, to work in sympathy. One consequence of this of interest in the present context concerns the plan we evolved to write a subjectivist economics textbook. He was unwilling to be deterred by the possible reluctance of our colleagues to accept the obsolescence of intellectual capital that such a text would require, and faced me with an ultimatum. Either we would write a joint textbook which assumed no more about knowledge of the future than ordinary men could have: or he would attempt the task alone. I was encouraged by his determination, and – as I suspect he knew – could not see myself left out of such a venture. We embarked upon it.

A central problem was the need to recast much of elementary economic theory: it is difficult for example to use such constructs as market demand curves in ways that do not contradict the underlying assumptions of the subjectivist-uncertainty model. But ideas began to emerge, and Littlechild began to use them in his undergraduate lectures. The reactions were interesting; the less the previous exposure to economics, the less the difficulty the student had with our ideas. We used the traditional simplifying device of a Robinson Crusoe world. This was technically valuable, but if sustained produced ennui among students expecting to be informed about the 'real world'. Although we were both committed to the enterprise, we came to recognise that we could not do a satisfactory job alongside our ordinary duties, by the medium of correspondence and irregular meetings. In any case, Littlechild was spending a sabbatical period in USA. Jim Buchanan, with whom I had maintained contact, had by now established the Center for the Study of Public Choice at Virginia State Polytechnic. He kindly provided us with facilities in Blacksburg through the summer of 1980, and we spent that summer trying to pull the book into shape. It was a stimulating, but ultimately discouraging experience. We finally became persuaded that there is at present no way to write such a textbook that would not depart from established norms to a greater degree than teachers would find acceptable, dissatisfied though many of them profess to be with what they now teach. It is sufficient for other books to be read by those whose views one respects; but a textbook that is not read by students is simply wasted effort. But our labours did not go without all reward. The Introduction to Chapter 13 describes the episode in greater detail: the work ultimately resulted in an essay in 'Crusoe Economics', published after long delay in a volume dedicated to George Shackle. (A fitting outcome. Shackle and I have never been colleagues or collaborators, and I came to know him only in the later part of our careers. But I have been greatly influenced by his work. He is in my view one of the most underrated of living economists; I think and hope that posterity will give him the place in the history of ideas that I believe his originality merits.)

It is easier to write about opportunity-cost than it is to allocate one's time efficiently. In retrospect, I don't think that I have ever been specially good at the latter, as my Berkeley experience and Chapter 8 illustrate. I console myself that the observation fits well with my intellectual commitment to the unknowability of the future, and also with my perception of the lifestyles of many colleagues whom I respect. Paish is the notable exception. I was lucky to have a wife who was not only tolerant of an unreasonable loss of leisure-time, but also unfailingly supportive and indeed disciplinarian in time of need. In the early years at York in particular, I was always conscious of the danger presented by my enjoyment of administration – or, more precisely, by the pleasure I got from the pay-off to successful organization. I had continuously, and perhaps not always entirely successully, to remind myself that the cost of promoting other people's research was likely to be the sacrifice either of my own, or of my private life. Similarly, time given to 'related activities': international organizations, policy issues, and the like, brings its own satisfaction. But it is time lost from the development of one's subject.

Yet I never saw myself other than as an economist concerned with the development of my subject. These related activities provided the environment within which my ideas about my subject have evolved. On balance, I believe it was a positively valuable environment, for I would regard the constraints of time as greatly outweighed by the gains from the testing of my ideas in the broadening context of my research and teaching. How else would I get from product pricing rules to rules of social organization?

The chronology of the papers from the York period included in this volume reflect this situation. In order of writing, the first one is the fiscal federalism paper prepared for the Carter Commission. Following this, a first venture into participative (group) behaviour, and, published in the same year, a paper returning to the problems of public production, but concerned with the specification of the decision environment in contrast with my earlier interest in welfare-efficient pricing policies. As the relevant chapter introductions explain, all of these are aspects of a growing conviction of the need to escape from the restrictive constraints of the neo-classical logic of choice. But I had not lost my narrower interest in the theoretical framework. As the introductions also explain, most of the papers in the Institute period were prepared in response to some specific stimulus. Their order to some extent at least reflects the evolution of my current preoccupations. After the three papers concerned with the broader issues, my preoccupation with the existent state of economic analysis surfaces in two papers which encapsulate my criticisms of neo-classical orthodoxy. These are the final papers in the collection which were published during my tenure as Director.

In retrospect, I timed my departure from the Directorship well, though the decision owed not a little to the new policy which facilitated my continued involvement with the University during partial retirement. The climate for research funding changed in the 1980s, and in course of time our success had begun to stimulate emulation and competition. There was a growing feeling of uncertainty about future funding: and our own interests had become increasingly dominated by the microeconomic problems of the public sector. It was time for new departures. Before my retirement, we had obtained agreement and funding for the establishment of a major Centre for Health Economics. The timing was good, for the anticipated stringencies in fact emerged. But thanks to my colleagues and successors, our research activities have grown more quickly than my own most optimistic forecasts.

I have said little about my colleagues of this period, and must remedy the deficiency before I move on. York changed my life in this respect as much as in others. At the School, there was a sense in which I thought of Robbins as my mentor, and of myself as a relatively junior (though hopefully maturing) colleague, even into my forties. In York, I was the senior member of the Department in years, and second only to Peacock in length of university service. The intellectual and social ambience had to be of our creation. It took a little getting used to: the

more so in that I had a special responsibility for the 'fledging' economists appointed to the Institute as research fellows. I am unsure that I
always did them justice. But I tried, and I relished the role. (I have no
greater treasure than a book dedicated to 'Jack' by a former research
fellow: and not just because I think it is a good book.)

In quite fundamental respects, the successful development of my
activities, intellectual as well as organizational, in York came from the
support and enthusiasm of my friends and colleagues of all grades and
ages. That I have not so far identified them is not a denial but an
affirmation of this. For I cannot name them all. Some were more
directly involved than others: to identify these implies no disrespect for
others. In the early days, the mutual efforts of Peacock and myself were
enthusiastically supported by our two professorial colleagues, Douglas
Dosser and Alan Williams. The Professor of Politics, Graeme Moodie,
was my collaborator in the development of the politics and economics
teaching programme and was active in policy-making, as in a different
way was Lewis Waddilove, Director of the Joseph Rowntree Memorial
Trust, which has been unfailingly supportive of our activities. By the
time Peacock left for new challenges, the Institute was firmly established, the Department and the other Social Sciences had grown in size
and reputation, and new faces and influences were emerging. Research
in political science began to develop through the particular influence of
Andrew Dunsire. Alan Williams became increasingly involved in health
economics, and in partial retirement has become the guru of that
research programme. Erstwhile young colleagues, 'grown up' in the
shadow of the Institute, were becoming more directly involved in policy-
making. Tony Culyer, already with a growing international reputation,
became my active Deputy Director. Keith Hartley and Alan Maynard
became heavily involved in both research and in policy-making (and
have now taken major responsibility for future development). I achieved my own objectives. But the subsequent growth has been phenomenal; I am sure my colleagues are enjoying themselves as much as I
did. It was a rewarding experience.

Looking forward (and still talking too much . . . ?)
When I took advantage of the government partial retirement scheme
from end-September, 1982, I continued as a Professor of Economics
physically located at the Institute. But I deliberately withdrew from any
formal involvement in the policy-making process: decisions are in general better made by those who know that they will themselves suffer
the consequences of error. I was now in a position to fulfil my teaching
and research obligations to the University in part of the year, and spend

the rest of my time as I wished. I wanted more time to write, and saw a way not only to find this, but to combine it with travel, which I continue to find intellectually stimulating. My wife Jeanne had a severe rheumatic condition, and we also hoped to arrange our travel to benefit this. Unhappily, she died suddenly before my retirement date. This book is dedicated to her memory; an inadequate recognition of the contribution she made to my life. I have since married again, to one of our old friends; I have been more fortunate than I deserve. I persisted in my plan, and have spent the last few years in travel and in writing; the last few papers republished here were written in this period. They reflect my increasing dissatisfaction with neo-classical economics, and, more positively, the evolution of my ideas about cost and choice to the point that I am ready to incorporate them into a comprehensive political economy. Over this period, I have enjoyed the hospitality and stimulation of a number of institutions around the world. One of them requires particular mention. The Center for the Study of Public Choice, now at George Mason University, has been kind enough to appoint me Adjunct Scholar. The opportunity to visit there from time to time (I am writing this during my third visit since partial retirement) and to renew my ongoing debate with Buchanan and his colleagues, has been invaluable.

I reached full retirement in 1987, becoming Emeritus Professor. I have plenty of unfinished business, and two spiritual homes at which to pursue it (and travel elsewhere if family circumstances permit). I can still hold a pen, and have begun to use a word processor. There is so much still to do: may there be time enough.

Academics are lucky people. What better life could there be?

References

Buchanan, J. M. (1958) *Public Principles of Public Debt*, Homewood, Ill., Richard D. Irwin.

Buchanan, J. M. and Thirlby, G. F. (eds) (1973) *LSE Essays in Cost*, London, Weidenfeld and Nicolson.

Buchanan, J. M. and Tullock, G. (1962) *The Calculus of Consent: Logical Foundations of Constitutional Democracy*, Ann Arbor, University of Michigan Press.

Peacock, A. T. and Wiseman, J. (1961, 1967) *The Growth of Public Expenditure in the United Kingdom*, Princeton and London, Princeton University Press, Oxford University Press, Unwin.

Wiseman, J. (1985) 'Lionel Robbins, the Austrian School, and the LSE tradition', *Research in the History of Economic Thought and Methodology*, (ed. Samuels, W. J.), Greenwich, Conn., JAI Press.

2 Uncertainty, Costs and Collectivist Economic Planning*

Foreword

This was the first paper that I published on economic theory. Although it was published in socialist Britain, the topic was intellectually unfashionable and the article attracted little immediate attention. Looking back, I find little that I would want to change, though my conclusions would now be more forceful. The identification of the 'only difference of economic importance between the two systems' derives from acceptance of aspects of the neo-classical specification of the problem that I would now reject. I had correctly identified the destructive consequences of subjectivity and uncertainty for the operational feasibility of the marginal cost rule, but, along with earlier writers, had not appreciated the wider intellectual consequences of the argument. Even so, I might perhaps have asked more questions about the mechanisms for selecting, rewarding and dismissing managers, the need for proceedings substituting for the role of bankruptcy as the ultimate reallocating mechanism of the market economy; and so on.

But even these questions, much less wider ones concerned with the definition of cost and choice, fitted uneasily into the simple competitive model around which the debate had developed. It would also have made for a longer article, and one which I suspect would have been difficult to publish in the intellectual climate of the time.

Introduction[1]

The purpose of this chapter is to consider the possibility, in conditions of uncertainty, of utilizing a marginal cost 'rule' to distribute resources between uses in an economy in which there is consumers' sovereignty, with freedom of choice of goods and occupations, but in which factors of production cannot be privately owned and exploited.[2]

It will be argued that in conditions of uncertainty (i.e. once the fact of time is admitted), the marginal cost rule, as normally framed, gives no clear guidance to those responsible for the organization of production in such an economy. Attempts to reinterpret the rule in such a way as to take account of uncertainty preclude the possibility of a

* *Economica*, May, 1953. Reprinted in Buchanan, J. M. and Thirlby, G. F. (eds) (1973) *LSE Essays in Cost*, London, Weidenfeld and Nicolson.

direct check on the efficiency of collectivist managers in obeying that rule. Any indirect, *objective*, check used as a supplement to the marginal rule will in fact supplant that rule as the directive for managerial effort, and in any case no completely objective check is possible. Further, whatever rule or check is adopted, imperfectly competitive behaviour is to be expected in the absence of detailed regulation to control it.

In these circumstances, the most satisfactory distribution of resources seems likely to be obtained by an instruction to collectivist managers similar to the profit maximization 'rule' of the market economy. Identification of the managerial and the public interest would then have to be sought through the detailed regulation of managerial behaviour, in much the way that the government in a market economy attempts to regulate imperfectly competitive behaviour by entrepreneurs.[3]

The nature of the rule

The competitive market economy

The 'rule' to be discussed derives from the classical model of the perfectly competitive market economy, and is best understood in relation to that model. It was elucidated in the course of controversy as to the possibility of distributing productive factors efficiently between uses in an economy in which such factors were owned collectively.[4]

In this competitive market economy, resources are privately owned and exploited. They are also, in the perfectly competitive model, perfectly divisible and perfectly mobile between uses. Producers are assumed to act in the light of known data, i.e. their task is the combination of factors of production with known prices in the production of products to be sold at known prices. The distribution of resources between uses is carried out by an administrative mechanism, the characteristics of which are profit-maximization and a system of competitive markets in which buyers and sellers compete. With such a mechanism, producers' decisions about the use of resources are determined by *opportunity cost*; i.e. the use of resources in the chosen way is the result of an assessment of the revenues to be obtained by their use in any other way, the greatest of these forgone alternative revenues being the opportunity cost.

With the conditions of the model, the process described must result in an 'efficient' distribution of resources between uses in the sense that, with given consumer incomes, no reallocation of factors or products between uses could increase the satisfaction of any one consumer without reducing that of another. Since all relevant factor- and product-values are assumed known, there is no *doubt* about the production decisions to be taken by individual producers. The subjective (opportunity) costs have an objective counterpart in lists of known factor prices, which are in effect the sole content of the opportunity cost decision. The producers' task is simply the pricing of money inputs (i.e. sums of known factor prices) and product outputs, in the case of some production plan, and the relating of this certain result to the money values of products forgone, the prices of these products also being known. Different individuals in similar circumstances should make identical assessments and reach identical decisions. That is, the opportunity cost concept in such conditions is merely a reassertion of the fundamental economic problem of *scarcity*; it contains no element either of uncertainty or of judgement.

The competitive model as normally set out nevertheless contains an indirect check on efficiency in resource distribution, implicit in the mechanism of competitive profit-maximization. It is a property of the ideally efficient situation that producers' total money revenues will equal their total money outlays (including payment for their own services). Inefficiency in production (and hence in resource distribution) results in a money loss which indicates a need to redistribute resources. That is, the final check on the efficiency of the individual firm would be the bankruptcy court. However, the idea that firms can be 'extra-marginal' (in this sense of money outlays exceeding money revenues) requires the introduction of time into the analysis in some form, since otherwise it is difficult to explain, in the light of the assumptions of the competitive model, how the resources came to be in that use, or why there is not an instantaneous readjustment removing all extra-marginal production. This difficulty is usually circumvented, not by introducing a problem of *judgement* by relaxing the assumptions about knowledge, but by retaining the assumptions about knowledge and introducing time only as a modification of the assumptions about mobility. Only some of the productive factors are now fully free to move; losses can therefore be incurred as a result of the use of temporarily immobile factors, if the data on which the decisions were taken change after that use was decided upon.

A solution along these lines is uncomfortable in two important and related respects. The producer plans his productive activities in terms of factor and product prices of which it is assumed he has knowledge. It appears that he does not take possible future changes into account in reaching his decisions. If this is because the assumptions imply *knowledge* of future prices, and these are the prices which influence decisions whenever relevant, then how can the data change so as to create extra-marginality, since the change was foreseen? If, on the other hand, future conditions are not assumed known, then how can the producer plan in terms of known prices? Associated with this problem is the difficulty of establishing a precise relationship between mobility and time: the concept of the long period as a period in which all factors are free to move seems to make sense only if regarded as a planning period – i.e. a subjective notion about future activity sufficiently distant for all resource uses to be replanned. But such an interpretation appears to imply the need for foresight and judgement, which are ruled out by the perfect competition assumptions.

The liberal collectivist economy
This, then, is the model from which the cost rule of the liberal collectivist economy derives. As has been said, a liberal collectivist economy is one in which resources cannot be privately owned and exploited. With this reservation, the same freedom of choice of goods and occupations pertains as in a competitive market economy.[5]

The administrative mechanism of profit-maximization is replaced in the liberal collectivist economy by a 'marginal rule'. This rule has several formulations;[6] the most general one is the rule that managers of collectivist enterprises, working through a system of competitive markets similar to that of the market economy, should produce that output which makes marginal (money) cost equal to price. The origins of this rule are to be found in the model of the competitive market economy. It is a property of the 'efficient' situation in such an economy that marginal money cost (i.e. the sum of known prices of marginal factor inputs) of producing each product must be equal to the price for which the product can be sold. This equality is merely another way of expressing the fact that profit is being maximized, since in the conditions postulated a maximum profit (excess of revenues over outlays) is made when marginal cost is equal to price.

This is a *property of the market economy model*, an incidental result of the operation of the administrative mechanism of profit-maximization in the rarified conditions of perfect competition. It is no one's purpose to make marginal cost equal to price. But in the liberal collectivist economy this incidental property becomes a principle of administration, by following which, it is argued,[7] a liberal collectivist economy could not only effect an efficient distribution of resources, but could do so more quickly and accurately than a market economy, because a broader survey of the data relevant to his decisions could be made available to each collectivist manager.

Time and uncertainty
Once we admit that the future is unknown, analysis of the behaviour
of producers in terms of adaptation to *known* future conditions becomes
irrelevant. It is therefore necessary to ask how the admission of time
and uncertainty affects the administrative mechanism of the market
economy and of the liberal collectivist economy. The task of the producer is now to decide, on the basis of *his own estimates* about likely
future conditions, between the possible alternative courses of action
open to him at any point in time. Present prices and conditions are
relevant only in so far as they provide a basis for judgements about the
future. There is now no reason to suppose that individuals in similar
circumstances will make the same assessments and hence reach the
same decisions.

The administrative mechanism of competitive profit-maximization
can still function in the market economy, but the 'efficient' distribution
of resources between uses must now take account of the use of *new*
resources and of the development of *new* products. An excess of money
revenues over money outlays, once the element of judgement inevitable
with uncertainty is admitted, is no longer necessary evidence of an
inefficient distribution of resources; it may be due simply to exceptional
skill in forecasting. But, at the same time, the fact of uncertainty makes
the association of competitive behaviour and profit-maximization, on
which the market economy model depends, less generally acceptable.
The desire to reduce uncertainty by gaining control of the uncertain
variables must be an important motive in attempts to eliminate competition. Uncertainty thus implies the need for positive government policy
to ensure *competitive* behaviour in pursuit of profit-maximization, since
only such behaviour conduces to an efficient distribution of resources.
The difficulty in framing such a policy lies in distinguishing those factors
which are the inevitable accompaniment of ignorance and uncertainty
and those which arise simply out of a desire to maximize net revenue
in an environment characterized by these things.

It is no longer possible, once uncertainty is admitted, to interpret the
opportunity cost problem as one of scarcity alone, to be solved by a
choice between alternative factor inputs and product outputs with all
prices known. That is, opportunity cost is no longer a simple question
of summation and comparison of known data. Prices and other variables
have to be estimated: opportunity cost decisions involve uncertainty
(and therefore judgement) as well as scarcity. The cost problem now
arises as a *choice between alternative plans of action*, i.e. a choice
between a series of estimates of the outlays likely to be incurred and the
revenues likely to be obtained as a result of the adoption of particular

alternative courses of action. Costs are in fact incurred when decisions are made; to understand the use of resources over time it is necessary to go back to the decisions which decided that use, and to understand cost, requires consideration of the *estimated forgone alternative revenue* associated with the decision when taken. These forgone alternatives (i.e. discarded plans) not then implemented may in fact never be implemented at all.[8] But in the circumstances of the market economy, errors in the alternatives considered by any one producer do tend to be adjusted by the ability of others to take advantage of his oversight.

Since opportunity costs cannot be treated simply as known money costs, but must be considered as estimates of forgone alternative revenues, it is no longer very useful in conditions of uncertainty to speak of equality of marginal money cost and price as a property of an efficient resource distribution. This is unimportant in a market economy, since the equality comprises no part of its administrative mechanism. Uncertainty creates conditions in which it is to be expected that the mechanism of profit-maximization in competitive markets will function imperfectly and will require positive government action to support it. But the final check on efficiency is still the bankruptcy court, and difficulties about the interpretation of the marginal cost price equation are unimportant to its functioning. In fact, the admission of uncertainty disposes of those difficulties of the competitive market economy model which arise out of the association of time with resource mobility only. Once the assumptions about knowledge are dropped, 'extra-marginality' becomes reasonable; it is a function both of accuracy in forecasting and of speed of reaction to change (i.e. flexibility in coordination and the replanning of activities).

The problem is of greater importance in a liberal collectivist economy: it follows from the nature of the opportunity cost problem that an instruction to equate marginal money cost and money price in conditions of uncertainty gives no clear guidance to collectivist managers as to their productive behaviour. Thus the rule requires reformulation. The most appropriate reformulation would appear to be in terms of *anticipated objective outlays*. The marginal cost of any decision must be the displaced alternative revenue which would have accrued from some alternative use of the resources concerned. To obtain this figure requires a comparison of alternative sets of *ex ante* budget calculations. Each set of calculations gives the expected revenues and outlays involved in the production of each of the two relevant outputs of some product. The *budgeted* marginal cost is the difference between the outlay and revenue calculations in the case of the best forgone alternative budget.[9]

The question is whether the rule, thus reinterpreted, can provide an unambiguous guide for collectivist managers, and whether it enables a check to be made on the efficiency of the distribution of resources between uses similar to that provided by profit in the market economy.

The rule as reformulated

If no rule other than the marginal cost rule is used,[10] and that rule is interpreted as a relationship between *budgeted* marginal cost (as defined) and *budgeted* price, is there any check on the efficiency of the distribution of resources between uses?

A *direct* check on efficiency requires a check on decisions in relation to results. But only one of the *budgeted* outlays becomes a *realized objective* outlay, since only one plan can in fact be decided upon. Thus the 'marginal cost' with which we are concerned rests upon a judgement by the manager as to the accuracy of his estimates about the revenues which would have accrued had the forgone alternatives in fact been chosen. That is, estimation of marginal cost involves an inevitable element of personal judgement. There may in some cases be a check upon the 'reasonableness' of estimates. This is the more likely to be so the more the alternatives considered relate to the production of known things by known methods. The imponderables, and with them the difficulty of a direct check on efficiency, become the greater the more unique or novel are the matters with which decisions are concerned. All decisions about new and major investments of resources seem likely to involve important imponderables of this kind; it appears that those decisions likely to be most important to efficiency will be those upon which no adequate check can be made with the rule as now interpreted.

There is a further difficulty not yet considered. How is it to be decided whether the plans considered are the relevant ones? Suppose, for example, there is a difference of opinion about market prospects between the manager and the checking authority. If the checking authority can impose its views on the manager, then decisions about resource distribution (i.e. about costs) inhere in the checking authority; the decisions of that authority become the ones relevant to a check on efficiency, and the same questions have to be asked about them as about the decisions of the collectivist manager. The removal of investment decisions from managers robs them of their primary function from an economic viewpoint: the concentration of decisions in another authority shifts the relevance of the analysis towards that authority. It becomes appropriate to consider the *joint* decisions of the two bodies, in so far as any decisions are left with the manager at all. In effect, the vesting of such powers in the checking authority carries with it the need to abandon rules of the kind considered here, and to adopt some kind of Centralist Scheme[11] for the distribution of resources.

If the check is made at intervals, it must also be taken into account by the checking authority that estimates are subject to constant revision; skill and speed in revision must in effect be recognized as factors in efficient behaviour. But the existence of, and need for, such revision of plans is a further obstacle to a sensible check by an outside authority.

Thus, if the only criterion used is a marginal-cost: marginal-revenue relationship, as now defined, there can be no possibility of an unambiguous check on managerial efficiency through the use of these magnitudes. The most that can be done is to check efficiency, in the limited sense of correct forecasting, in the plan actually chosen. If both the manager's *planned* results and his *realized* results can be stated in unambiguously objective (empirical) terms, and if the plan is unambiguously his own, the comparison of planned and realized results provides (*ex post*) a check on *forecasting* efficiency *in respect only of the plan actually chosen*. But this provides only a very partial check, since it cannot explain whether that plan should have been chosen at all.

There seems little possibility of a direct check upon whether the marginal-cost rule has been obeyed: can the liberal collectivist economy then function without such a check? There are two possibilities: abandonment of any attempt to check obedience to the 'rule', and the use of some other 'indirect' check, in the form of a relationship between total revenues and total outlays, *ex post*, arising out of the plan actually implemented.

The rule without a check
The rule as reformulated does not carry with it any relationship between total revenues and total outlays. In the absence of some further instruction there seems no reason why a manager should not obey it while producing continuously at a loss.[12] The manager can check his own efficiency (i.e. the extent to which his activity conduces to an efficient distribution of resources, as defined), or can have it checked by someone else, only through the fulfilment or non-fulfilment of the plans he elects to implement. And even the meaning of the results of this limited check is not unambiguous: what degree of non-fulfilment should suggest to a manager (e.g.) that he should cease producing?

The manager is not told what things to take into account in drawing up budgets. As a result, it is to be expected that he will often base his policy partly upon judgements about the policy of his close rivals, since he considers this to be realistic budgeting, unless he is instructed to ignore such related policies when compiling his own. But how could such an instruction be formulated or enforced? Would it be conducive to efficiency, in any case, to attempt to make managers act on the basis of assumptions they believed to be unrealistic? But, in the absence of any guidance or control beyond the 'rule', it is a short step from this 'oligopolistic competition' to attempts to make budgeting easier by reaching policy agreements with rivals – that is, to collusive, imperfectly competitive behaviour.

Knowledge of rivals' reactions gained in this way is not, of course, what is envisged by those who suggest that a liberal collectivist economy could reach an equilibrium more quickly and efficiently because more data on which to base decisions could be placed at the disposal of each manager. Their argument is quite other: its basis is the idea that more information could be made available to all managers by the use of some kind of central information service. But there is a logical fallacy here. What each manager wants is knowledge of the firm plans of other managers, on which to base his own plans. But, plainly, not *all* managers can have such information unless either all plans are imposed from above (a possibility already rejected) or the plans are made *jointly* through some form of collusive (non-competitive) behaviour.

If there is to be no check on the efficiency of managers in attempting to obey the 'rule', the choice of the managers themselves becomes particularly important to efficiency. The market economy depends, for the correction of errors of judgement, upon the ability of any producer to take advantage of the oversights of others. From this point of view, any restriction of the field of choice of managers is a restriction upon possibly useful entrants and hence a curb upon efficiency. On the other hand, if *anyone* can be a collectivist manager, how are the managers of banking institutions to decide who is to have control over liquid resources, and how much?[13] Presumably they would have to try to judge whether the applicant was capable of equating marginal cost and marginal revenue, although once the funds have been granted and used, those granting them become dependent upon the applicants' view as to whether this has been done or not.

It has sometimes been suggested, as an alternative, that managers should qualify by some kind of competitive examination.[14] Apart from the difficulty of formulating a suitable test, it still has to be decided what those who have qualified become entitled to. Can they all demand control over the same volume of liquid resources, or does the volume controlled vary with seniority, or is there some other means of deciding?

In the absence of a check on the *outcome* of managerial behaviour, then, managers will be uncertain as to the implications of the consequences of their own acts, no other authority will be in a position to check the efficiency of those acts, oligopolistic and collusive behaviour is to be expected, and there is no clear criterion for the allocation of control over resources between managers. Therefore, while there can be no direct check on efficiency in resource distribution through the marginal relationship, an indirect objective check is plainly desirable; the problem is to discover one.

Checks through net revenue
Since the marginal check is ineffective, the only possibility remaining lies in a check on efficiency depending upon the relationship between total money revenues and total money outlays. There are two possible relationships between total revenues and total outlays which might be accepted as a standard of efficiency: equality of total outlays and total revenues, and maximization of the excess of receipts over outlays.

The equality criterion is indicative of an efficient resource distribution only in the conditions of the perfectly competitive model. Uncertainty introduces the possibility of a difference between revenues and outlays due to exceptional ability in forecasting, and such a difference cannot be considered incompatible with efficiency. Thus to use such a check might entail the abandonment of plans which producers would expect to yield greater revenues for the same outlays. Since such plans would be implemented if the marginal rule were followed, a criterion of equality of total revenues and total outlays is incompatible with the marginal rule, as reformulated to take account of uncertainty. A check on the equality of total revenues and total outlays would not operate as a supplement, for the checking authority, to the marginal rule to be followed by managers, but would in fact replace that marginal rule as the directive to managerial effort.

The most likely result of the use of an equality criterion is secret budgeting for revenue surpluses on the part of managers. These surpluses can then be 'lost' if they seem likely to materialize, so that the required equality is always achieved. There is also an inducement to non-competitive behaviour. Oligopolistic situations arise for reasons already argued, and the realization of interdependence must lead to a realization that the equality of total revenues and total outlays is more easily budgeted for and achieved if some variables can be ruled out of account by collusive action.

The seeming objectivity of a check on the equality of total receipts and total outlays is in any case misleading. The check must by its nature be periodic, and to obtain the requisite receipt and outlay figures for any period, it is necessary to place a valuation upon the *physical resources* of the organization at the beginning and end of the period concerned.

This valuation rests upon a judgement about possibilities of future revenues from the use of the resources in question – a judgement incapable of complete check by another person or body.[15]

An instruction to managers to maximize the excess of money receipts over money outlays raises fewer problems. It is compatible with the marginal rule, in that the latter would lead to the same choice of plan as does the instruction to maximize net revenues. But the marginal rule is no longer needed; once net revenue is accepted as the guide, the marginal rule is no more important to a check on efficiency than it is in the market economy. On grounds of convenience it is therefore better dispensed with. There is with this revenue rule some kind of check on efficiency, in the size of the net revenue, and some possibility of formulating a criterion for the allocation of resources between producers, probably in terms of the size of past net revenues. The utility of the net-revenue rule does, however, depend upon two preconditions.[16] First, there must be similar opportunity for individual producers to take advantage of the oversight of others as was the case in the market economy, so that absence of net revenue is a clear indication of a need to redistribute resources and its persistence in the case of any one manager an indication of the inefficiency of that manager. Second, the behaviour of managers in maximizing net revenue must be conducive to efficiency, i.e. it must be competitive. But since, in conditions of uncertainty, the net-revenue rule provides the same kind of incentive to imperfectly competitive, collusive and monopolistic behaviour as in the market economy, the net revenue rule could only hope to function reasonably efficiently given detailed government regulation of revenue maximizing behaviour of kinds incompatible with efficiency in the distribution of resources.

Conclusions

The most effective general rule for managers of enterprises in a liberal collectivist economy would seem to be one similar in nature to the profit maximization 'rule' of the market economy. This appears to be the only rule offering the possibility of any external check on managerial efficiency; the 'marginal' rule is of no value in this respect. The 'net-revenue' rule also makes possible the formulation of a criterion for the allocation of resources to producers in the future, in terms of achieved past net revenues. The use of the 'net-revenue' rule (or, for that matter, any other of the rules examined) provides an incentive for non-competitive behaviour on the part of producers, which would need to be tackled by detailed regulation similar to that required in a market economy.[17]

It may be that imperfectly competitive behaviour would be less of a problem in a liberal collectivist economy, because the link between personal income and net revenue is less direct and the desire to act in the public interest more important. But it must be borne in mind that in the case of joint-stock organization the link is also indirect, and also that it is implicit in the whole liberal collectivist pattern that the incentive to obey the rule (in this case to maximize net revenue), whatever that incentive might be, is such that producers treat it seriously.

If the preceding argument is sound, and the need for a net revenue rule is accepted, then the only difference of economic importance between the two systems lies in this possibility of greater simplicity in the control of imperfectly competitive behaviour in the liberal collectivist economy, balanced against the loss of the 'unparalleled simplicity and force' of the motive of private profit in the market economy. It becomes relevant at least to consider whether a competitive market economy might not function more efficiently even while accepting such impairment of the force of the profit motive as resulted from policies of income redistribution satisfactory to collectivists.

Notes

1. I am particularly indebted to the valuable suggestions and criticisms of Mr G. F. Thirlby, and to my colleagues who commented on the article in draft.
2. Such an economy will be referred to hereafter as a 'liberal collectivist' economy.
3. While the argument presented is related to the functioning of a liberal collectivist economy, it has a direct bearing on problems arising in a 'mixed' society such as our own. It is relevant, for example, to a consideration of the pricing policy of public utilities which is normally discussed in relation to similar 'rules'. This is a question the writer hopes to take up in a later paper.
4. Much of the early discussion has been brought together in two sets of reprints of relevant articles: *Collectivist Economic Planning*, ed. F. A. Hayek (which includes L. von Mises' pioneer article, 'Economic Calculus in the Socialist Commonwealth'), and *On the Economic Theory of Socialism*, ed. Benjamin E. Lipincott (which includes reprints of articles by O. Lange and F. M. Taylor suggesting and elaborating the use of marginal criteria). A number of other papers on the subject were published in the *Economic Journal* and *Review of Economic Studies* during the 1930s, and a marginal 'rule' was elaborated by (*inter alia*) A. P. Lerner in *Economics of Control* (1944).
5. An economy of this kind is discussed (e.g.) by A. P. Lerner, *Economics of Control*, and E. F. M. Durbin, *Problems of Economic Planning*.
6. e.g. Lerner (ibid.) formulates five conditions relating marginal private and social benefit, cost, etc. Durbin (ibid., Paper VIII), has suggested the use of marginal-value products. These differences do not affect the substance of the argument.
7. e.g. Lange (ibid., pp. 89–90), Durbin (ibid., p. 50), P. M. Sweezy, *Socialism*, p. 231.
8. A decision to build a particular type of bridge over a river, for example, is likely to mean that alternative plans concerned with other types of bridges, considered *ex ante*, will never be implemented.
9. This formulation is based upon that used by G. F. Thirlby, 'The Ruler', *South African Journal of Economics*, December 1946.
10. i.e. no relation between total revenues and total outlays is postulated.

11. Cf. H. D. Dickinson, 'Price Formation in a Socialist Economy', *Economic Journal*, December 1943, and *The Economics of Socialism*, pp. 104–5, and M. Dobb, *Political Economy and Capitalism*, ch. VIII. Dobb advocates such a scheme in preference to the competitive solution using a marginal rule; Dickinson merely suggests it as a possible practical alternative.

12. i.e. if . . . no plan considered is expected to yield a surplus of revenues over outlays.

13. I leave aside the question of where *these* managers come from, and whether they can interpret the marginal rule, if they are expected to follow it.

14. e.g. Durbin appears to envisage 'Planning' of this kind being taken care of by extension of the civil service – ibid., Paper VI.

15. A valuation problem similar to this arises, of course, in a market economy. In either economy there is more possibility of an approximate check than was the case with the marginal rule, since wide fluctuations in successive valuations of particular assets appear reasonably clearly and need to be explained.

16. It also depends upon a reasonably satisfactory solution of the valuation problem, which is still relevant (see note 15 above).

17. Where, in the nature of things, competition cannot function (e.g. for technological, reasons), revenue maximization with detailed regulation may be unsatisfactory; a combination of regulation and some given net-revenue objective might operate more efficiently. This is the public utility pricing problem of the market economy.

3 The Theory of Public Utility Price: An Empty Box*

Foreword

The affinity of this chapter and the previous one is clear; it is referred to there, and existed in conception in 1973. The reasons that it saw the light only some years later are curious. I had problems with the 'club principle'. I had been introduced to the idea as an undergraduate, and heard many subsequent references to it. But since my purpose was critical, I thought it desirable to cite sources, since I did not wish to appear to be setting up a straw man. This was the one occasion on which the LSE grapevine failed me. A poll of colleagues produced general support for the principle; it was clearly not the product of my imagination. But no one could suggest an accessible reference; it seemed to be part of the 'oral tradition'.

The principle caused further difficulty. The piece was rather long, and I chose to send it to *Oxford Economic Papers*, which appeared sympathetic in this respect. The editor returned it with a note saying that he had found it interesting, but did not fully understand it. Why did I not expand the argument to book length? Instead, I replied asking him to indicate the areas of difficulty. The essential one turned out to be the club principle. I tried to improve the argument, and re-submitted the article; it was accepted.

I did not take the advice to write a book seriously, and have since wondered why. I think the answer must be that I did not feel that I had enough to say of a positive kind. The argument is essentially destructive of a widely held view. This is a sufficient justification. But to develop it at greater length required the positive expansion of the position taken in the final paragraph: that, failing some generally acceptable theory of the *public* economy, 'decisions . . . must be a reflection of the particular attitude of the government concerned'. I was not ready to develop such a theory then. Indeed, it is only now, some thirty years later, that I begin to feel confident of the shape of the answer, and ready to write the book that I was being encouraged to write then.

* *Oxford Economic Papers*, February 1957. Reprinted in Buchanan, J. M. and Thirlby, G. F. (eds) (1973) *LSE Essays in Cost*, London, Weidenfeld and Nicolson, and in Rowley, op. cit. (translation): 'La Teoria dei Prezzi delle Imprese di Publica Utilita', *Economia Internazionale*, (February 1958).

The subsequent history is also interesting. The theme was more topical than liberal collectivism, and the article produced some immediate debate, which in my view did nothing to destroy the essential rejection of the practical (policy) relevance of marginal cost rules. Since that time, the article has been republished three times (once in translation). But its argument is still not generally accepted, perhaps because neo-classical economists are reluctant to accept the need to distinguish between the value of the marginal idea as an intellectual tool, about which there is no dispute, and the translation of that idea into a decision rule relevant to a real-world operational context.

At the conceptual level, Rowley (1972) described the argument as demonstrating that in a world characterized by uncertainty 'a direction to marginal-cost price is little more than an empty order', which 'represents a fundamental challenge which no amount of mathematical ingenuity can really answer' (p.xxv). Subsequent attempts to overturn the logic have in my view contributed little new: the 'fundamental challenge' goes unanswered, though often unheeded. Resort to evidence is also unconvincing. For a period, UK nationalized industries were instructed to price at marginal cost. There is no published evidence to support the view that this generated any systematic change in behaviour, much less as to whether managers had ever failed to obey the 'rule'. Indeed, there was never any relevant public discussion after the rule was introduced. The case of Electricité de France is superficially more interesting, in that those concerned themselves claimed that they made their decisions in accordance with a marginal cost rule. In an accounting sense this was true. The decision-makers were economists, and were given wide discretion in the pricing of their (monopoly) product. They decided upon a marginal opportunity-cost formula that seemed plausible, and set prices by reference to it. However, when I discussed the content of my own paper with them, they did not dissent from the argument. They did not deny that a different group of decision-makers might have adopted a different formula or used different estimates, nor did they claim to have any 'scientific' way of demonstrating the superiority of their own margins or numbers. Such alternative calculations could equally have satisfied a 'marginal rule' and been equally acceptable to their political masters.

In a different context, readers may find it interesting that the argument of the paper develops an (unrecognized) special case of the still unarticulated general theory of second-best.

Introduction[1]

Criticism of the analytical validity of public utility pricing 'rules' has resulted over a period of years in the introduction of successive modifications to the original simple (though not unambiguous) marginal-cost 'rule', culminating in advocacy of the two-part tariff and of the 'club' principle.[2] While these pricing rules have been regarded with scepticism as practical guides to public utility pricing policy,[3] however, there has perhaps been a less general appreciation of the cumulative weight of the theoretical objections to all such rules; there is still interest in the discovery of a 'right' rule, and in the estimation of the 'marginal' or other costs of particular public utility enterprises.

It will be argued in this chapter that no general pricing rule or rules can be held unambiguously to bring about an 'optimum' use of resources by public utilities, even in theory. Indeed, failing some universally acceptable theory of the public economy, the economist can offer no *general* guidance at all to a government having to decide a price policy for such utilities. To demonstrate this, it will be necessary to begin with a brief survey of the criticisms of the simple marginal-cost rule. This will provide the basis for a demonstration of the possibly less familiar (though no less decisive) analytical shortcomings of the two-part tariff rule, both in its simple form and as modified by a 'club' principle. In conclusion, the effect of uncertainty on the analysis will be examined, and the broad implications of the whole argument for public policy will be suggested.

The marginal-cost rule

Any discussion of a 'right' price presupposes criteria of the public interest against which alternative suggested prices can be judged. The criteria from which the marginal-cost rule stems are derived from the analytical model of a perfectly competitive market economy, in which entrepreneurs are assumed to have perfect foresight[4] and it is a property of the long-run equilibrium situation that, given the distribution of income between consumers, no transfer of factors between uses could increase the satisfactions of one consumer without reducing those of another. The optimum conditions of 'economic welfare' are consequently said to be fulfilled by the model. For the competitive firm, it is an incidental property of the long-run situation that marginal cost (money outlay on factors) = average cost = price of product. Consequently, this equality can be regarded as evidence of the existence of an 'ideal' situation, and pricing at marginal cost has accordingly been proposed as a general pricing rule (e.g. as the 'principle of administration' of a collectivist economy).[5] But public utility enterprises are not perfectly competitive firms. By the usual definition, an important part of the factors they employ are not perfectly divisible; they can be obtained only in large physical units, or in a durable or specific form, or both. Also, the technically efficient production unit is large relative to the possible size of the market, and the utilities are public bodies, often with considerable powers of monopoly protected by law. In such circumstances, there may be no possible price equal both to marginal cost (the money outlay required to increase output marginally) and average cost (which includes outlays on the 'indivisible' factors excluded from marginal cost). It therefore appears to be necessary to decide whether price should be fixed equal to the one or to the other.

The argument for pricing such public utility products at average cost is simply that 'each tub should stand on its own bottom'; all money outlays which would have been avoided if a product had not been produced should be recovered in the price charged by the utility. But the advocates of marginal-cost pricing find this unconvincing. Some of the outlays included in average cost, they argue, are not current opportunity costs but are either payments for technically indivisible factors or past out-payments for durable and specific factors. The inclusion of these outlays in the price charged therefore prevents the achievement of the optimum welfare conditions, which (it is said) require that additional consumption of a good or service should be possible at a price not greater than the additional costs (money outlays) necessarily incurred in providing for that consumption. Accordingly, such outlays should be ignored, and the product priced at marginal cost, even though the enterprise runs at a loss as a result.

Clearly, the proposal for pricing at marginal cost requires an explanation of how the consequent losses are to be financed. Hotelling, who originated much of the discussion,[6] suggested the use of particular types of taxes. The inclusion of charges for 'overheads' (past outlays on indivisible factors) was itself, he said, of the nature of a tax. But there were other and preferable taxes (lump-sum taxes on inheritance, income taxes, etc.) which did not offend against the welfare criteria since they affected only the *distribution* and not the *size* of the national income. If such taxes were used, and public utility prices were equated with marginal cost, the optimum welfare conditions would be achieved. Later writers have been justifiably sceptical of the possibility of a tax system that would meet Hotelling's conditions.[7] In particular, income taxes (on which he expected to have to rely) can be shown to affect the marginal welfare conditions directly. In any case, the proposal is open to an even more fundamental objection: the welfare 'ideal' relates to a *given* distribution of income, and that distribution of income must be altered by the proposed taxes (unless these fall on consumers of public utility products in proportion to their consumption, which is effectively a return to average-cost pricing). Thus to advocate marginal-cost pricing and the meeting of losses out of taxation is to advocate acceptance of income redistribution from non-consumers to consumers of public utility products. The welfare criteria provide no justification for an inter-personal comparison of this kind. In other words, any government deciding upon a pricing policy for public utilities has to take simultaneously into account the effects of its decisions upon the fulfilment of the welfare optima (and hence the size of the national product) and upon the distribution of incomes, and there is nothing in the welfare analysis that provides guidance as to the 'right' policy about the second of these.[8]

The reason why marginal-cost pricing raises these difficulties is to be found in the fact that the arguments for the marginal-cost rule are logically unsatisfactory in that they attempt to apply welfare criteria derived from an analysis concerned with marginal variations in factor use to a problem whose essence is discrete change; the whole basis of the public utility discussion is the indivisibility of the factors employed by such utilities. The results of this attempt are not only of dubious relevance to policy; they are also uncertain in themselves.

The type of indivisibility most emphasized in the discussion is that created by the durability and specificity of factors (*temporal* indivisibility).[9] It is enlightening to examine the nature of such indivisibility more closely. It has been shown that the marginal-cost 'rule' distinguishes between 'current' and 'past' opportunity-cost problems. Once the sacrifices necessary to create a durable and specific asset have been made, it is argued, no further opportunity costs are created by its later use. The opportunity costs having been borne in the past, no account should be taken of them in deciding current prices,[10] even though, as has been demonstrated, this results in losses and in income redistribution. Such an argument rests upon a dubious interpretation of the welfare criteria. The long period, from which the welfare postulates derive, is a situation in which all factors of production are considered to be perfectly mobile; this would seem to imply consideration of a time-period at least as long as the lowest common multiple of the lifespan of all the factors of production concerned. If the marginal-cost rule is conceived in terms of a time-period shorter than this, then not all the opportunity costs requisite to the manufacture of the product concerned can be imputed to that product, and the time-period chosen must itself be arbitrary, so that the marginal-cost rule becomes simply a statement that outlays on factors of some specified durability should be ignored in deciding prices (i.e. should be treated as 'past' outlays). The figure treated as marginal cost will thus depend upon the time-period selected.[11]

The division of outlays into 'past' and 'current' is clearly unsatisfactory, and the implications of durability and specificity become less obscure if such a division is abandoned and the problem is presented in the form of a planning process through time. All opportunity-cost decisions, taken at one moment in time, fix the use of factors during some future period of time. All factors embodied in plans implemented by entrepreneurs, that is, become durable and specific to some degree; new opportunity costs arise in respect of them only when their use can be replanned. This being so, it is not possible to separate opportunity costs into two groups, 'past' and 'current'. The most that can be said is that some kinds of factor lend themselves more readily than do others to frequent replanning. There is a difference, for example, between the extent to which factor-use will be 'fixed' over time by the implementation of a decision to build a railway bridge and by a decision to hire a railway porter. But the difference is one not of kind but of degree; it is possible to conceive of an 'ordering' of opportunity-costs decisions in accordance with the length of time for which they commit factors to particular uses (i.e. create specificity and durability), but it is not possible to divide such decisions into a group that involves a commitment over time and another group that does not.

Marginal (opportunity) cost in these circumstances is represented by a forgone revenue. The use of factors of production in the entrepreneur's selected plan excludes them from use in some other plan; marginal cost is the forgone marginal revenue from the best plan necessarily excluded because the chosen plan is selected. But the alternative uses to which factors can be put, and hence the opportunity-cost valuation imputed to them in the planning process, will depend on the time-period in terms of which the entrepreneur's plans are themselves conceived; marginal cost will consequently vary according to the time-span of the production plans considered. Thus, the meaning and results of an instruction to equate marginal cost and price will be determined by the length of the planning period to which the marginal cost is intended to refer. At one extreme, the period chosen may be as long as the lowest common multiple of the life-periods of the assets required to produce the public utility product, and the marginal-cost rule would then give a price that took into account the whole of the sacrifice of alternative consumption caused by the implementation of plans to manufacture the utility product. At the other extreme, the consideration of 'current' opportunity costs only, if interpreted rigorously, would seem to require that products should be given away. Between these two extremes, there is a range of possible marginal cost rules, differing from each other in the planning time-period chosen as appropriate and hence in the 'durable' assets they ignore and in the opportunity costs they treat as relevant to decisions about price and output.

The only time-period in which all factor-use can be clearly attributed is one as long as the lowest common multiple of the life-periods of the assets concerned; the designation of any other (shorter) time-period as the one appropriate to the rule must involve both an arbitrary decision that that period is one relevant to the computation of marginal cost and a value judgement that income should be redistributed over time towards the consumers of goods produced with relatively durable assets. The marginal-cost principle thus becomes, not the assertion of a general welfare 'ideal', *but the expression of a particular value-judgement, that certain long-run opportunity costs for the community as a whole should be ignored in the interests of the greater short-run utilization by consumers of specific factors of some stated degree of durability.*[12]

The only defence offered against criticism of the marginal-cost rule on such grounds lies in the introduction of a supplementary criterion: the investment principle. This requires that marginal-cost pricing should be used to decide the selling prices of public utility products once the utilities are in existence, but that the public investment necessary to create a utility initially should be considered justified only if a perfectly discriminating monopolist could (notionally) recover its cost by charging prices that would maximize his returns. The need for such a supplementary principle to a 'general' rule is implausible. In any case, the investment principle does not answer the criticisms. It still has to be decided which economic decisions are to be treated as 'investment' decisions and which as subject to the marginal-cost rule, and no principle has been suggested by reference to which such decisions might be made. Further, since the prices actually charged are to be determined by the marginal-cost rule, the discussion of the effects of that rule (e.g. on income distribution) is unaffected by the introduction of the supplementary principle. It is worth pointing out, further, that the investment criterion itself has redistributive implications: certainly it does not appear to meet the welfare conditions in the same fashion as would a perfectly competitive market.[13]

The foregoing criticisms of marginal-cost pricing have been fairly widely accepted, although the precise nature of the value judgements implied in the treatment of temporal indivisibility is perhaps not generally recognized. Despite this acceptance, there still seems to be considerable support for marginal-cost pricing from those who feel that policies affecting only the *distribution* of the national income both are possible and are in some sense superior to alternative policies that would also affect its *size*. In the absence of some generally acceptable basis for preference between different income distributions, it is clear that such a position cannot be supported by logic. The two issues cannot be separated, and policies desirable in terms of the welfare criteria may therefore reasonably be rejected because a government chooses to obtain a 'preferred' distribution of income even at the cost of some diminution of its total size. There is no escape from the very special value judgements that marginal-cost pricing implies.[14]

The multi-part tariff and the 'club'

The two- (or more) part tariff is intended to avoid the anomalies of marginal-cost pricing, in that it is designed to meet the marginal 'welfare' conditions and also to avoid problems of interpersonal comparison by raising revenues large enough to cover all outlays. The essence of the proposal is that the price to be charged should be the sum of two parts:[15] a 'marginal-cost' element determined by the increase in costs necessarily incurred in providing further consumption for an individual consumer, and a 'fixed charge' to cover costs which do not vary with consumption but which must be incurred if the consumer in question is to be enabled to consume at all. In this way, total costs are covered and the payments made for additional consumption are kept equal to the extra costs of provision (marginal cost) alone. The problem appears to be solved, since the 'welfare' conditions are satisfied and no income redistribution seems to be implied.[16]

Unfortunately, multi-part pricing provides an unambiguous solution only if the two types of costs concerned can be clearly imputed to individual consumers. In fact, when this can be done the two 'parts' of the price can logically be treated as the prices of separate products, each capable of clear determination by a normal market process. When these conditions do not obtain, however, the situation becomes very different. This can be seen by introducing the possibility of common costs. If problems of time are disregarded, these are simply current costs that do not vary with total output, but are necessarily incurred if *any* output is to be produced at all and are not *imputable directly to individual consumers*.[17] How should these current 'fixed and common' costs be shared between consumers? In principle, limits can be set to the charges that individual consumers can and should be asked to pay, by reference to the cost of providing the indivisible service for them if other consumers ceased to consume, on the one hand, and the minimum possible cost of providing their addition to total consumption on the other.[18] But there may still remain a variety of possible methods of charging, and some non-arbitrary means of choosing between them is required if the multi-part tariff is to provide an unambiguous solution to the public utility pricing problem.[19]

There is a suggested means if meeting this common cost problem that seems to be fairly widely accepted. This is the use of the 'club' principle. This principle is not usually stated with precision; its essence appears to be the proposition that the consumers of the utility product can be treated as a 'club', created by the consumers to arrange both the amount of the good each individual shall consume and the amount that he shall pay for it. Then, if all 'members' (potential consumers) are asked what they would voluntarily pay as a fixed charge rather than go without the possibility of consuming a particular product at a price per unit equal to marginal cost (money outlay), and if the sum of the amounts offered would be great enough to cover the total outlays required, the service should be provided and each consumer charged that part of the common cost that he has stated his willingness to bear. It follows that the 'club' principle is likely to give rise to price discrimination, in that different individuals need not be required to pay the same amount for a similar volume of consumption. That is, the principle must imply a redistribution of real income, since consumers with given money incomes purchase a technically homogeneous product at money prices differing from one consumer to another. But, it is argued, the 'club' principle allows consumers themselves to make a voluntary decision whether to accept the good and the consequent income redistribution in preference to having neither. If they, as consumers, take the first course, then this must produce a more satisfactory situation from the point of view of consumers' choice, and the optimum 'welfare' conditions must therefore be better satisfied as a result of the use of the 'club' principle despite the consequent redistribution of income.

The 'club' principle has deficiencies serious enough to make the extent of its acceptance a matter for some surprise. The deficiencies are of two kinds. First, the value judgements being made in relation to income redistribution are difficult to justify. Second, the 'club' proposals require as unusual (and peculiar) interpretation of the concept of voluntary choice.

Income redistribution and the 'club' principle
No one suggests that the 'club' principle avoids the need for value judgements about income distribution.[20] Rather, what is implied is that 'welfare' can unambiguously be said to have been improved by a policy which meets the marginal welfare conditions, even though there is a consequent change in the distribution of income, *provided that the*

*changed income distribution is the consequence of the 'voluntary' action
of consumers.* This extension of the welfare criteria is less innocuous
than might at first appear. Economic welfare, as normally defined, is
concerned solely with the optimum conditions of individual choice,
given the distribution of income; the objective of the public utility
discussion might be described as the discovery of a pricing policy to
meet those conditions, in the special circumstances of public utility
production. But if a suggested principle of pricing would affect economic magnitudes other than the conditions of choice, then it becomes
necessary to establish further policy criteria concerned with these other
magnitudes, by reference to which the proposed principle can be
assessed. In the present case, since income distribution is affected by
the 'club' principle, criteria for choice between income distributions are
required. Moreover, these criteria must take the form of a statement
about the·*income-redistributive objectives of a government,* since it has
to be recognized that the public utility discussion (although itself conceived in relation to the conditions of individual choice) is concerned
to recommend policies to be implemented by a government. *That is,
income distribution is a question of public policy, and it is the attitude
of the government to it, and not the attitude of particular groups of
consumers, that is of significance for policy.* The value judgement
implied in the 'club' principle in that if the members of the public
utility 'club' agree to a particular redistribution of income, then the
government must necessarily think such a redistribution desirable. This
is not plausible; there are likely to be many cases in which the 'voluntary' redistribution would be of a kind that the government disap-
proved.[21] In short, once a government is committed, by the creation of
a utility and the existence of common costs, to a decision about income
distribution, there is no reason why it should prefer public utility pricing
polices that cover total costs by use of the 'club' principle to other
policies which may or may not cover costs, but which accord better
with its own attitude to redistribution. A government permitting utilities
to use the 'club' principle in effect substitutes the authorities of the
utility for itself as the final arbiter in matters of income distribution in
this particular context.[22]

'Voluntary' choice and the 'club' principle

The argument for the 'club' principle depends upon the fact that the
charges to which it gives rise are 'voluntarily' agreed by consumers. In
general, this agreement will be 'voluntary' only in the special sense that
a malefactor voluntarily goes away to prison after a judge has sentenced
him; he chooses the best alternative still available. To appreciate this,

it is necessary to look more closely at the form these 'clubs' can take and at the nature of their 'regulations' (i.e. the powers they have to take and enforce decisions about such matters as the payments to be made by members). Three broad types of 'club' can be envisaged.

The first type might be called the *direct production club*: it is created and administered by the consumers themselves. Thus, if factor services are available for purchase in free competitive markets, groups of consumers may find it convenient to join together to hire certain services whose products will be consumed by all the group, although it would not be worth the while of individual consumers to hire them separately. Effectively, the consumers *ask themselves* whether it is worth their while to create a 'club' to provide the good concerned, and agree together (in deciding to create it) upon the volume of their individual consumption and upon the payments each shall make. The illustrations given of the 'club' principle are usually of this direct-production character.[23] Provided that there are alternative competing means of satisfying the demand in question without recourse to a 'club', then the possibility of forming a 'club' simply represents a widening in the range of choices made available by the competitive market, and so increases satisfactions ('welfare').[24] This is true even though members of the 'club' pay different amounts for what is technically the same service. However, such cases of direct production would seem unlikely to be of widespread importance, though there may be special instances in which the conditions are quite well satisfied.[25]

The second form that the 'club' might take is one in which the organization of production is undertaken, not by the eventual consumers, but by independent producers, who find the use of standing charges advantageous but whose freedom in deciding the charges that consumers ('members') shall be asked to pay is restricted by the presence in the market of other, similar clubs competing for the consumer's membership. An example of this type of 'club' (the *competitive producer club*) is provided by the book clubs, offering supplies of books at differential rates related to total guaranteed consumption, but with the discretion of any one club in deciding its rates circumscribed by the policies adopted (or able to be adopted) by the other book clubs, and by the ability of consumers to transfer their 'membership'. There is a case for the existence of this type of 'club' also, on grounds of economic welfare. But it must be noticed that the consumers are not now taking decisions about how much they are willing to contribute to a venture in joint production; their 'voluntary' decisions are concerned solely with the nature and amount of their personal consumption at the prices thrown up by the market. The production decisions are taken by independent producers, and the fulfilment of the welfare conditions depends upon the protection provided for the consumers by competition between these producers.[26]

The third type of 'club', the *discriminating monopoly club*, occurs when neither direct production (with factor services provided by a competitive market) nor competition between 'club'-type producers is present. Only one 'club' is in a position to provide the good or service, so that consumers must join this 'club' and pay the discriminatory charges asked, or go without the good. In such cases, where the producer has a considerable degree of monopoly power, it is difficult to see how discriminatory charges can be justified by appeal to the 'club' principle. The differential charges are fixed by the producer without reference to consumers, who must accept them as a datum when deciding how much to consume – the only 'voluntary' decision left with them. Consumers in these circumstances are protected neither by direct association with pricing and production decisions nor by the existence of competition among producers of the good concerned. The distinction between this last formulation of the 'club' principle and the earlier ones is clear; it is the difference between my offer (choice) to pay two-thirds of the cost of a particular taxi shared with a friend, in preference to travelling by bus, and my choice whether or not to consume electricity at the particular set of discriminatory prices that a monopolistic electricity utility decides to apply to me. Cases of the latter type are clearly not justifiable on 'welfare' grounds; if all that is required to satisfy the 'club' principle is that some consumers should pay rather than go without, then any private discriminating monopolist might meet the conditions.

Unfortunately, it is only the last and most unsatisfactory type of 'club' that is likely to be relevant to the pricing policy of public utilities, whose products often have no close substitutes and whose monopoly power is protected by law, so that the 'club' becomes effectively a method of coercion operated by a sole producer.

In summary, there are clear arguments for a multi-part pricing rule only where the services of the indivisible factors (and therefore the 'standing charges') can be imputed directly to individual consumers. In such conditions the method avoids the need for interpersonal utility comparisons. This is not so if there are common costs, which is likely to be the general case. In these cases, the decision taken about the prices to be charged must involve a value judgement about the distribution of income, and this cannot in general be avoided by an instruction to make use of the 'club' principle.

The welfare model and uncertainty[27]

In the simplified conditions of the competitive model so far postulated, the pricing 'rules' could be implemented simply on the basis of objective cost computations made by utility managers. The assumptions about knowledge that lie behind the model are such that it does not matter who takes the decisions about the use of factors in production, nor is there any need for economic activity concerned with the discovery of information, framing of expectations, or considering and choosing between alternative and speculative courses of action. Any departure from the 'ideal' situation in which the price of any factor (including 'entrepreneurship' as rewarded by normal profit) is equal to its value in another use or to another user must be explained solely by reference to the short-term immobility of factors of production.

A simple model of this kind is inadequate for the derivation of pricing rules intended to have relevance to practical policy. This can be seen by considering the effects of uncertainty.[28] Once uncertainty is admitted, it becomes necessary to distinguish between the process of decision-taking by which the use of resources is determined (the *ex ante* planning process), and the *ex post* distribution of factors between uses that is the consequence of that process. The opportunity-cost problems arise at the *ex ante* planning stage: costs are incurred when decisions committing factors to particular uses are taken. With uncertainty, this *ex ante* planning process must involve judgement as well as a capacity for arithmetic; there is no longer any reason why different individuals, working as they must in an atmosphere of doubt and with incomplete information, should make the same assessments or reach the same decisions even in the unlikely event of their acting on the basis of identical data. That is, the *ex post* distribution of factors between uses at any time is determined not only by factor-mobility but also by the skill of those who plan the use of those factors *ex ante*.

In these circumstances, the entrepreneurial function cannot be treated simply as a factor of production rewarded in similar fashion to other factors. The decision-taking process is concerned with the selection and implementation of the production plans which, in the view of those taking the decisions, offer combinations of riskiness and expected net revenue superior to those offered by any alternative plans considered. But the implementation of any plan at all involves a risk that the actual revenues and outlays achieved *ex post* will differ from the *ex ante* forecasts that provided a basis for action. This risk is borne by those whose resources are utilized in implementing the plan (the 'owners'). The 'owners' and the 'decision-takers' need not be identical. The possible combinations of the functions of ownership and planning control (decision-taking) are clearly very numerous, and the returns to risk-bearing and to the planning function are difficult if not impossible to separate in practice, since individuals may share both functions in varying degrees. But the separation is clear in principle.

The reward of the decision-taking function will be that part of the earnings of decision-takers that is not directly dependent upon the *ex post* success of their *ex ante* planning activities. So regarded, the return to such decision-taking can be treated, like normal profit in the competitive model, as an outlay on a productive factor. But the rewards offered to individual decision-takers will reflect the view taken by owners of their relative abilities; there can be no question of their being treated as homogeneous. The return to risk-bearing, on the other hand, cannot be treated as an outlay at all; its reward is the *ex post* (achieved) excess of revenues over outlays (net revenue) in plans actually implemented. It is in no sense a hire-payment for a factor, depending as it does upon the ability to obtain a return from the utilization of factors greater than the hire payments that have to be made to those factors. The size of the return obtained is directly determined by the efficiency with which planning decisions are taken *ex ante* and by the attitude of risk-bearers to ventures of different degrees of riskiness.

Since net revenue is the return to the essential economic function of risk-bearing, but cannot be treated as an outlay on a factor, it follows that, if factors of production are to be ideally distributed between uses, the total revenues obtained by firms (*ex post*) should be greater than their total outlays and not equal to such outlays as in the conditions of the perfectly competitive model. Also, the 'normal profit' principle cannot be satisfactorily replaced, as a condition of the welfare 'ideal', by a requirement that the net revenues obtained by different firms should be equated *ex post*. The competitive process does provide a check on the undue divergence of the net revenues actually obtained from different kinds of productive activity, by directing activity towards avenues in which large net revenues seem likely. But even with complete freedom for potential producers to enter any market they wish there is no reason to expect that competition will, or (from the point of view of an 'ideal' factor-distribution) should, result in a general equality of achieved net revenues. Net revenue depends upon the individual skill of risk-bearers and decision-takers and upon their attitude to risk. If the abilities and risk-attitudes of these individuals differ, then net revenues must also be expected to differ. A welfare principle of net-revenue equalization, in accord with the general principle of factor-price equalization, would thus be valid only in a society in which risk-bearers and decision-takers were of precisely equal ability and took the same attitude to risk. Such a situation being unlikely, it seems better to substitute the more realistic, if less precise, formula that some net revenue must be obtained if the employment of factors of production in any use is to be justified, and that some means (such as the competitive process) is necessary to limit the extent of the divergences between the net revenue obtained from different kinds of productive activity.

If this argument is accepted, then a new dilemma arises for public utility pricing policy. The need for skill in making production plans, and the risks involved in implementing those plans, are not peculiar to one form of economic organization. They do not disappear because an industry becomes a public utility; simply, the risks are transferred from private owners to the community as a whole. In respect of decision-taking, no insuperable difficulties need arise; so long as there is a large private sector, suitable individuals can be hired at prices determined by their earnings in private industry, and their hire-prices treated as outlays. The only difficulty in this respect is the discovery of an incentive to efficient *ex ante* planning activity that will replace the association of reward with achieved net revenue generally used in private industry. But risk-payments cannot be treated in this way; they are not simply factor-outlays. If public utilities are not expected to earn some net revenue, as is the case with the 'rules' so far discussed, then factors of production will be utilized in plans that would not be implemented in private industry because the expected returns were too small. On the other hand, public utilities will often have considerable powers of mon-opoly, so that the competitive process is not available as a check upon the means utilized to obtain revenues. Consequently, if they are required to earn a net revenue, utilities may do so simply by using their monopoly power to raise prices. Some increases in *ex ante* planning efficiency may (but need not) also be stimulated, by the need to reach a more difficult target. Thus there would appear to be some justification for the view that if a public utility, required to achieve a specified net revenue, did so solely by exercise of its monopoly power over prices, yet the need to raise the revenue might serve a useful 'welfare' purpose by checking the over-expansion of the public utility enterprise relative to enterprises in private industry of a similar degree of riskiness. But there seems to be no 'right' net revenue that all utilities should be required to earn in all circumstances, since public utilities differ both in riskiness and in the extent of their monopoly power.

The introduction of considerations of uncertainty also draws attention to the problems that would arise for utility managers concerned with interpreting and administering 'rules' of the type so far discussed. These problems are particularly important in the case of rules that do not require costs to be covered. For example, the investment principle, interpreted in *ex ante* planning terms, requires that managers, when deciding whether or not to create an asset, should base their revenue estimate upon the system of prices (discriminatory or not) that they would expect to maximize such revenues. The asset should be created if any plan shows a potential (*ex ante*) excess of revenues over outlays. But if no charge is made for the use of the asset once created, then the plans that prompted its creation will never be implemented. There will therefore be no means of checking upon the efficiency with which the investment decisions are made. This position will be aggravated by the fact that once charges for the use of durable assets cease to be made, no guidance can be obtained from the success of *ex post* (implemented) plans when considering newly current (*ex ante*) plans, since the revenues obtained from implemented plans are not an indication of the valuations placed upon the durable factors by consumers. It is difficult to believe that such a situation would be conducive to efficiency in planning the use of factors and hence in the *ex post* (achieved) distribution of factors between uses. Similar problems arise with the marginal-cost rule. The marginal-cost–price relationship becomes a manager's opinion about the results of a marginal increase in factor-use in the alternative *ex ante* plans considered by him.[29] There is consequently no possibility of any outside authority checking upon whether a general instruction to implement the marginal-cost rule is being followed, quite apart from the other shortcomings of such a policy. Considered together with the proposition advanced earlier, that what is treated as marginal cost must depend upon the length of the planning period specified, this suggests that the marginal-cost rule could only be made intelligible in an environment of uncertainty if the general rule were replaced by specific individual directions to managers. Such directions would take the form of an instruction to ignore the estimated replacement costs of particular specified durable assets when deciding price policy, which should otherwise aim at the recovery of all outlays. But this would amount to the replacement of the marginal-cost rule by average cost (or multi-part) pricing, associated with a specific subsidy.

Summary and conclusions
It must be concluded that the welfare criteria give rise to no unambiguous general rule for the price and output policy of public utilities, such that for the given distribution of income to which the welfare model refers obedience to that rule must achieve an ideal use of resources by the utility. An instruction to price at marginal cost, if it was to be intelligible, would need to be supplemented by a specific statement of

what costs were to be ignored when fixing prices, in the case of each utility, so that the general 'rule' would effectively be replaced by average cost (or multi-part) pricing and specific subsidies decided separately for each utility. Furthermore, value-judgements about income distribution are unavoidable with marginal-cost pricing. Average cost or multi-part pricing can solve some of the problems, but only if there are no important common costs, or if the 'club' principle can be justified in individual cases. In any case, any policy 'rule' adopted would need adjustment to take account of uncertainty; an optimum use of resources requires that utilities should earn an excess of revenues over outlays, and there is no simple principle by reference to which the appropriate net revenue to be earned on account of the risk-factor can be decided. Failure to require an excess of revenues over outlays encourages the use of resources by utilities that could be better employed elsewhere, but a net revenue requirement may be met by the exploitation of the monopolistic position of the utility concerned. Consequently, uncertainty considerations also require the abandonment of general 'rules' and the separate determination of pricing policy in respect of each individual utility.

These negative conclusions have an important positive aspect. The failure to establish general pricing rules does not mean that the government need take no pricing decisions. Rather, given the existence of public utilities, it has to consider each utility individually, and decide policy in respect of some or all of the following matters in respect of each one:

1. The net revenue that the utility should be expected to earn.
2. Whether it is considered desirable explicitly to encourage the short-period use of particular durable and specific factors and, if so, what form the requisite subsidization shall take.[30]
3. The nature and extent of the discriminatory pricing to be permitted. That is, if there are common costs, whether these can be satisfactorily allocated by the free use of a 'club' principle without this implying a compulsory and undesirable redistribution of income by the utility managers. If the 'club' principle is not appropriate, then a decision has to be taken as to what system of charges would best accord with the government's general policy in regard to income distribution.
4. Whether, quite apart from the considerations at (2) and (3), the industry concerned is thought suitable for use as a means of redistributing income, as a part of the general system of indirect taxes and subsidies. In this regard, of course, public utilities differ from other

industries only in that they are more likely to become the subject of government policy for other reasons,[31] and in that they provide a convenient method of achieving these 'indirect' income redistributions that some economists consider must be one of the purposes of public finance.[32]

Clearly, the decisions taken in the case of each utility must be a reflection of the particular attitude of the government concerned. It would therefore appear that, failing some universally acceptable theory of the *public* economy by reference to which policy could be decided (and the possibility of such a theory is doubtful), economists would find their efforts better rewarded if they ceased to seek after general pricing rules and devoted attention to the examination of the policies actually adopted by governments, in order to discover their effects and make clear to the government and to the electorate the nature and consequences of the policies actually being pursued. That is, the economists' *general* recommendations need to be concerned not with general pricing rules, but rather with the availability of information about policy and with the methods adopted to keep that policy under review.[33]

Notes

1. I am grateful to Professor H. G. Johnson, to Mr. T. Wilson, and to colleagues at the London School of Economics for reading and criticizing drafts of this Chapter.
2. There is a good deal of literature on this subject. For a useful first list the reader is referred to the end of the lucid survey of the topic by Professor E. H. Phelps Brown in chapter viii of his book, *A Course in Applied Economics*. Cf. also G. F. Thirlby, 'The Ruler', *South African Journal of Economics*, December 1946; William Vickrey, 'Some Objections to Marginal Cost Pricing', *Journal of Political Economy*, 56 (1948); Gabriel Dessus, 'The General Principles of Rate Fixing in Public Utilities', *International Economic Papers*, No. 1 (translation of a report presented to the Congress of the Union Internationale des Producteurs et Distributeurs d'Énergie Électrique, 1949); and T. Wilson, 'The Inadequacy of the Theory of the Firm as a Branch of Welfare Economics', *Oxford Economic Papers* (February 1952). This list is not comprehensive.

    The historical development of the rules and their analytical origins is set out in two articles by Nancy Ruggles: 'The Welfare Basis of the Marginal Cost Pricing Principle' and 'Recent Developments in the Theory of Marginal Cost Pricing', *Review of Economic Studies*, Nos. 42 and 43 (1949–50).

    Specific references have been given in the text only where articles are of particular relevance to the issue concerned.
3. The scepticism is by no means universal: e.g. The *Report of the Committee on National Policy for the use of Fuel and Power Resources* (Cmd. 8647), 1952 (Ridley Report), considered the question of whether coal should be priced at marginal cost, and half the members of the Committee in fact favoured the use of some form of marginal-cost pricing.
4. This assumption is of course highly unrealistic; there are also tenable arguments for the view that it is internally inconsistent (cf. e.g. J. Wiseman, 'Uncertainty, Costs, and Collectivist Economic Planning', *Economica*, May 1953, p. 120). For the purposes of this article, the model is accepted for the present and criticism is developed

within its assumptions. The consequences of relaxation of the foresight assumption are discussed below.

5. For a critique of this collectivist 'rule' and of the model from which it derives, cf. Wiseman (ibid.).

6. H. Hotelling, 'The General Welfare in Relation to Problems of Taxation and of Railway and Utility Rates', *Econometrica*, 1938. Hotelling's paper was stimulated by the much earlier work of Dupuit, around 1844. The relevant papers have been collected and reprinted with comments by Mario di Bernardi and Luigi Einaudi, 'De l'Utilite et de sa Mesure', *La Riforma Sociale*, Turin, 1932. One of the most interesting papers, 'On the Measurement of Utility of Public Works', *Annales des Ponts et Chaussees*, 1844, is published in translation in *International Economic Papers*, no. 2.

7. Cf. (*inter alia*) J. E. Meade, 'Price and Output Policy of State Enterprise', *Economic Journal*, 1944, pp. 321–8, and 'Rejoinder', pp. 337–9; P. A. Samuelson, *The Foundations of Economic Analysis*, p. 240; R. H. Coase, 'The Marginal Cost Controversy', *Economica*, n.s., 1946, pp. 169–82; H. P. Wald, 'The Classical Indictment of Indirect Taxation', *Quarterly Journal of Economics*, 1945, pp. 577–97; I. M. D. Little, 'Direct *v*. Indirect Taxes', *Economic Journal*, 1951, pp. 577–85.

8. There is implicit in Hotelling's argument (and in that of writers who have supported him) the view that the welfare criteria can be extended to cover situations involving changes in the distribution of income. Some attempt has been made to support this position by reformulating the compensation principle (that a decision about a particular measure can be made only if all who would lose by it can be, and in fact are, compensated for their loss) in such a way that only the *possibility* and not the *fact* of compensation is necessary for an economic policy to be accepted as beneficial. However, it has been amply demonstrated that interpersonal comparisons cannot be avoided in this way (cf. M. W. Reder, *Studies in the Theory of Welfare Economics*; I. M. D. Little, *Critique of Welfare Economics*; W. J. Baumol, *Welfare Economics and the Theory of the State*, and the references cited therein). The debate will not be discussed in the text; all that has to be established is that the simultaneous decisions referred to therein are unavoidable, and that the welfare criteria provide guidance about only one of those decisions.

9. The distinction between this type of indivisibility and *technical* indivisibility is not always made clear in the literature (for a clear separation, cf. e.g. Phelps Brown (op. cit.) and Coase (ibid.)).

   In contrast with the present section, the discussion of the 'club' principle in the next section will be conducted with reference mainly to technical indivisibility. Such indivisibility amounts to no more than the fact that the whole of a productive factor must be employed in order to obtain *any part* of the total product of that factor, so that if the factor is an economic good it must have *current* alternative uses, and therefore a price (e.g. if a railway carriage can be attached to different trains, opportunity costs are incurred in attaching it to any one train. But no opportunity costs may be incurred in allowing one more passenger to travel once the carriage is attached).

10. Dupuit's argument against bridge tolls (op. cit.) is the *locus classicus* of this argument.

11. Cf. Wilson (ibid.).

12. It will be appreciated that arguments based on *technical* indivisibility raise similar considerations.

13. In the competitive market case, all consumers are faced with the same system of prices: in Wicksteed's phrase, the 'terms on which alternatives are offered' are the same for all. In the other, since discrimination is admitted, each individual is considered to be faced with a different price for the purpose of deciding whether or not to make the investment. If such prices were subsequently charged, they would involve a change in the distribution of real income, and would fall under the same strictures about interpersonal comparison as the marginal-cost rule. That is,

a decision taken in accordance with the investment principle might be considered as being partly concerned with the consequences for consumption of the public utility product in question of a change in the distribution of real income. But it would appear that in this respect, as with the advocacy of marginal-cost pricing, the income redistribution is treated as a problem separable from, and in some way inferior to, that of income size (as expressed in the welfare 'ideal').

14. An illustration may help to make the point clear:

A government, having decided to build a bridge out of revenue raised by taxation, might offer the services of the bridge free and ignore the source of the initial revenues in framing subsequent tax policy. Alternatively, it might decide to charge tolls for (say) twenty years, accepting the reduction in use (i.e. in total income) in the interests of compensating those who had to make the initial sacrifice, or it might decide upon some other combination of current financing and compensation. The economist is without adequate criteria to judge between these alternatives.

15. There could of course be more than two parts, depending upon the nature of the fixed factors. To introduce more simply adds complexity without affecting the logic of the argument.

16. A model used by R. H. Coase (ibid.) gives the essentials of the argument very clearly. The model is concerned with current (technical) indivisibility only, problems of time and of common costs being abstracted therefrom. In the model, a number of roads radiate from a central market, and there is one consumer on each road. All costs are assumed to be currently incurred, and each consumer purchases a combination of the market product and the transport service necessary to deliver it. Transport units are sufficiently large to carry any one consumer's requirements. Thus, while the transport service is *indivisible*, in that extra units of product can be carried without cost, yet there are *no common costs* since one van serves only one customer and the transport cost is attributable to that consumer. In these conditions, Coase argued, the price charged should comprise a fixed charge for the transport service and a price per unit for the product. Total costs are then covered, and the additional payment for extra consumption is equal to the price of the product only (i.e. to marginal cost).

17. Indivisibility need not imply the existence of such costs, though their presence must imply indivisibility.

The nature of the complications caused by common costs can be illustrated by replacing Coase's road-system (n. 16 above) by a ring road, with the market at the centre and one van serving a number of customers around the circumference, which the van can join at any point. Clearly, the pricing problem now becomes much more complex.

18. In the conditions of the modification of the Coase model (n. 17 above), these limits (for any one consumer) would be the total cost of providing the service ('indivisible' transport cost plus cost of goods purchased), on the one hand, and the cost of the goods alone on the other. If there were also variable costs associated with the transport service (e.g. petrol cost), then the lower limit would have to be increased by the minimum cost of transport between the consumer in question and the next nearest consumer.

19. The problem becomes even more intractable if time is introduced into the analysis, so that the 'common costs' being considered can become past outlays on *temporally* indivisible assets. This kind of question cannot suitably be discussed without relaxing the assumptions of the competitive model. The present section therefore ignores those questions of time, which are more fully treated in the following section of the article. It will be appreciated that the criticisms of the two-part tariff and the 'club' principle in the present section are in no way invalidated by this simplification.

20. The 'club' argument might indeed be stated in the form that there is some distribution of income, different from the existing one, which would induce consumers to cover the costs of the utility without the need for differential charges, and that this distribution must be superior to the existing one because consumers will

'voluntarily' bring it about if allowed to do so. This form of statement brings out the similarity between the 'club' principle and the investment criterion and compensation principle (n. 8) discussed earlier; it is therefore not surprising to find that they have similar weaknesses.

21. An illustration used by Phelps Brown (op. cit., p. 260) makes the point very well; poor families in an area may be willing to pay more towards the provision of a playground than richer families in the same area, but there is no presumption that a government will agree that they should. The welfare criteria provide no guidance in such cases since they offer no means of choice between income distributions.

22. These criticisms are the more striking when the restrictive assumptions of the analysis are recalled; the 'offers' made by consumers must be quite independent, since otherwise there may be no possibility of an 'agreed' set of prices because 'club' members insist on relating their own offers to the amounts others will be expected to pay. Further, there is no *logical* reason why only one system of prices should satisfy the 'club' principle; what happens, e.g. if the amounts offered to meet standing charges are greater than the total of common costs, but only total cost is to be recovered? In these cases, where more than one set of prices would satisfy the conditions, someone will have to choose between them. Value judgements must be made in the process, and it is difficult to understand why the government should accept those of the utility as superior to its own.

The false plausibility of the argument for voluntary redistribution through the 'club' arises from the application of a logical system concerned solely with individual choice and taking no account of the existence of a government with coercive powers, to a situation where governments have to take decisions involving economic matters outside the scope of individual choice. Some attempt has indeed been made to 'fit' the behaviour of the public economy into the individual choice (welfare) analysis, by treating the whole of the economy as a 'club'. This brings out the weakness and unrealism of the 'club' argument even more forcefully than the discussion above; it leads to advocacy of an 'ethically neutral' system of government income and expenditure, such that the size of the taxes paid and the public services consumed by individuals would be determined by the free agreement of the citizens (taxpayers and consumers) themselves, and to the suggestion that those unwilling to pay such taxes should be treated as 'pathological' (see F. Benham, 'Notes on the Pure Theory of Public Finance', *Economica*, 1934, pp. 453–4, and, for a critical discussion, Musgrave, 'The Voluntary Exchange Theory of the Public Economy', *Quarterly Journal of Economics*, November 1949).

23. If, for example, a man wishes to fly to Scotland to visit a sick relative, but cannot quite afford to charter an aeroplane at £30 for the trip, it may be possible to find a prospective rail traveller who is willing to pay £10 to share the air trip. The same (physical) service thus costs each traveller a different amount, but each prefers to make the payment and take the service rather than take the services to be obtained by using the market in any other way.

24. e.g. in the illustration given (n. 23) the travellers could themselves decide whether to travel separately or together, could choose between a variety of competing means of transport, and could decide between various offers of aeroplanes for hire.

25. A good example is given in Part III (pp. 94–145) of R. S. Edwards, *Co-operative Industrial Research*. Here the common service is research for a group of firms with a common interest in the results. Firms can, within broad limits, control the direction of research activity, the distribution of benefits between members, and the methods by which common costs are covered. There is also a possibility of using the market as an alternative to the 'club'. But it is also not without interest, in view of the earlier argument about the role of government (see p. 58), that a decision had to be made as to whether membership should be made compulsory, because the benefits of the co-operative research are not always easily confined to members of the 'club'.

26. The difference between the two types of 'club' might be put in this way: in the

second type, unlike the first, the members of the 'club' are not automatically members of the committee, although they are still in a strong position to influence its decisions.

27. The method of analysis adopted in this section is similar to that used by G. F. Thirlby, (ibid.). Cf. also Wilson (ibid.) and Wiseman (ibid.).

28. It is not suggested that the unsatisfactory treatment of uncertainty is the only reason for objection to the perfectly competitive model and to the welfare criteria. In particular, there has been considerable and cogent criticism of the validity of the simple welfare model as an explanation of the process and nature of individual choice (cf. e.g. I. M. D. Little, op. cit., and W. J. Baumol, op. cit.). However, such criticism need not concern us here. There is still point in discussing the use of resources in terms of choice, and the logic of the 'rules' can be destroyed even accepting the conceptions of the simplest welfare analysis.

29. For further discussion of this cf. Wilson (ibid.), and 'Price and Outlay Policy of State Enterprise', *Economic Journal*, December 1945, Thirlby (ibid.), and Wiseman (ibid.).

30. In general the desire of governments to give this type of encouragement seems likely to be greater the longer the relevant planning period and the more random and imprecise the distribution of the benefits and losses concerned.

   An example of a suitable case might be a change of a permanent nature in the geographical environment, as through the diversion of a river.

31. A question of this type inevitably arises, e.g. when a utility ceases to be able to cover costs at its present size as a consequence of changes in the economic environment, so that a decision has to be taken as to whether it should be subsidized, or should simply cease to be treated as a public utility at all, and competition allowed to determine its future size and operations. This is perhaps a not unrealistic way of describing the current position of the British railway industry.

32. Cf. e.g. J. Margolis, 'A Comment on the Pure Theory of Public Expenditures', *Review of Economics and Statistics*, November 1955.

33. The preceding analysis would appear to furnish sound arguments, for example, for treating British public utility pricing policy as part of indirect tax policy, and (possibly), for providing opportunity for review and discussion of the policies of important utilities along with the rest of tax policy at the time of the annual budget.

References

Rowley, C. K. (ed.) (1972), *Readings in Industrial Economics, Vol. 2, Private Enterprise and State Intervention*. London, Macmillan.

4   The Political Economy of Federalism: A Critical Appraisal*

Foreword

This chapter was written in 1964, but first published in 1987. When I took appointment at the University of York (January 1964), I was already committed to spend some months in Ottawa, as a consultant to the Canadian Royal Commission on Taxation. The chapter was written for the Commission. A couple of years later, long after I had returned to York, it was decided that the Commission could not publish it because it breached their terms of reference, which precluded discussion of the principles of federal–provincial relations. Although free to do so, I did not prepare the paper for submission elsewhere. In its original form, it needed shortening to meet journal requirements. I felt that other material was already appearing dealing with the formal analytical issues; and I had myself moved on to other things. But the treatment of the political decision process, and the idea that policy objectives should themselves emerge from it, did not appear elsewhere. For this reason I kept it 'alive' in manuscript form, and used it in particular with graduate students. It provided the structure for Bernard Dafflon's thesis, subsequently published, which develops for the Swiss federation the kind of interlocking committee structure proposed in the paper (Dafflon, 1977).[1] The paper was finally published when I sent a copy to a colleague who had come to share my interest in the problems of multi-tier government. He read it also with an editor's eye, and decided that, however archaic the formal analysis and references, the discussion of decision processes, far from being out-of-date, would be

* *Government and Policy* (1987), Vol. 5.
Editor's note: This paper was originally prepared for the Canadian Royal Commission on Taxation (1965). It has obtained very wide citation and currency, but has never been published and hence has never been available in a definitive or easily accessible form. It is reproduced here in an edited and amended form, in order to provide easy access and to allow its arguments to reach a wider audience than has been hitherto possible. The author and editor acknowledge that the intellectual debate in this field has now moved forward very considerably. But since the main issues of debate in this paper are still relevant to contemporary concerns, Wiseman has been coerced into making the paper more generally available in a form close to its original format. The author is, however, preparing as part of a book a much longer discussion of the debate contained in this paper.

regarded as novel by many. It was at his instigation that the article was published (see Editor's Note).

I have placed the paper in chronological sequence of writing, both because it reads more naturally there, and because it more adequately reflects the evolution of my own thinking. I came to an interest in federal problems by way of a more parochial concern: the finance of local government in the UK. Interest in this topic was a natural consequence of my teaching in public finance. But I found the literature perplexing. Financing of local authorities came from a local property tax (the local rate) and central government subsidies, the size of which was determined by complex grant formulae. I found myself faced with a whole new jargon and conceptual framework, and with prevalent notions such as 'equalization' which, while clearly concerned in some way with notions of equity, were difficult to fit into the orthodox language and habit of mind of neo-classical economics. The (largely American) literature of fiscal federalism, to which I turned for enlightenment, provided more new questions than it did answers, and opened up a whole new field of intellectual interest.

At the time this paper was written, I was clearly concerned to integrate my interest in cost and decision into the study and teaching of the problems of public finance which were my present obligation, and saw that this might be the route to the theory of government behaviour that I was beginning to see to be needed. But while the explicit introduction of the decision process is a clear advance, there is still a good deal of ambiguity. My dissatisfaction with the normative prescriptions of economists for fiscal federalism is manifest; the goals of the federation are to emerge from the deliberations of the decision-makers themselves, working through the proposed committee structure. But I have clearly not freed myself from the endemic, if usually unrecognized, paternalism of neo-classical economists, which permits the individualism of choice-through-markets to co-habit with the authoritarian specification of the proper goals of economic policy. Thus, I am willing to enunciate, in sympathy with the orthodox literature, the general nature of the equity and efficiency goals with whose details the committees are to be concerned.

I would be more careful (modest?) now. But I still think that the essential proposal was a sound one, and one that would perhaps get a more sympathetic hearing today than when first put forward.

Introduction
The purpose of this chapter is to survey the economic literature which is concerned with federal public finance, with a view to illuminating

the relation between the politico-economic characteristics of federal countries and their public finance arrangements. It is conceived in the belief that federal policy in public finance cannot plausibly be divorced from the nature of federal–regional relations in general: the first is a particular manifestation of the second.[2] Furthermore, this is not a problem that can be escaped by considering federal public finance, for example, 'within the context of existing federal–regional relations'. It is not easy to envisage any significant changes in public financial arrangements that do not have implications for such matters as regional autonomy and the separation of powers. The most that can be expected of a sensible but 'neutral' approach, therefore, is that it should be focused upon discovering the implications of tax proposals, etc. for the economic well-being of the federal community, while it draws attention to the relation between the proposals discussed and the political and constitutional characteristics of the federation. That is, federal–regional relations cannot be ignored. But it is possible to avoid normative propositions about them, to try simply to show what types of relation are implied by the sorts of proposals economists have made for federal public finance, and to show how the economic and the political and the constitutional aspects of federalism are related.

In the event, we shall find that it is as difficult to derive policy-relevant normative propositions about the economics of federalism as it is to make similar pronouncements in the field of federal–regional political relations. For this reason, I shall conclude with a set of proposals in which I do not make firm recommendations for public finance policy, but simply suggest a procedure which it is believed might improve the efficiency with which policy decisions are taken. Since this procedure is comprehensible in itself, it might be asked whether the long survey of the literature which precedes it is really necessary. It has two strong justifications. First, many ideas will be discussed that have fairly common currency, so that a clear understanding of their nature and limitations, and a recognition of the complexities of the relevant issues, are essential for an understanding of the policy problem. Second, although the procedure described in the conclusion is simple enough in form, the reasons for its adoption, and the relevance of the suggested structure of committees to the important issues of policy, can be understood only if the underlying problems are themselves understood.

To put the matter in another way; for purposes of policy-making it is as important to be precise about the areas of disagreement as it is to identify the points of accord. If a reading of the text helped no one else, therefore, it is hoped that it would be of value to the members of the proposed policymaking committees; in reducing the time spent on irrelevancy and in directing their attention towards the substantial issues that must be resolved by the federal policies in the field of public finance.

Coverage and procedure

The first comprehensive discussion of federalism as a special problem of public finance was provided by Adarkar (1933). His and other early treatments were descriptive and normative in character. The approach was embracing in that it attempted to incorporate all aspects of federal finance – political and administrative as well as economic – that might bear upon public policy. Not surprisingly, this comprehensiveness was accompanied by a lack of precision. Thus Adarkar lists six 'essential features' of federal public finance, ranging from equity, and efficient use of resources, through to financial independence of the regions and administrative efficiency. These features of federal public finance are said to be the '*sine qua non* of its workability', but they are agreed to be 'divergent in character' and to provide no neat guide to public policy: 'it is difficult to set up a definite norm for a federal fiscal system from *a priori* principles.'

Later discussion has tended to concentrate upon economic aspects in a narrower sense, and particularly upon equity and economic efficiency in the federal context. This has provided illumination (though not agreement or plausible normative propositions), but at the cost of a formulation of the federal problem that is unduly narrow for purposes of practical policy.

For procedural convenience, the narrow context that is postulated in the economic literature which is developing will be accepted in the first instance, and the problems which arise will be considered within that context. It should be made clear that no attempt will be made to review all the literature; my concern is only with the development of the main strands of thought and the authors that are discussed are chosen because they exemplify relevant aspects of that development. The study will then be complicated by the introduction of problems associated with the economic dynamics of federalism, and then by the reintroduction of some of the essential political aspects of federalism that the economic literature which is conceived more narrowly either ignores or contradicts.

This procedure does some violence to the earlier studies just described, as they will be specifically considered only in relation to their contribution to our understanding of fiscal equity, which in their earlier treatment was one part of a larger whole. On the other hand, in the later sections of the paper I am explicitly concerned with some of the broader considerations to which these early studies gave emphasis, so that the whole exercise might, in some sense, be regarded as a rehabilitation of their general approach.

Economic aspects of federalism

The literature of federal public finance has evolved around the twin concepts of equity and economic efficiency. I shall consider in turn the development of ideas which concern each of these concepts. This separation is somewhat misleading. Few writers concerned with formulating an equitable system of federal public finance fail to pay lip-service to the need for economic efficiency, and vice versa. But much of the writing does have a distinct emphasis, which makes the separation plausible, and any resultant deficiency will in any case be remedied later, when equity and efficiency ideas are brought together.

Federalism and fiscal equity

The Pigovian approach   Adarkar and some later writers took their concepts of fiscal equity from the utilitarian approach to public finance that was developed by Pigou. More recently, Bhargava (1953, 1956) has suggested a more thoroughgoing application of the same ideas.

Essentially, the formulation extends the concept of diminishing marginal utility to the behaviour of governments. The community is treated as a unitary being whose government is its brain. As in the case of an individual, its concern is to relate the satisfactions obtained from its expenditures to their cost. To do this it is necessary to know what sacrifice is imposed upon individuals (and the community) by taxation. For this purpose, the writers being examined here extended the concept of diminishing marginal utility to embrace individual income; they invoked a 'law' of diminishing marginal utility of income, in which it was postulated that the satisfaction obtained by an individual from an increment of income diminished as his total income increased. They argued further that satisfactions could be compared – essentially, that individuals had an equal capacity for enjoyment of income.

These propositions serve to specify a role for government. The 'principle of least aggregate sacrifice' requires that the sacrifice involved in raising any volume of taxation, should be minimized, and this must occur when the *marginal* sacrifice for all individuals is equated, as the *rate* of sacrifice increases as the individual tax burden is increased. Equally, individual benefits from expenditures should be so distributed that the benefits from marginal expenditures are equated between persons – otherwise, aggregate benefit from any total expenditures could be increased by shifting expenditures from some (lower marginal benefit) recipients to others. Finally, the optimum aggregate tax-expenditure programme is given by the equalization of marginal sacrifice from the total tax yield with the marginal benefit from total expenditures.

As we shall shortly see, the intellectual foundations of this formulation are shaky. It was recognized to be artificially simple by most of the writers who used it, but was argued to be conceptually valuable. In fact, they did not carry its application to the problems of federalism very far. We can illustrate from a work of Maxwell (1946). Maxwell recognized that the 'unitary being' approach has deficiencies – for example, in dealing with public goods consumed in common. But he argued that it showed how, even in a unitary state, tax or expenditure functions might be performed at a local level, simply because, for example, the minimization of sacrifice implied the provision of services at lower cost, and this could be best ensured by local administration. This was equally true when one considered a federation, but there is no reason to expect that efficiency in raising revenues and in providing services will be coincidental. Thus, even in a federation in which all regions had the same natural endowments and the same level and distribution of incomes, implementation of the Pigovian principles might still require transfers of tax revenues from the federal government to the individual regions. The transfers would be *within* local areas, in the sense that the taxes raised in a region would pay its own 'subsidies'. The central government, that is, would act, on grounds of efficiency, as a sort of tax collecting and distributing agent on behalf of each region.

The problems multiply as the limiting assumptions are removed. Thus, Maxwell points out that the problems of economic heterogeneity among regions are compounded by federal constitutions, by political arrangements, and particularly by the requirement that each region shall count as one when decisions about common policy are made. The significance of these constitutional–political arrangements is discussed in some detail. For example, division of political powers cannot be regarded as 'unsatisfactory', he says, simply because it makes for policy difficulties. It is the essence of federalism. Lack of balance, and the general existence of log-rolling, back-scratching, and 'political' negotiation may be unfortunate, but they are the natural consequence of the constitutional form, and their existence must be accepted as part of the policy environment. Maxwell is led from this into discussion of such questions as the possibility of the use of grants to deal with the kind of problems he has raised. This discussion, although illuminating in itself, depends hardly at all upon the original Pigovian formulation for its conclusions; the unitary being remains curiously unaware of the politico-constitutional peculiarities of federal countries.

In this regard, Maxwell's is typical of the approach to federalism used by most of the writers being considered here; they are never willing to ignore what seem to be relevant issues in order to reach a conclusion. Bhargava tries to go a good deal further in the application of general principle.

The special problems of cooperative federalism in implementing a suitable public finance programme, he says, result from the coordinate and, to some extent, the independent powers of the regional governments. If the federal and the regional governments each obeyed independently the Bhargava rules (which follow broadly the Pigovian formulation just described), the result would be less than optimal for the federation as a whole. For it follows from the postulated principles of interpersonal utility comparability and of diminishing marginal utility of income that with a similar level of taxation the sacrifice imposed by an additional unit of taxation would be less in a richer state than in a poorer one. Similarly, the benefit from an increment of public expenditures would be smaller, as the need for public services is smaller when private incomes are higher. Consequently, the federal government must act in a 'coordinating capacity' to achieve 'economic equilibrium' by increasing the tax burden on the citizens of richer regions and by raising the level of expenditures in poorer regions. Federal taxes and expenditures must discriminate between regions, in order to make marginal benefits from combined federal and regional expenditures, and make marginal sacrifices from combined federal and regional taxation, the same for all federal citizens.

Bhargava accepts that these principles would be difficult to implement in a precise and practical way. He accepts also that the proposals would be unwelcome to those living in richer regions. But neither difficulty is regarded as overwhelming. As regards the question of implementation, there are a number of federal arrangements that he believes would facilitate suitable policies, these include: constitutional authority for the federal government to levy taxes on all citizens, including both direct and some indirect taxes, the possibility of a scheme of federal grants-in-aid, assignment of some sources of revenue to the regions, and constitutional provision for shared taxes, with quotas defined by reference to the specified general principles. Also, the expenditures of the federal government would have to be supplemented by discriminatory grants, in order to ensure, throughout the federation, equimarginal benefits from expenditures. In respect of the richer regions, they must simply be required to recognize that their objection to the scheme is invalid when the regions are considered as a group.

The contrast between this use of the Pigovian approach and the earlier uses is marked, and it derives effectively from a difference in attitude to the nature of federalism. Earlier writers took the politico-constitutional aspects of federalism as a constraint, and were unwilling to ignore them in formulating policy proposals. Bhargava sees the federal structure primarily as an instrument for the implementation of his normative rules. Regions may differ in customs, structure, aims, and endowments, but the federation is 'an association of states which cooperate like members of a family'. The federal government is quite clearly the head of the family and the master of its purse; for Bhargava, it is an essential requisite of satisfactory federalism that there shall be no constitutional hindrance to the implementation of the programme, which his analysis has shown to be necessary. As is shown below, Bhargava has not been alone among economists in his fitting the ends of constitutional federalism to the convenience of his normative economic model – or, indeed, in finding it convenient to adopt a strongly 'centralist' interpretation of the powers and the duties of the federal government.

The whole Pigovian approach, in any case, rests upon some assumptions that make it a dubious guide to public policy. At the general level, Buchanan and others have pointed out that the 'unitary being' is in fact a euphemism for an organic theory of the state. This must make the formulation unacceptable to those who reject such a theory, with its implication of a state with a being independent of, and taking primacy over, the wishes of the individual.

The argument is open also to objections at a more technical (economic) level. The general nature of these objections and their specific federal aspects are well known. It will be enough for present purposes to indicate the general nature of the difficulties.

The Pigovian approach requires acceptance of the propositions: (a) that there is a plausible concept of diminishing marginal utility (satisfaction), which can be applied to the satisfaction obtained by individuals from different sizes of money income; and (b) that different individuals have identical (or similar) capacities for the enjoyment of income. Both propositions are essential for the derivation of tax policies from the Pigovian approach, and to support argument for the use of the federal tax system, for example, to equalize income-distribution or to pursue regional equalization policies of the Bhargava type.

Many economists find both propositions unacceptable. Whereas they might be willing to accept (with reservations), some concept of personal, diminishing marginal satisfaction from consumption of individual commodities, they would be unwilling to generalize the proposition in order to allow it to embrace income as a whole. Diminishing satisfaction, from particular forms of consumption, is perfectly compatible with the scope of human wants as a whole remaining broadly unlimited. Additionally, even if this first proposition is accepted, there is still room to question the plausibility of the second which requires not only agreement that the wants of different individuals are the same kind of thing, but also that they are felt with similar intensity, and in a fashion that must always make an increment of income yield less satisfaction to a richer than to a poorer man, irrespective of differences in character, personality, background, etc.

Whatever view is taken of these objections, it is clear that, as Robbins (1935, p. 120) first pointed out, the Pigovian proposition about behaviour cannot be subjected to any kind of scientific test. Nor can the position be defended, as Adarkar attempted to, on grounds that the assumptions of the argument do not need to be verifiable in order for its conclusions to be valid – the conclusions are also incapable of empirical verification.

Ultimately, therefore, the Pigovian approach, whether in its older or more recent formulations, yields no propositions about tax equity that amount to more than the assertion of a particular attitude to social equality; tempered, in the case of most of the writers concerned, by recognition of the need to take account of other goals of public policy, which include in our context the goals (whatever they might be) of fiscal federalism. Thus, the approach can provide no useful guidance to practical decisions about federal tax policy, save for those who are willing to accept that attitude as an act of faith.

The equalization of fiscal pressure   A distinctive approach to equity in federal taxation was being formulated by Buchanan (1949, 1950) and Clement (1963) even before Bhargava's attempts to resuscitate the Pigovian concepts. Buchanan argued for an individualistic approach to the public sector and public finance, in which the state was not treated as a 'sentient organism'. Buchanan has attempted also to develop the argument, discussed here, to incorporate allocation as well as equity. These allocational implications will be taken up later in the appropriate context. The equity problem for Buchanan was one of devising a tax-and-expenditure system that ensured that individuals situated similarly (families, households) shall be similarly treated. If policy is guided by a benefit theory of taxation, he argued, then such equal treatment must take both taxes and public expenditures into account. If only taxes were considered, a progressive tax system might be argued to be the one to use, in order to produce a more equal distribution of income, but this need not be true if the benefits of public services are greater for the rich than for the poor. Similarly, a regressive tax can be egalitarian if used to preponderantly provide benefits for lower income groups.

Equalization of the tax-and-expenditure treatment, of individuals situated similarly, raises special problems in a federal context because of the separate taxing and spending activities of the individual states and of the federal government. To deal with this, Buchanan uses a concept of 'fiscal residuum' – that is, the individual's tax burden less the benefits he or she receives from public services. Buchanan argues that this residuum is the relevant magnitude for decisions about tax policy. Equity requires that the central fisc be used to equalize fiscal pressure (in this residual sense) on individuals situated similarly, irrespective of the particular region in which they might live.

Buchanan's equity argument, then, would provide a justification for what are effectively income-transfers through the agency of the federal government. It should be noted, however, that the transfers that he proposes are between *individuals* rather than between political units. The object of equity in federal fiscal arrangements is the equalization of the fiscal position of *individuals* whatever their location, and not, in any sense, the equal fiscal treatment of different political units.

Buchanan's formulation appears to avoid at least some of the difficulties of the Pigovian approach, but it does it by leaving them aside. Buchanan sees the equal treatment of equals, or what has come to be called *horizontal equity*, as 'an essential guide to the operation of a liberal democratic state, stemming from the same base as the principle of the equality of individuals before the law'. It should consequently be the 'specific long-run goal' of federal fiscal policy. He argues that it is therefore sensible to leave aside considerations of *vertical equity* (the equitable treatment of unequals), about which there is ample scope for disagreement, in order to concentrate upon the achievement of horizontal equity. But this distinction has no logical foundation. If it is agreed that there is no way of reaching agreement on the equitable treatment of unequals, how can we know that those agreed to be equal in other respects should be treated equally for tax purposes? If the proposition is not to be interpreted as a simple tautology, then it must rest upon a value-judgement about interpersonal capacities for enjoyment of income, which is of precisely the same character as the value judgement, about interpersonal utility comparisons, that underlies the Pigovian approach. It is a value-judgement that has a wide appeal, but this should not be allowed to obscure its lack of scientific foundation. It also must be recognized that a part of its appeal derives from obscurity, to be against equality is a little like not being against sin. Much more scope for disagreement arises when we try to agree the *objective charac-teristics*, in respect of which people should be equal for purposes of a decision on how to tax them. Nor is this position saved by Buchanan's analogy with the rule of law. The quotation given brings out that the law treats individuals equally despite differences between them in other respects – the analogy in the treatment of tax would seem to be the equal treatment of unequals!

Further problems arise when one turns to the treatment of benefits. It is of the essence of the public provision of goods and services that individuals cannot take decisions about their consumption in the same fashion that they decide between goods made available privately through the market place. First, decisions about how much and what kind of public goods to provide, and on what terms, are made by legislators rather than by private individuals. Second, many public goods (defence, national parks) are by their very nature consumed in common, so that there is no obvious or agreed way to impute their cost to individual citizens (this is also discussed in more detail later). But the outcome of Buchanan's computation of residua must be arbitrary on failure of agreement on this question; one will obtain quite different results, for example, if the benefits of public services are treated as being enjoyed equally by all members of the relevant fisc (regional or federal), or if these benefits are treated as accruing in proportion to individual income.

Even more difficult to deal with is the fact that if all levels of govern-ment levy taxes solely by reference to benefits received, then there can be no fiscal residua and hence no need for differential tax treatment of individuals by the central fisc. Such differential tax treatment can only arise, therefore, if the tax structures of states differ not because of different provision of benefits but because of different ideas about income-distribution (vertical equity). It follows that the need for correc-tion of fiscal residua derives solely from the different progressiveness of the tax systems of the individual states, and from the acceptance of the view that it is appropriate for the central fisc to compensate for such differences and so override the income-distributive ideas of local units. This reinforces the point made earlier with regard to the character of the federalism under discussion; although Buchanan rejects the utili-tarian approach, partly on grounds of its authoritarian overtones, his own formulation is also centralist in character. He is concerned with the fiscal treatment of *individuals*, and would use the powers of the federal government to subordinate or to offset different regional notions of fiscal equity. Thus, Buchanan has more in common with Bhargava, in this respect, than is at first apparent – they both postulate a 'weak' (centralist) form of federalism because such a form fits their theoretical construct. In so far as federal constitutions are explicitly designed to protect the rights of regions *per se*, and in so far as equity is interpreted as a matter of the relative treatment of different regions as well as of individuals, such a treatment must be inadequate as a guide to the policy of public finance.

Buchanan's position, as here described, has been modified in later discussion (see, for example, Musgrave, 1961). I return to this when I consider the allocational implications of his position. However, no substantial counter has been made to the criticisms of the equity aspects of the fiscal pressure approach, which are being made here.

Ethical neutrality   In a third approach to the equity problem, it is asserted that the economist has no authority to pronounce upon the objectives of federalism, and so should confine himself to *technical* advice, as to how specified objectives might be reflected in fiscal programmes. The most comprehensive treatment of this type is that of Musgrave (1961).

Musgrave restricts his discussion of ends to the suggestion of some possible federal objectives whose implications seem worthy of examination. Specifically, he distinguishes two broad approaches to the federal problem:

a.   that which treats the central problem of federal public finance as being the relation between the central fisc and the *groups of individuals* that comprise the various political regions within the federal fisc;

b.   that which concerns itself with the relation between the central fisc and *individual citizens*, irrespective of their residence.

Musgrave discusses the second approach only in a summarized form, primarily in order to bring out its centralist character and to offer critical comment upon the Buchanan approach to fiscal federalism.

The first approach requires that the federal government respect the tax policies decided upon by the regions, and that they leave the individual taxpayer at the fiscal mercy of his own region. But the federal government can, of course, by its own operations, influence the terms on which public services are provided at the regional level. For example, it may 'equalize' the fiscal operations of the various regions, where equalization is defined in any one of a number of possible fashions, or it may provide incentives to increase the general level of services provided by the regions, or it may use the central fisc to ensure minimum levels of (regional) services, irrespective of the contribution of regional finance, and so on.

Musgrave puts forward a set of 'plans' (grant-formulae) which relate the activities of the central fisc to the individual regions. The purpose of these plans is to influence the fiscal performance of the member regions, in one or other of the fashions just described. The plans have to be considered both from the point of view of their distributional and of their incentive implications. Additionally, to be analytically consistent the plans must allow for the federal taxes and transfers that are needed in order to implement any particular equalization scheme, etc., and for the clearing of the central budget which includes those taxes and transfers.

Musgrave describes six plans (grant arrangements) concerned with (income and need) equalization objectives and also a 'pure incentive' plan, variants of which could be integrated with one or other of the equalization plans. They are to be regarded as illustrative of the possibilities (since Musgrave implies no normative judgements), rather than as specific guides to policy. But it is this last aspect that is of interest here; to what extent, if at all, can this 'ethically neutral' approach contribute to policy-making?

It has certain obvious limitations. In the first place, the fact that the ends are given 'from outside' means that at least some part of the policy issue must already be settled before the grant-formulae can be discussed. This is hardly a criticism, as the restriction is deliberate, but it may not always be easy, in practice, to distinguish between questions of principle which are concerned with the *context* of a formula and questions of measurement. There is considerable room for disagreement as to the 'right' measure of comparative regional income for the purposes of grant equalization, and even more scope for argument as to the proper method of measuring regional need. These disagreements do not concern simply the statistical efficiency of different techniques of measuring a defined attribute, but are also because of different conceptions of what it is that is being, or should be, measured. Thus, the debate about ends is not as easily separated from the techniques of implementation in practice, as it can be in formal logic.

Additionally, Musgrave developed his specimen formulae under some very restrictive technical assumptions. Since these would need to be removed if the formulae were to be used as a basis for policy decisions, it is worth setting them out and commenting upon the problems they raise. Musgrave lists six significant limiting assumptions:

1. that there is only one type of regional service;
2. that taxes are borne by citizens of the collecting regions – that is, there is no exporting of the tax burden or shifting;
3. there are no 'spillovers', between regions, of the benefits for public services, in the sense that services paid for by some regions confer unrequited benefits on other regions;
4. there is no finance by borrowing;
5. there is full employment;
6. regions do not pursue 'strategic' policies, but try only to do as well as they can for themselves, within the framework that is specified.

What possibilities emerge as these assumptions are removed? In turn:

1. Musgrave believes this introduces complication but nothing more; there would be a requirement to use more than one index of need. But Musgrave may be overoptimistic about the facility with which this statistical exercise can be separated from the discussion of ends.
2. The possibility of shifting the taxes imposed by regions to other regional areas destroys much of the simplicity of the formulae. If taxes are so shifted, it would be necessary to determine the fraction of regional taxes that imposed a burden within that region, and use only this fraction as an index of regional tax effort. Musgrave argues that, unless there are matching 'spillovers' of benefits between regions, exported state taxes are an anachronism. But shifting may have to be taken into account as a practical problem – this involves laborious problems of measurement and new possibilities of the confusion of ends and means.
3. If there are spillovers, then the states must be able to tax outside their jurisdiction, or a central tax-transfer system must be used to make the necessary adjustments. The purpose of this procedure would simply be to prevent regional redistribution through spillovers, and in this sense it lies outside the problems presently being considered.
4. The possibility of loan finance is not regarded as important. If contributions are measured in terms of 'own' finance, whether from taxes or from loans, then the loan problem would work itself out in the long run.
5. Introduction of stabilization problems would complicate the analysis, says Musgrave, again without destroying its essential features. It might be necessary, for example, to permit the central budget to be cleared over the period of the economic cycle, rather than annually. But the complications, created by shifting and by stabiliz-

ation policies, would become much greater in the (not unlikely) event of these policies being treated as having an equity aspect (that is, as involving ends). I shall discuss this possibility further in the next section.

6. Musgrave recognizes that strategic behaviour by regional governments must be expected in the real (policymaking) world, particularly in the case of plans in which a region's own policies may produce significant reactions. This possibility must, of course, reinforce the practical ends/means difficulties just described.

These limitations should not, however, prevent recognition of the positive possibilities of the 'ethically neutral' approach. Particularly, the bringing together of several objectives in a common formula which itself must be consistent with the overall budget, is a valuable way of broadening the context of policy debate, and so of minimizing the extent to which discussion runs at cross purposes, because those concerned have different ends in mind, and do not appreciate the relation between them. At the same time, the formulation can perform the important function of bringing out the *actual implications* of particular proposals, for such things as regional income redistribution – Musgrave demonstrates convincingly that these are by no means always obvious.

Musgrave suggests that the approach has practical relevance for the assessment of the existent grant systems of federal countries. Moreover, it is valuable in suggesting a (nonnormative) *formalization* of the policy-making process of federal public finance, which might provide a suitable context for efficient decisionmaking. This is no trivial matter; it will be argued later that it is at the core of the economist's contribution to the policy problem.

Federalism and resource allocation

Programmes for optimum allocation   The discussion of allocation can be suitably opened from Buchanan's 'fiscal pressure' approach. Buchanan argued in his original paper that his proposals not only would ensure fiscal equity, but also would be compatible with efficient use of resources, as failure to equalize fiscal pressure (and to relate it to income from capital as well as from labour) must result in the different tax-expenditure treatment of individuals who are otherwise distinguishable only by their geographic location. The consequence would be factor movement towards areas of least fiscal pressure, which would be less productive areas from the point of view of the community.

A different view was taken by Scott (1950), whose 'pure' treatment of the problem of the allocation of federal resources generated a debate of some interest (see Scott, 1952; Buchanan, 1952a, 1952b). Scott takes a particular, and narrow, view of the objectives of federal public finance. Thus, the 'financial dilemma' of differing expenditure responsibilities and differing revenue sources, to which such writers as Maxwell and Adarkar direct their attention, Scott dismisses as a short-term problem which should not be allowed to obscure the question of long-term policy. All federal countries, he says, have areas of low average income per capita. The usual explanation of this is by reference to differences in resource endowment, and this seems to incorporate endowment both of natural resources and of other forms of capital. Federalism implies the local administration of some functions, whether for reasons of efficiency, history, tradition, ethnic differences, or whatever. In respect of these functions, each province sets its own standards and levies its own taxes. As there are poor and rich regions, the low personal incomes of the poor regions will prevent the provision of as high a level of services as in the rich regions because it will be impossible to levy the necessary taxes. The poorer regions cannot afford the same level of amenities as the richer regions; there are large differences in the *general* possibilities of consumption, and this includes consumption of public goods. Such a situation is not abnormal for a group of separate countries living in a 'Balkan' relationship, but it is generally considered to be incompatible with the idea of nationhood. The problem of federal finance is that the extension of the relevant communal services to poor regions must involve a departure from the requisites of efficient government finance, as it is seen from other points of view. In particular, it must involve a loss of central revenues to other uses or an undue intervention in local affairs. The difference between a federation and a single unitary state is that in the second, transfer from richer to poorer areas can be made by methods which do not incorporate a geographical criterion, whereas in a federal country the use of conditional or of unconditional grants to regions must inevitably be done by methods which do.

The inefficiency with which Scott is concerned does not relate to tax administration or financial responsibility, but simply to the use of community resources. Inter-governmental transfers of the kind described are, he argues, incompatible with the maximization of income per head for the community as a whole. Ideal allocation of resources requires that capital and labour be combined in such a fashion that the marginal product of similar labour is equalized everywhere. For this to be so, transfers of labour from place to place, or from job to job, should be controlled by differentials in real wages (and this includes relative amenity). (For our purposes, this real wage can be thought of as the sum of the other returns to labour, plus the workers' rights as a local citizen in the relevant area.) Transfers of government income from place to place must reduce the incentive to mobility, and by doing so must reduce the size of national product. The argument may be valid as stated; a federation can in fact help mobility in a way that the unitary state cannot, as the second is obliged to provide the same level of amenities everywhere, and this also must weaken the influence of wage differentials. But the more appropriate contrast would be with the 'Balkan' area. There, no fiscal transfers occur from rich countries to poor countries. Emigration thus becomes sensible and, in the absence of barriers, will occur. Confederation, as such, alters nothing fundamental in this situation, but it does produce fiscal systems which incorporate arrangements for covering the deficits of poorer areas. These arrangements must reduce the pre-existing incentives to labour migration. Furthermore, the problem is likely to be self-perpetuating, insofar as the pressures to transfer income to the weaker regions will increase with an increase in the political power of those states, whilst the very provision of amenities for them, may increase the birth rate in the poor relative to that in the richer states.

It is apparent that the conflict between the Scott proposals and the Buchanan formulation turns at least partly upon differences in the postulated ends of federal fiscal activities. Scott himself recognizes this, but believes his own emphasis to be appropriate: 'the material end of a *federal* nation . . . must surely be in these days the production of a higher income collectively than could be achieved on a fragmentary basis.' Buchanan criticized this as unduly restrictive. He pointed out that no one else suggested that considerations of income distribution could be ignored when the federal fiscal arrangements are decided. Such a procedure would be contrary to accepted ethics; particularly as the transfers that Scott found objectionable would be to the poor.

Scott's argument raises also some interesting technical questions. He specifically excluded 'infant industry' situations. Although this exclusion preserves the logical validity of his argument, it also restricts greatly its relevance. The reasons for the existence of low-income states within a federation are clearly of primary importance when one attempts to decide whether income-transfers will be corrective, neutral, or distortive, in their effects on the use of resources. I shall return to this question below. Before this, we must turn to another aspect of the allocation problem.

The regional distribution of public services It will, by now, have become apparent that one of the central difficulties that writers on fiscal federalism have to face, is that of separating the 'benefit' aspects of the fiscal activities of governments (that is, those parts of the tax system that can be regarded as simply payments by the citizen for his consumption of public goods and services) from the rest. In this section I consider a recent attempt by Tiebout (1956), to relate the benefits received by citizens from public services to the costs incurred, and so to produce an 'optimum spatial patterning' of these services. The exercise is more useful in that it indicates the character of the problem, than in that it furnishes impeccable solutions.

Tiebout identifies fiscal federalism with the existence of multilevel governments. A normative approach to the problem must either study the economic consequences of a given political structure, or rank political structures by their 'economic efficiency'. He uses the second approach; political federalism is assumed neutral between different arrangements, and the purpose is to discover how to produce a system of taxes and benefits, that shall be ideal from the point of view of the provision of public goods. This approach involves some very restrictive assumptions. Tiebout starts from a situation in which there are no public authorities other than central government, and no public goods, and draws on the work of Lösch on industrial location, in order to specify the resultant spatial patterning of the production of private goods. The problem then becomes one of discovering how this patterning will be affected by the introduction of public goods. It is further assumed that the set of goods to be publicly provided, and the cost conditions of their production, are known, that the central government can establish such agencies as it wishes to produce them, and that there is no taxation, save by reference to benefits received; there are no tax-transfer redistributions between individuals or between regions.

The spatial aspect of the problem is important not only because there are transport costs in moving goods from points of production to points of consumption, but also because the benefits from public goods and services may not accrue equally to all the residents of a particular region. Thus, the benefits of some services (for example, those provided by soldiers or by police patrol cars) may accrue equally to all within the region served. The benefits of others may taper from the point of production – for example, firehouses, air raid sirens. Either of these types may have spillovers, in the sense that the provision of the service for a particular community provides benefits for or imposes costs upon citizens outside the community.

Tiebout sets out to discover how many 'branch governments' are needed to produce, in these various circumstances, an 'ideal' patterning of the production of public goods. He provides a formal solution for the case of a single 'pure' public good which provides uniform benefits, in circumstances in which individual tastes and incomes are uniform. Cost conditions will be affected by the size of the precinct served, and for any given precinct, actual costs of provision will be a function of the amount of service provided. From this information it is possible to specify an ideal size of precinct, and a volume and unit cost of the provision of the service. If the service is then 'priced' at average cost, all costs would be covered, all citizens would pay the same tax, the residuum (in Buchanan's sense) would be zero for all taxpayers, and the benefit principle would be fully satisfied.

The solution is less simple if the benefit of the service under consideration diminishes with distance from the point of production (the firehouse case). In this case, Tiebout suggests that all residents be asked to place a value on having a firehouse within specified distances of their home. It is not obvious, however, why all citizens need be interviewed, given the assumption made about tastes and incomes – one citizen could answer for all. From this information, together with data for the cost of the output of the different types of firehouse that could be built, one can compute a surplus of value over cost for each resident in respect of each type of firehouse. For each type, this surplus will be at a maximum with a particular size of precinct. But how to decide between the available types of firehouse? We might select, for example, that with the largest *total* surplus, of valuation of service, over cost, or that with the largest surplus in proportion to the cost per resident. Tiebout plumps for the second, for reasons that are not entirely clear. What is clear, however, is that the principle being used is different from that used in the previous exercise, and even more different from the principles affecting allocation of resources in the private sector of the economy, which are concerned with the equation of *marginal* cost (sacrifice) with *marginal* benefit (satisfaction).

Furthermore, even when this criterion has been decided upon, there remains the decision as to how to tax. The benefit principle requires that one tries to leave the taxpayer with a zero fiscal residuum, as well as covering the relevant costs. In fact, Tiebout fails to provide such a scheme. Rather, he suggests two possibilities: tax in proportion to shares in the total benefits (which diminish with distance from the firehouse), and tax so that surpluses are equalized for all. The first method makes individual surpluses proportional to taxes paid. The second equalizes the result of benefits less taxes. Neither is equivalent to a zero fiscal residuum. The solution takes also no account (as Tiebout recognizes) of the interdependence of the costs of the provision of services, and of the size and structure of population. Increases in population do seem to bring increased expenditures per capita, for particular purposes. But in the case of 'pure' public goods (which by definition are consumed in common) there is no agreed method of how to calculate whether the standard of service has changed when population changes, and if so, how. Tiebout cannot solve this problem, but argues that it should not be allowed to distract us from the other problems being considered here.

If answers can be found to the questions posed so far, a pattern of the provision of public services can be developed. There will be as many branch agencies for any one service as the exercise indicates to be optimal; national defence, for example, might have one, fire protection many local branches. Spillovers would not affect the solution, as the taste and income assumptions must cause them to cancel out.

The discussion becomes increasingly tenuous as these restrictive assumptions are removed. Even if we relax only the assumption about tastes the earlier solutions become unacceptable, and we are driven back upon such possibilities as the maximization of the total surplus relative to taxes. Additionally, this solution is implausible operationally, in that it requires the comparison of all possible cost structures for the production of public goods in all possible locations with the summation of the resultant benefits (marginal or total valuations?) for all individual citizens. As an alternative, Tiebout suggests that a varied pattern of public goods might be provided, and that citizens could be left to move towards those local combinations that they liked best: 'that people with similar tastes move together is a first principle of fiscal federalism'. Some similar solution is necessary to deal with the problem of variations in income. If people can choose their community, they will do so in the light of the pattern of services provided, and of their own expected share of the tax bill. Given a sufficient range of choice, and the costs of particular levels of service provision, Tiebout argues that an approximation to the optimal patterning will result from people of similar fiscal tastes moving together. In the real world, the 'solution' may be affected by deliberate attempts to inhibit movement and to create 'tax colonies' protected, for example, by zoning laws. All these possibilities are enhanced by the fact that those considering movement need not take the existing pattern of provision of public goods as given; but can negotiate to change it.

There remains the problem of spillovers. Residents of area B may benefit, for example, from mosquito spraying in area A, and so can reasonably be asked to pay some part of the cost. On the other hand, no one asked them whether the spraying should be done, and given heterogeneity of tastes and incomes, there is no way of assessing the value of the service for them. For such reasons as these, compensation for spillover normally has to be dealt with by higher levels of government, and by such rough-and-ready measures as the imposition, on all local areas, of minimum standards of provision (so that none can rely solely upon spillovers from their neighbours); associated with freedom for the local communities to exceed this standard, if they are willing to accept (or negotiate about) the consequent spillovers.

Although it is true that the problems of the provision of public goods may be easier to deal with if people of similar tastes and incomes are free to move into similar local areas, it might be questioned as to whether an argument as complex as that put forward by Tiebout is needed in order for the point to be taken. Furthermore, the very way the problem is formulated makes it difficult to apply the conclusions in the policy context of a constitutional federation. Tiebout's model allows for only one government with *political* authority; other public bodies are simply its instruments in the provision of public goods. Given this absence, from his formulation, of any legal separation of powers between political authorities, it can be reasonably argued that Tiebout is concerned with a special aspect of the problem of industrial location (relating to the production of public goods), rather than with the political economy of fiscal federalism.

Despite these deficiencies the article merits careful consideration, for two reasons. First, in its emphasis upon the problems of assessment of benefits and of costs, it directs attention to an aspect of the problem of resource allocation that otherwise would receive too little emphasis. This aspect is concerned with the fact that the separation of functions between layers of government has a technical (economic) aspect, as well as raising questions of administrative efficiency – the two are not independent but are correlative. At the same time, in a federation the policy problem concerns the division of functions and powers not between two levels but among at least three (federal, state, municipal), and the weight given to particular criteria may differ in accordance with the functions and levels of government under discussion. Although Tiebout himself effectively postulates the absence of a federal constitution; there is clearly a problem of the reconciliation of the issues of economic efficiency in provision, as he defines them, with the facts of political and constitutional (including constitutional–federal) life. Studies of this kind are available, and Tiebout has himself contributed to the literature (see, for example, Ostrom et al., 1961).

Second, the discussion of Tiebout's argument brings to light difficulties about the nature of public goods and the measurement of benefit, which bear upon the next problem to be discussed – the reconciliation of efficiency and equity.

The reconciliation of equity and efficiency

The Buchanan proposals   From the point of view of the guidance of public policy, the studies of equity and efficiency considered so far adopt a restrictive and, in significant ways, a misleading definition of the federal problem. Before I consider how the context of the discussion might be broadened, it will be useful to examine how far the equity and efficiency arguments adduced are capable of reconciliation within the specified framework. This will both provide a background, necessary for what follows, and indicate some of the ways in which a broader approach might be developed.

It has been seen that Buchanan took exception to Scott's exclusion of equity considerations from his discussion. In Buchanan's view, it would be more appropriate to give weight to the resource effects of federal fiscal policy, at most, alongside other considerations such as interpersonal equity and the preservation of minimum standards. He pursued the indicated exposition in terms of multiple objectives, however, only to the extent of attempting to reinforce his own position; that equity and efficiency could be reconciled within the context of his 'fiscal pressure' formulation, by the entire tax-expenditure structure being made geographically neutral. The amended argument is not free from obscurity. Its central point is that regional differences in income, etc. could arise for a number of reasons, and in at least some of these cases transfers of the Buchanan type would improve, rather than detract from, the efficiency of the use of resources in the federal community at large. The implications and limitations of a reconciliation of this kind can be summarized as follows.

The technical conditions and their implications   Essentially, the position of Buchanan is that transfers designed to equalize fiscal residuum might generate a more rapid growth both in the income of backward regions and in the income of the federation as a whole. This is the 'infant industry' argument, excluded by Scott. Buchanan illustrated it by reference to conditions in the states of the southern USA, and by examination of the consequences for labour, etc. efficiency of particular sorts of expenditures (for example, on health and on education). This involves an uncomfortable extension of his earlier model which was concerned with the achievement of 'geographical neutrality' of the tax system by the equalization of the tax-benefit treatment of individuals, and not with the stimulatory effects on backward regions of expenditures of particular kinds.

In fact, Buchanan's reformulation cannot rehabilitate entirely his earlier position, as he does not claim that the transfers required to satisfy the claims of equity *must* be efficient, only that they *might* be. Clearly, much will depend upon the technical conditions and relationships that are being assumed. Essentially, Scott assumes regions to be unequal in their natural endowments, and labour to be mobile between them. Buchanan argues that labour, capital, and natural resources may be capable of improvement *in situ*, and for this reason mobility may be contrary to purpose; the need is to correct an existing inefficiency by the use of transfers to raise marginal productivities, and not to compound it by the movement of resources out of a region which is already relatively poor. To use the concept of optimum allocation, common to the works of both Scott and Buchanan, the first is arguing that a 'neutral' fiscal system must not impede the movement of resources to locations of highest marginal productivity, the second that such a situation of optimal general equilibrium may *require* the use of transfers, in order to inhibit unnecessary factor movements.

If the two views were considered to be equally acceptable as guides for public policy from other points of view, the choice between them would thus turn upon matters of *fact* about resource-endowment, labour and capital mobility, and so on, in different regions, and upon the results of these facts for regional incomes, etc. There is consequently no reason why both views should be given the same relative weights in all federal situations. It is of interest to note that one writer, Graham (1940), has, in fact, treated the two approaches as those which are practically relevant, and made an interesting attempt to use both in dealing with the actual issues of federal policy in Canada. Graham treats the ideas of Scott as of diminishing importance, the less mobile resources between regions, and vice versa.

But there is need for caution. The concept of economic efficiency used by the writers, which provides the theoretical framework to which the facts must be fitted, is narrow, and this must restrict its direct relevance for policy problems. Ostensibly, they are concerned with the achievement of Pareto-optimality – the 'ideal' use of currently available resources in the satisfaction of the wants of consumers. This formulation was natural, if not inevitable, when they were writing, but it provides a narrow analytical framework which is unsatisfactory for the examination of such relevant problems as the effects on regional incomes of partial factor-mobility. In any case, it is evident, in retrospect, that the writers were not interested simply in efficiency in this static sense; much of their argument really concerns the broader question of the relation between federal fiscal arrangements, and the rate of growth of the incomes of the federation and its constituent provinces. The nature of efficiency (and its reconciliation with concepts of equity) becomes a good deal more complex when explicit account is taken of growth problems, and of the associated problems of economic stability and inter-regional trade.

Some unsettled questions   The attempts at reconciliation leave unsettled some of the issues raised in earlier sections, and particularly those concerned with equity and with the characteristics of public goods.

At the general level, it must be reiterated that the Pigovian (utilitarian) approach to fiscal equity has to be rejected on a number of grounds: it requires acceptance of an organic theory of the state, its policy prescriptions derive from implausible and untestable propositions about the capacities of persons, and the approach can throw no light upon the special fiscal problems of federations, unless the federal government is endowed with effectively authoritarian powers. More important from our present point of view, the attempt of Buchanan to overcome this problem, by the concentration of attention upon questions of horizontal equity, is logically untenable; the proposition that equals should be treated equally, if it is not a tautology, is dependent upon the same kind of value judgements as the approach it replaces. Neither can these difficulties be avoided by interpreting equity simply as a *geographical* concept. What aspects of the environment are relevant? Should the tax system be neutral, for example, as between Florida's sunshine and Alaska's ice?

These problems are compounded by those which relate to the benefits received from public goods; there is no agreement about how to measure benefit, or about the plausibility of relying (or relying only) on a benefit theory in order to decide tax policy.

The discussion of Tiebout's attempts to discover an economically optimal pattern of the location of public goods production, in particular, brought out the fundamental importance of finding an agreed measure of the valuation by the individual of his consumption of public goods, and the no less fundamental difficulties of devising such a measure in the (realistic) situation of differing individual tastes and incomes. It is not easy to see how this problem is to be solved, given that it is an essential characteristic of many public goods that they should be consumed in common.

If one assumes that benefit could be measured, there would remain the logical problem posed by Musgrave: how can there be fiscal residua if taxes are related solely to benefits received? Buchanan has tried to escape this dilemma by taking up Tiebout's proposition that differing individual incomes and tastes for public goods will, in the absence of obstacles, result in the 'clustering' of people of similar characteristics. This enables those concerned to reap the benefits of the externalities (spillovers) discussed by Tiebout, and the fiscal residuum should be redefined to include such 'neighbourhood effects'. But Buchanan provided no convincing reason why the fact that local services are spatially limited, should be a reason for making equalizing grants. He has come to accept that such a situation is a part of the economic map which determines resource allocation, and that no case of this kind, can be made out on economic grounds, if there are no artificial obstacles to the movement of persons between neighbourhoods, and if an adequate choice of public goods, and an adequate choice of state and local fiscal systems is available. Even these last qualifications are dubious. The use of transfers to offset 'protectionist' policies by local groups must be supported by equity rather than by efficiency arguments, and it would seem more to the point to direct policy to the removal of the foundations of the protection, by such means as the amendment of property laws.

It must be concluded, then, that Buchanan's position cannot be rehabilitated by reference to 'neighbourhood effects'; the 'clustering' of groups of like tastes and incomes is not in essential conflict with the efficient (geographic) allocation of resources, save to the extent that the relevant migrations impose costs (external diseconomies) upon the (immobile) resources which remain behind.

In summary, the discussion so far has drawn attention to a number of fundamental problems, and those concerned especially with the technical characteristics of the geographical distribution of resources, with the implications of tax equity as between the individual citizens of a federation, and with the nature of public goods. But, in the writings discussed, there has been more success in the discovery of significant questions, than in the finding of agreed answers to them. One must now see how this situation is affected by the introduction into the present context, which is relatively simple, of some further relevant complexities.

Further economic considerations: the dynamics of federalism
In this section I shall try to show, in a very general way, how the development of economic thought suggests a modification of the conclusions reached so far. Within a single country, growth and stability, as efficiency objectives, can be reconciled with resource allocation, at

least at the formal level, by way of a budgetary process in which the policy concerned with each objective is determined on the assumption that the other aims will be successfully achieved. It is not suggested that this formulation can provide solutions to all the problems discussed earlier (for example, those concerned with equity and with the valuation of public goods); only that any postulated set of objective solutions to those problems, can be incorporated into a general system of simultaneous equations (budgetary process) that will permit them to be reconciled with the aims of growth and stability (see, for example, Musgrave, 1959). The introduction of a federal form of government into this situation produces one essential change – we must recognize the existence of more than one level of government which has at least some budgetary independence. Thus, stabilization policy needs to be concerned with the aggregate effects of all the relevant budgets.

It is tempting to suggest that one can provide a formal reconciliation simply by extending the single-country model. Conceptually, this might be done by the use of Buchanan's definition of the federal problem, that it is concerned with the relation between the *individual* and the overall fisc. In consonance with the 'equity' role of the federal government, in offsetting differences in the fiscal treatment of equals, one would then have a federal stabilization policy concerned with 'compensating' or offsetting such (aggregate) changes in provincial budgets as would be considered 'perverse' from the point of view of economic stability in the whole federation.

But this has some uncomfortable implications. It was pointed out earlier that the Buchanan formulation implied a 'strong' federalism, in which both income distribution and resource allocation were effectively determined by the central government. The present proposal would further extend this federal authority, to incorporate adjustments in the overall size and structure of (federal and provincial) revenue–expenditure programmes, in particular regions, for purposes of federal stabilization policy. It is not unreasonable to ask whether this sort of solution does not solve the federal problem by assuming away the separate powers of the provincial governments. Furthermore, the incorporation of a stability programme raises some new questions about the nature of equity. It is a not unlikely possibility that, for example, federal stabilization policy may be concerned with the reduction of the general level of the aggregate demand of money, whilst the inflationary pressure that necessitates such a policy originates in a particular region or regions. Is it plausible to suggest that (in a federal environment with no regional trade barriers and with a common currency) stabilization policy could be so arranged that the regional (and individual) burden is placed precisely upon those who make that policy necessary? And must not any other solution raise awkward questions about fiscal equity?

These complexities are compounded if policy considerations are extended to include growth as well as stability. This needs an analytical structure which incorporates regional growth and interregional trade, and into which federal and regional tax and expenditure policies can be fitted. If fiscal equity is treated as an *individual* concept, the model would also need to provide a dynamic theory of tax incidence, as it must show the effects of policy upon the time process of income distribution.

No fully comprehensive analytical structure has yet been developed. There is, however, a considerable body of literature which bears upon aspects of the problems of regional economics, trade and growth, dynamic tax incidence, and tax harmonization. There is no space here to survey all this literature, nor is it necessary, for my purposes, to do more than summarize, in three propositions, the state of the debate:

a. Both the available facts and the theoretical discussion encourage the view that, despite trade and some factor mobility, factor incomes can continue to diverge between (geographical) regions.
b. The dynamic effects of tax policies on factor incomes and on growth are only just beginning to be studied [in 1963]. It is apparent, however, that the use of a benefit theory of taxation, in order to avoid incidence problems, becomes even more unsatisfactory than it was already found to be, when taxation and public spending have a time dimension and can affect both the size of national income and the time-evolution of factor income.
c. The existence of trade between regions may or may not result in a convergence of regional growth rates, it depends upon the technical conditions and behaviouristic patterns that are assumed. But there seems to be no reason to expect that, in the real world, the different regions of a federal country will automatically move towards the same levels of income per head, or even the same rates of growth of income per head, solely because there is free trade between them, and irrespective of the particular conditions of factor mobility or immobility, of federal and regional tax policies, and of expenditure policies.

The introduction of dynamic considerations, then, resolves none of our earlier problems and adds some new ones. It is now necessary to decide what attitude to take to the equity implications of stabilization policy, and to the possibility of divergent regional-growth rates. Particularly, in the (realistic) situation in which equity is considered to be concerned with growth as well as with current distribution, a choice may have to be made between (fiscal) policies that would maximize the rate of growth of income per head for the federation as a whole, and policies that would bring the rates of growth of different regions closer together, but at the cost of reducing the average growth-rate. This kind of choice cannot be simply a technical matter, but must involve a judgement about ends; there appears to be as much disagreement (and of a similar kind) between economists here, as in the earlier discussion of ends. A parallel to the Scott–Buchanan differences, for example, is to be found in the contrast between the emphasis given to the 'growth efficiency' objective by J. R. Hicks (1961) and that given by Higgins (1963).

It should be noted, finally, that 'interregional growth equity' does not automatically imply 'interpersonal growth equity'. The policy of federal public finance has to be concerned with both, as (as the next section emphasizes) the political and constitutional realities of federal government underline the importance of regional relationships, and the relevance of interpersonal equity is already clear.

The political characteristics of federalism

The separation of powers
The problems of federal fiscal policy may seem to have become so complex already, that to seek further complication would be pointless. However, some of the fundamentals of political federalism have not yet been recognized. It will be found that these do indeed complicate the question further, but they also bring one nearer to policy requirements.

The distinguishing political feature of a constitutional federation is the formal reservation of particular powers to the regional governments. There is regional discretion in policymaking, at least in respect of some kinds of decision. Of course, the contrast should not be overemphasized. Unitary states commonly have local governments to whom authority of particular kinds is delegated, *de facto* if not *de jure*, and there has, in recent years, been a growth of cooperative arrangements among independent states upon particular matters (for example, common market arrangements), which fall short of constitutional federalism but have some important characteristics in common with it. At the same time, the constitutional federations do not regard the actual separation of powers, which exists at any time, as ineluctable; they quite normally spend a good deal of time in debate about constitutional change, and

I shall suggest later that this is in the nature of federalism in a changing world.

Nevertheless, the formal (constitutional) reservation of powers to regional authorities is of sufficient importance to make the separate study of federal fiscal policy pointful. In particular, the existence of such separate powers places the conflict of policy *aims* in the centre of the picture; the constitutional bickering just referred to, is not an aberration of federalism but is its essence, and this alone adds a dimension to policy that is less significant in other political environments. The policy prescriptions of economists are frequently weakened by the fact that they derive from economic models in which the government is ignored or is treated as a sort of aberration – the otherwise passive instrument for the implementation of the economists' *obiter dicta*. But this is perhaps nowhere so unfortunate as it is in the context of federalism.

The relevance of the economists' debate

The recognition that regional governments with discretionary powers of their own are the political essence of federalism, makes it pointless to ignore the possibility that their policy views may differ from those of the federal government, or to treat them as no more than a part of the administrative machinery, whose decisions the federal government can and should adapt to serve the general objectives of federal policy. This does not mean that the kinds of problems that have been discussed are irrelevant to the policy-making problems of federations, but rather that it must be accepted that policy has an explicit *regional* as well as a *federal* dimension. Thus, the concepts of equity and efficiency, with which I have been concerned, may be variously interpreted by the federal government and by the individual regional governments; and I have already found good reason to believe that there is considerable scope for difference of view, both about policy ends and about technical questions. It is illuminating to look again at the two concepts in this new and broader setting.

Equity   The concept of *individual* equity, which is concerned with the treatment of individual citizens in different (geographical) locations, is still of interest in this new and more realistic environment, if only because too great a difference in 'fiscal pressure' between regions, may encourage the citizens of some regions to 'vote' against their government by moving to other regions where they believe themselves better treated. But there is no reason why regions should agree upon what constitutes equity in such matters as, for example, the progressiveness of the tax system; all regions may well prefer to accept some differences in overall fiscal pressure on particular groups, if the only way to get rid of those differences requires acceptance of Buchanan's or Bhargava's 'strong' federalism which in fact allows the central fisc to negate the regional governments' ideas about individual equity. The crucial issue concerns who is to have the last word on which distributive questions, and this is not a question to which there can be a *technical* answer (see, for example, Musgrave, 1961).

New problems arise also in respect of equity as a *regional* concept. From the point of view of current income-distribution, equity might be thought to be concerned with the equalization of the average income per head of different regions, perhaps constrained by some concept of relative need. But in the absence of agreed criteria there is no way to settle *a priori* what degree of equalization is 'correct', and regions in different positions must realistically be expected to disagree about it. Equally, regions may be expected to hold views, which differ from one another and from those of the federal government, about equity as a growth concept. The question of what degree of curtailment of the average (federal) growth rate, is justifiable to keep the spread of regional rates within acceptable limits, and of how should the implied burden be shared must be expected to produce disagreement, both about facts and relationships, and about objectives. Equally, there will be a need to reconcile differing ideas about the relation between equity and economic stability, especially in the (not unlikely) circumstances that regional policies can be used to attempt to shift the burden, for example of local unemployment, on to 'outsiders'.

Again, equity may be interpreted as a matter not simply of regional income or regional growth, but of the standards at which particular services should be provided to citizens throughout the federation. The 'standard of service' concept has affinities with that of income equalization, in so far as it is concerned with the relative ability of different regions to meet the specified minimum levels of provision, but differs in that it involves the specification of general standards for *particular forms* of public provision, so that the pursuit of this type of equity implies a special encroachment upon the freedom of decision-making of regional governments, and hence upon regional autonomy.

Last, equity may be interpreted in yet another fashion which is in potential conflict with all the others. This asserts that public revenues should be spent in the regions in which they originated. In its extreme form, this *principle of deprivation* reduces the federal government to the status of a tax-collecting agency for the regional governments. At most, it would permit the federal government to determine the *form* but not the *size* of its expenditure by regions. In either case, its use is compatible only with a 'weak' federalism, at the opposite extreme from the 'strong' (centralist) federalism implied by some of the economic literature discussed earlier.

Economic efficiency Apart from disagreement about efficiency of resource use in the federation at large, one must recognize that policies, based upon efficiency criteria alone, will be in potential conflict not only with equity in the senses so far discussed, but also with the political objectives of federalism. To take an extreme case, it will usually be unrealistic to expect a region to acquiesce readily in its own depopulation, simply because it is believed elsewhere that economic efficiency requies that the labour move to other parts of the federation. The importance of this particular conflict of aims is underlined by recognition that population groupings are not normally dictated by economic motives of any simple kind. The 'clustering', discussed by Tiebout and Buchanan, is frequently influenced by ethnic, religious, etc., motives, as well as by more directly economic ones; regions consequently exhibit differences in these matters as well as in economic characteristics, and policies proposed on grounds of economic efficiency will thus, quite normally, appear to suggest discrimination, not only between regions but also between social groups. Once more, there can be no simple or agreed answer. Policy must be conceived as a 'pay-off'; how much 'efficiency' (resource mobility, etc.) need be and should be sacrificed to preserve the political fabric of federalism?

In addition, policy must take account of the fact that the regions of a federation are frequently the product of politics and history rather than of economic geography. A glance at the map of North America provides a sufficient illustration. Thus, for policy purposes it is not enough to distinguish between regions in terms of their 'general' resource endowment. There may be differences within regions as great as those between them (so that policy decisions need to be related *inter alia* to the needs and problems, not only of two but also of at least three tiers of government), and the 'natural' geographic areas, for particular decisions about economic policy, may cut across the boundaries of political geography. An illuminating and practical illustration concerns the development of a river and its catchment area. Economic efficiency requires that the problem be studied, and the policy determined, by reference to the economic magnitudes affected. But the geographic region which is relevant for this purpose may incorporate parts of several political regions. There is no reason why the policies that each of these political regions believe would serve their own economic interest, should approximate the general needs for economic development of the whole geographic area. Thus, the achievement of efficient use of resources must be constrained by the (political) need to reach agreement between the federal units affected. Neither can it be asserted that the 'right' solution 'must' be one that enables optimal overall development of the geographic area, and be one which leaves 'horse-trading' to decide the sharing of the proceeds, for this must involve the substitution, in the case of some regions, of income from outside sources ('grants') for income collected by the regional government itself. In this and in other contexts, it cannot be assumed that the regional governments will be indifferent to such a change. Fiscal independence may be seen as an end in itself (or grants viewed as a threat to autonomy), and if this is so a lower direct income may be preferred to a larger one which accrues indirectly from a shared activity, and perhaps involves also the separation of the *financing* of the activities in question from their *administration*.

Political dynamics
To conclude this section, I must take note of the fact that the process of economic change in a federation influences and is influenced by its political and constitutional evolution. Thus, economic change (growth) brings with it changes in the *technical* possibilities which are open to a federal community – the 'optimum patterning' sought by Tiebout must be expected to change over time.

In so far as technical change carries with it improvements in transport and in communications (which has certainly been the case historically), the effective result of this process must be to produce a 'widening of the market' – an increase in the (geographical and technical) scale at which public goods and services can be provided efficiently. This, in turn, must alter the 'costs' that may be imposed on the (federal) community by insistence upon regional autonomy (for example, by regions persisting in themselves providing services, on a scale that has become too small for technical efficiency or for the efficient raising of the necessary revenues or for both). It is not suggested, of course, that such a dynamic evolution *ought* to shift the provision of the services concerned to higher administrative levels; to mention only one countervailing influence, it is in the nature of the process described that the federation is growing richer, and so can better afford the (economic) sacrifice that may be implied by insistence upon regional autonomy. But one can expect the process of change to produce a *tendency* for effective control of services to move to higher levels of government. This process may be in conflict with views about regional autonomy;

the outcome cannot be predicted, and must be frequently expected to take the form of regional changes in the way responsibilities for the finance and for the provision of services, respectively, are divided, rather than of outright or abrupt changes in the level of government generally responsible for particular forms of provision. In regard to this, it must also be remembered that the geographical size and other characteristics of the regions being considered are also relevant to the form in which the problem shows itself in any historical time period. The counterpart of a (technical) pressure for the shift of particular functions from local authorities towards central government in Britain, for example, might be a similar pressure for a shift from other levels towards *regional* governments, in, for example, USA or Canada.

The tendency may be reinforced by another aspect of dynamic change; the very process of change may alter the ideas of individuals and of governments about the weight they wish to give to particular economic and politico-social objectives. Two aspects of these changes in social attitudes are of special interest.

The first is the constitutional aspect. The process of creating a federation can be not implausibly described as a sort of 'horse trade'. The hitherto independent units are concerned with the gains they might make from being part of a confederation (for example, by obtaining free access to a larger market), and with the associated sacrifices by way of reduced autonomy, limitation of tax powers, obligation to make income transfers, or grants, to 'compensate' other regions enough to persuade them to join, and so on. In part then, at least, a federal constitution is going to be a reflection of this 'horse trade', although it may, of course, reflect other things too, such as authority or ability of third parties to impose conditions. It will provide for only such sacrifice of powers as the independent units find it necessary and worthwhile to accept – though it is of interest to note that, even at this initial stage, some system of transfers (grants) is likely to be an unavoidable part of the bargain, if those regions which stand to lose (for example, by losing their ability to levy tariffs) are to be persuaded to join.

Once the federation has been created, however, the process of change may be expected to produce differences between regions (for example, in the value of their residual tax powers), and also changes in community attitudes to social and to economic policy in general, and to the purposes of federal policy in particular. As a natural consequence, the constitution is likely to become out of consonance with the developing situation, and pressures arise for constitutional amendment. Here is a more complete explanation of the proposition that constitutional debate is of the essence of political federalism; but there is no neat formula to deal with the problem. There can be no 'right' answer which is derivable from economic theory or political philosophy. On the other hand, I shall argue that, from the point of view of efficient policy-making, it is valuable to have recognized the problem for what it is.

Second, it has been noted that technical changes, and particularly changes in transport and in communications, do not only alter the production possibilities, both of public and of private goods, but also alter the *geographical* parameters of the social attitudes towards equity, standards of service, and so on. The point is obvious enough to need little illustration. In particular, the geographical interpretation of 'minimum standards' or 'equal standards', as an equity idea, bears a clear relation to the region with which individuals are able to identify themselves. Thus, in many (federal and other) countries, equity (or equality) in standards of educational provision begins as a local concept, develops into a wider (regional) one, and then (at least at particular levels) begins to be discussed as a matter of national concern. The relation between this kind of evolution of ideas and the changes in men's knowledge of their fellows, induced by improvements in communications, can hardly be denied. It reinforces the conclusion towards which the discussion of the whole of this section has been moving; that the policy problems which I have been concerned with earlier in this paper, are not, in the nature of things, capable of an ultimate, once-and-for-all solution. The most one can hope for is to use an understanding of the nature of the issues in order to devise a *policy-making environment*, that will enable decisions to be made in a context appropriate for reconciliation of the objectives with which we have been concerned, and that will at the same time be flexible enough to allow the processes of economic and sociopolitical change to be dealt with (see also U. K. Hicks, 1961). It remains to consider, in the final section, what concrete proposals are suggested by the survey as likely to conduce to this end.

Conclusions and proposals

The outcome of this lengthy exposition must be disappointing for those who seek a normative framework that would guide decisions about the tax and expenditure policies of federations. I have not established such a framework; on the contrary, I have drawn attention to a number of important unsettled questions which concern both the ends and the means of policymaking, and have found reason to doubt whether it can ever be pointful to try to derive useful policy generalizations from the corpus of economic analysis.

But it does not follow that there is nothing of value to be said. In the first place, something has been established about the *nature* of federalism: it surely has less resemblance to Bhargava's 'family' (good-will-towards-men) relationship than to Carnell's description:

> With its rigidities, technicalities, inefficiency, excessive legalism and conversatism, federalism is only for peoples of mature political experience capable of playing the complicated game of circumventing such restrictions. (Carnell, 1961)

In so complicated a game it is essential to formulate the rules in a fashion that minimizes the possibility of misunderstanding, and it is here that political economy should have some contribution to make. For although the survey may not have produced agreed solutions, it should, at least, have brought out the nature of the issues of public finance policy on which agreement needs to be reached, and also have improved understanding of the possible causes of disagreement. Can this knowledge not be used, if not to make prescriptions, then to improve the policy 'ground rules', by the better relation of the *procedures*, by which tax and expenditure policy is determined, to the present understanding of the *problems* which need to be solved?

Any attempt to do this must begin from the existing constitutional and political environment. This is not to suggest that environment cannot or should not be changed – a case has already been made for the opposite view. But, for present purposes, constitutional reform can be thought of as arising out of the other evolving ends and possibilities of the federal community. If it is possible to provide an appropriate context for decisionmaking about these, the need for constitutional reform (where it exists) will be brought into the picture automatically, through the directing of attention to the inhibitions (costs) that the constitution imposes upon the pursuit of desired policies. Indeed, a by-product of the proposed procedure might be to improve the efficiency with which decisions about constitutional reform are taken, by emphasizing the *general directions* in which change is required rather than by emphasizing the immediate and specific needs.

The next task is to set out the relevant end-objectives. It has been established that there is room for different opinions, as to the weights that 'should' be attached to particular objectives, as well as about the technical consequences of particular policies of federal public finance. But whereas it is not possible for the economist to *prescribe* weights, the earlier discussion does at least make it possible to *list the characteristics* of the system, to which weights will somehow have to be attached by those concerned, if the policymaking process is to work efficiently. Thus, within the context of constitutional law and of political (autonomy, etc.) attitudes, the considerations that the discussion has suggested to have 'end-content' are as follows.

Considerations of fiscal equity
There are the following relevant aspects of 'federal' equity:

a.   equity in the (tax-and-benefit) treatment of individuals, by the federal and regional fiscs;
b.   equity in the federal treatment of the different (political) regions;
c.   equity in the formulation of policies for economic stability;
d.   equity in the use of public finance to improve regional growth rates;
e.   equity in the equalization of (federal) standards of provision of particular types of service;
f.   equity in the 'derivation' sense – the distribution of federal expenditures, by reference to the (regional) origin of federal tax revenues.

Considerations of economic efficiency
Several interpretations of efficiency have been suggested earlier. Those likely to be important to policy-making are:

a.   efficiency in the current allocation between uses of community resources;
b.   efficiency in the maintenance of (short-run) economic stability – that is, in the avoidance of too rapid or sustained changes in the level of unemployment and/or prices;
c.   efficiency in the generation of economic growth (defined as the rate of growth of average federal income per capita).

Last, a policy environment must be created in which the different views (whether on technical questions, or on ends) can be brought together. This requires, first, that all groups (governments) concerned with particular decisions should be able to bring their views to bear fully, and, second, that individual policy decisions should be taken in the light of an apprehension, not only of the specific problem, but also of its relation to the general body of tax-and-expenditure policy that is being evolved. The implication of this second proposition can be clarified by a return to the illustration used earlier in relation to stabilization policy. There, it was pointed out that regions might pursue budgetary policies which offset the stabilization policies of the central government. But it is misleading to label such regional policies 'perverse', if they are implemented with knowledge of the relevant facts, and if they originate simply in the different emphasis given to particular objectives by the federal and regional governments. But if the regional policies are formulated in ignorance of their possible effects upon (federal) economic stability, or without knowledge of the content of federal stabilization policy, then there is likely to be perversity, in the more meaningful sense that a better appreciation of the relevant issues would result in a change in regional or in federal policies. The policy-making structure needs to be designed to minimize perversity in this second sense.

It might, of course, be argued that all the aspects of equity and efficiency listed above affect all the citizens of the federal community; so that the above requirements amount to a need to associate all federal and regional governments with all decisions. But the sense in which the federal government is concerned with policies for stability and growth, is clearly quite different from the sense in which it is involved with the detail of garbage collection in one village inside one region. The policy framework needs to make provision for such different policies to be kept consistent; but they do not all need to be talked about at once, or by the same policy-making groups. The need is first to provide a context in which the broadest issues can be discussed, and, then, to associate with this an appropriate number of other groups which are concerned with significant but narrower (more specific) issues. A possible set of instruments for this purpose might be a set of committees of interlocking membership, designed to cover the whole group of policy objectives, and constituted so as to keep the distinct 'special' policies consistent with one another. The precise structure will, of course, differ with the particular needs and characteristics of individual federations. The important *generalization* is that the overall constitution of the group should (a) cover the relevant policy problems, and (b) provide for efficient intercommunication about them. The groups would not be *ad hoc* in character, or be created solely because of recognition of the need to deal with some specific emergent problem. Rather, in consonance with the findings about the political and economic dynamics of federalism, they would be quasi-permanent, and flexible enough to accommodate the shifts in policy emphasis, and changes in technical environment, that I have argued to be the essence of federal budget-making.

There is clearly more than one set of committees that might be devised for such a purpose, but the discussion in this paper has provided enough information, particularly about the technical aspects of the problem, for it to be possible to conclude on the general benefits that such a structure would allow. The suggested structure is as follows.

A budget coordination committee (committee A)
This would be the most general committee, and would contain representatives both of federal and of regional interests. It would be concerned with the general *structure* of the federal and provincial budgets. Thus, this committee would take the final decision on the size of the excess of federal revenues over federal expenditures, available for the purposes of other individual committees. In the process, it would determine and keep under review the tax *sources* available to the different governments, for example, by establishing procedures to decide upon tax sharing. At the same time, it would be at this committee that decisions about individual equity (p. 106, equity objective (a)) and current resource allocation (p. 106, efficiency objective (a)) would need to be taken, as it is only at this general level that there can be assessment of the impact of the 'combined fisc' upon the individual.

The final set of budget plans, as negotiated at this committee, would of course also incorporate, and be consonant with, the proposals of other relevant committees, which each have their own implications for efficiency and equity.

A regional equalization committee (committee B)
As its name implies, this committee would be concerned with the combined budgetary process, from the point of view of equity between regions (p. 106, equity objective (b)). Ideally, its deliberations would be intended to derive Musgrave-type formulae to use to guide regional redistribution by means of federal grants. The size of these grants would, of course, have to be consonant with the overall budgets negotiated at committee A, but the content of the grant formula would be a matter for inter-regional negotiation, in which the federal government might perhaps play a less significant role. It is at this committee also that the relevance (if any) of the 'derivation' concept of equity (p. 106, equity objective (f)) would need to be decided.

It is clear that regional variations in income and in wealth would be of fundamental importance to the decision-making of this committee. These variations are not inherently incapable of measurement, at least sufficiently well for agreement to be possible as to the appropriate index to use in a grant formula. More difficulties may arise in the attempts to agree upon a concept and a measure of *need*; should the committee wish to extend regional equity to encompass variations in need. True, it is possible to bring income and need together in a common formula which is designed, in some sense, to 'equalize' the 'burden' on different regions of providing particular service levels. And it is valuable to try to do so, in order that the joint consequences of the two shall be clear to the policy-maker. In order, however, that disagreement about the relevance and the measurement of need shall not inhibit the policy-making process elsewhere, it may be useful to separate the committee which is concerned with regional income-equalization, from the distinct (sub)committee concerned with standards. This has the additional advantage that the income-equalization formula can be used as a guide by committee E, as shall be shown.

A common standards committee (committee C)
Committee C (or a subcommittee of B) would be charged with the task of establishing minimum *federal* standards of service,.for the forms of public provision for which this was agreed to be appropriate, and with recommending methods of finance that would permit or ensure the provision of such standards, in a fashion that seemed equitable between regions (p. 106, equity objective (e)). While this might involve a service-by-service approach in the first instance, the relation between the activities of this group and those of committee B is clearly very close, and the committee should consequently have in mind, as its eventual purpose, the evolution of a generally acceptable measure of relative need, that might be incorporated in the equalization grant-formula.

A stabilization committee (committee D)
This committee, as its name implies, would be concerned with the maintenance of a satisfactory level of aggregate demand, and for this purpose would need to relate the federal and regional budgetary pro-posals to a general forecast of the development of the economy. That is, it would provide raw material for the budget coordination commit-tee, which would be designed to ensure that its proposals were conson-ant with the maintenance of full employment and stable prices. At the same time, this committee might initiate proposals for remedying actual, or potential, deficiencies or surpluses of aggregate demand; the equity aspects of these proposals then would become a matter for the budget coordination committee (committee A). This committee would need also to be suitably constituted so as to provide a link between budgetary and monetary policy.

An economic growth committee (committee E)
This committee would work closely with the stabilization committee, as it would be concerned, at least in part, with the same magnitudes. But as its prime concern is to facilitate a satisfactory rate of economic growth (p. 106, efficiency objective (c)), it will need to take a longer-

term view than may be requisite for purposes of short-term stability. Another reason for keeping its activities distinct concerns the concept of equity (p. 106, equity objective (d)). As has been shown, the desire to distribute growth between the regions may be an important federal objective. At the same time, there are severe technical difficulties to be solved in any attempt to assess how particular proposals are likely to affect (federal and regional) economic growth rates, and information about this is essential to an assessment of the 'costs' of equity (in terms of sacrificed growth). In addition, there is a close relation between the activities of this committee and those of committees B and C. Thus, success in equalizing economic growth rates might well reduce the importance which is attached to the need for equalizing grants for the purpose of maintaining standards of service. At the same time, the income-deficiency formula, devised to meet the needs of committee B, might provide a basis for the equity proposals of the economic growth committee. For example, it is likely that the committee will regard the stimulation of public investment as one means of improving the economic growth rates of the more backward regions. An appropriate way of doing this might be by means of encouragement grants, by which the federal government provides a proportion of the total cost of investment. The grant formula of committee B can then be used to decide the proportionate contribution, in respect of each region, as it measures the current 'spread' of income distribution between regions. If policies for 'growth with equity' are successful, then the federal contribution to regional public investment would diminish automatically.

The description I have given might be formalized in a set of simultaneous equations which relate the various activities of the individual committees. This would make for neater (and shorter) exposition, but it would also obscure the essential problem; to write the equations one has to assume the answers to questions about which there is less than complete agreement. In the absence of an agreed normative structure, the budgetary coordinating committee must expect to have a difficult task, and the political economist must be well satisfied if he is able to improve the efficiency with which policy decisions are arrived at, by clarifying the nature of the relevant ends–means relationships.

Notes

1. Dafflon, B. (1977) *Federal Finance in Theory and Practice, with Special Reference to Switzerland*. Berne, Paul Haupt Verlag.
2. The terms 'federal' and 'federation' will be used to denote the whole area encompassed by the federal constitution, and its government. 'Region' denotes the geographically smaller political units.

References

Adarkar, B. P. (1933) *The Principles and Problems of Federal Finance* (George Allen and Unwin, Hemel Hempstead, Herts).

Bhargava, R. N. (1953) 'The theory of federal finance', *Economic Journal*, **63**, 84–97.

Bhargava, R. N. (1956) *The Theory and Working of Union Finance in India* (Allen and Unwin, Hemel Hempstead, Herts).

Buchanan, J. M. (1949) 'The pure theory of government finance: a suggested approach', *Journal of Political Economy*, **57**, 496–505.

Buchanan, J. M. (1950) 'Federalism and fiscal equity', *American Economic Review*, **401**, 583–97.

Buchanan, J. M. (1952a) 'Federal grants and resource allocation', *Journal of Political Economy*, **60**, 208–17.

Buchanan, J. M. (1952b) 'A reply', *Journal of Political Economy*, **60**, 536–8.

Carnell, F. G. (1961) 'Political implications of federalism in new states', in *Federalism and Economic Growth in Underdeveloped Countries*, ed. U. K. Hicks (Allen and Unwin, Hemel Hempstead, Herts), pp. 16–59.

Clement, M. O. (1963) 'Interstate fiscal equity and federal grants-in-aid', *Southern Economic Journal*, **29**, 279–96.

Graham, J. F. (1963) *Fiscal Adjustment and Economic Development* (University of Toronto Press, Toronto, Canada) Chapter 3.

Hicks, J. R. (1961) 'The nature and basis of economic growth', in *Federalism and Economic Growth in Underdeveloped Countries: A Symposium*, ed. U. K. Hicks (Allen and Unwin, Hemel Hempstead, Herts) pp. 70–80.

Hicks, U. K. (1961) *Federalism and Economic Growth in Underdeveloped Countries: A Symposium* (Allen and Unwin, Hemel Hempstead, Herts).

Higgins, B. (1963) Review of *Federalism and Economic Growth*, ed. U. K. Hicks, *Pacific Affairs*, **63**, 460–3.

Maxwell, J. A. (1946) *The Fiscal Impact of Federalism in the USA* (Harvard University Press, Cambridge, MA).

Musgrave, R. A. (1959) *The Theory of Public Finance* (McGraw-Hill, New York).

Musgrave, R. A. (1961) 'Approaches to a fiscal theory of political federalism', in *Public Finance: Needs, Sources and Utilization*, ed. J. M. Buchanan (Princeton University Press, Princeton, NJ).

Ostrom, V., Tiebout, C. M. and Warren, R. (1961) 'The organization of government in metropolitan areas: a theoretical inquiry', *American Political Science Review*, **40**, 831–42.

Robbins, L. (1935) *The Nature and Significance of Economic Science* (Macmillan, London).

Royal Commission (1965) *Royal Commission on Taxation (Canada)* (Queen's Printer, Ottawa).

Scott, A. D. (1950) 'A note on grants in federal countries', *Economica*, **17**, 416–22.

Scott, A. D. (1952), 'Federal grants and resource allocation', *Journal of Political Economy*, **60**, 534–8.

Tiebout, C. M. (1956) 'A pure theory of local expenditures', *Journal of Political Economy*, **64**, 416–24.

5 Some Reflections on the Economics of Group Behaviour*

Foreword

In recent years, I have on occasion been taken to task for publishing this paper in what is regarded as a relatively inaccessible source (a multilingual *Festschrift*). The immediate reason for doing so was that an editor of the volume was a former graduate student, and the paper was provided at his request. But it is questionable in any case whether the article would at that time have been acceptable to a mainstream journal, and I could give it wider currency among specialists by circulation in the *York Reprints Series*. Even so, it attracted little immediate attention. Interest has evolved more recently: the article anticipated subsequent developments to a greater extent than I myself anticipated, though I saw the argument as having wider implications than I was able to pursue (which explains the title).

The paper is an explicit statement of the need for an extension of the logic of choice, which was an implicit assumption of the federalism paper. In this sense, it is the first deliberate attempt to 'marry' my two interests in cost theory and in 'social behaviour'. What I now find interesting is the extent to which this attempt identifies what have proved to be fruitful themes of future development, as well as hinting at others.

The normative study of groups obliges consideration of a philosophical problem: what do, or can, groups 'maximize'? I had no hesitation in adopting the libertarian postulate: only individuals have goals, group participation being simply an instrument for their pursuit. This was not of course a blinding new insight. But it is my own first explicit attempt to incorporate a libertarian notion into my evolving cost-and-choice ideas. Even so, I do not develop this large issue, but award it only a paragraph.

In relation to cost, the important innovation is the extension of the notion of subjective opportunity-cost to the explanation of group participation, the cost of such participation being the value attached to the constraint of submission to group rules, the benefit the (expected) better achievement of personal goals.

* Caroni, P., Dafflon, B. and Enderle, G. (eds) (1978) *Nur Oekonomie ist Keine Oekonomie*, Berne, Paul Haupt Verlag.

This general specification leads directly to some useful inferences. It permits explanation, for example, of individual participation in diverse social groups, some of whose objectives may be in apparent conflict. It also facilitates a taxonomy of groups that does not require them to be single-objectived: it is in the nature of things that groups will act to maximize the welfare of members within the existing 'social rules', and also act to change those rules in desirable ways, though of course the importance of different objectives will differ from one group to another. Recognition of this in turn directs attention to the complexity of the notion of freedom of choice, which must always be subject to the constraints of extant social rules, including the 'rules of society'.

Groups are seen as generating hierarchical decision structures with power (freedom to choose) being surrendered ('delegated') to managements or bureaucracies. The system of group rules and delegations become determinants of individual opportunity-costs. But groups differ in the constraints they impose. In particular, 'societies' and 'families' are different from other groups in that initial membership is involuntary and they have different costs of exit.

The complexity of the notion of freedom of choice in the context of group behaviour is seen essentially as a special instance of the 'liberal paradox' (rules 'forcing people to be free'), though the broader implications of the insight are inadequately recognized. Similarly, the dynamic and hierarchical aspects of the relations between costs and rules is incompletely explored. The recognition of the differences between the group comprising society-as-a-whole and smaller, within-society groups, leads me only to a taxonomy of groups and comment upon their relationships at a point in time. It foreshadows the broader implications for the hierarchical nature of social rules, the need to distinguish 'within-period' and 'between-period' freedom of choice (Brennan and Buchanan, 1985), and impermanence of social rules in the face of endemic uncertainty (unknowability of the future). Finally, the distinction between 'voice' and 'exit' as cost-categories (characteristics of rules) is used illustratively, but without recognition of the central value of the concept for the general logic of the group behaviour model (Vanberg, 1986).

But these are new developments, still not fully integrated in my subsequent papers. The way they fit into my present scheme of thought is summarily explained in the concluding chapter.

Introduction

This *Festschrift* for Professor Biucchi affords an opportunity to 'look forward' at the development of a topic which has been of concern to him: the study of the public sector. I have called these comments 'reflections', because the ideas are by no means fully worked through: what I have is a set of observations concerning the behaviour of social groups, which seem to me to need integration into any satisfactory explanation of the decision-making process in organized society.

There is now a considerable body of literature in economics which in one way or another acknowledges decision processes other than individual transactions through market exchange. The study of *political* decision-making (voting) is well established, as is its offshoot, *administrative* decision-making (e.g. in the theory of bureaucratic behaviour). Within 'orthodox' economic analysis, the existence of 'firms' which are something more than profit maximizing individuals is here and there recognized, though there is also a tendency to treat the multi-person firm as a simple extension of the lone entrepreneur – 'Maximize one thing at a time, please (though it can be sales with a profit constraint): and no quarrelling'. We acknowledge layers of government and potential conflicts between them: but we are only at the beginning of the development of theories of fiscal federalism that provide for group conflict resolution as well as individual maximizing behaviour. We need to integrate pressure groups into our models – associations whose objectives include the changing of the 'rules of the economic game' in their favour.

In addition to these specialized recognitions of non-market group behaviour, there is of course a literature concerned with group behaviour *per se*, the *locus classicus* of which is Mancur Olsen's *Logic of Collective Action* (1965). This present contribution might be interpreted as an extended footnote to Olsen's own work. I do not believe that I have anything to say that would surprise him, and indeed much of it is implicit or explicit in his own arguments. The difference is rather one of emphasis: where the focus of his interest is on such matters as the role of groups in the supply of public goods and the influence of size on group behaviour, my own is upon the extension of individualistic behaviour to include group participation, and within this context upon the symmetries between widely divergent types of group activity such as the 'society' and the family, and the potential implications for the development of both positive and normative economics.

Individual objectives and group action
It is necessary to make clear from the outset that the attempt to incorporate group activity into the study of the behaviour of individuals does not imply any particular 'theory of the state', and, in particular, does not require that groups must have objectives that are in some sense

'outside' (additional or superior to) the objectives of their members. It is as well, however, to recognize the importance of this question. If one adopts an organic theory of the state, for example, with the implication that what individuals 'really' or 'should' want is better known to the 'group' than to its individual members, there is then little point in attempting to evaluate the 'efficiency' of groups by their relative success in implementing the individual wishes of their members. Failure to recognize this philosophical problem produces much confusion in the debate about the virtues of alternative systems of socio-economic organization. I draw attention to the problem here solely in order to make my own position clear: in the societies I am considering, groups exist to fulfil the wishes of their members, and all relevant 'values' are 'values' as felt and interpreted by the individuals concerned.

It is in this context that we address the questions: Why do groups exist? Why should individuals join groups? Are there any criteria of 'socio-economic efficiency' that can be applied to groups?

My own interest in seeking answers to these questions stems from the fact that, in diverse contexts of concern to me, I have found myself both unable to explain observed phenomena within the intellectual framework provided by 'orthodox' economic analysis and become aware that a common reason for this appears to be the existence of group activities that operate 'outside the market' and in any case do not 'play the game' – they appear to be maximizing things other than those a Pareto-type model would allow. All individuals participate in some of these groups as well as in market transactions. Examples of diverse problems of which this is true (chosen solely because they have interested me personally) are:

The growth of government activity   There is now a proliferation of 'explanations' of the share of government in the economy, but no plausible means of choosing between them. Some run in 'orthodox' economic terms (e.g. the demand for public goods), others offer (e.g.) 'political' explanations. In a paper in 1979, Professor A. T. Peacock and myself have begun to explore the idea that a model of group behaviour may be the integrating concept needed to bring these various approaches together.

Subsidy policy   When one observes the bewildering variety of industrial and social subsidies that exist in many countries, it is not easy to believe that they all exist for purposes of 'market correction' or 'equity', and not for the achievement of other objectives on which the economist's orthodox models throw no light.

I do not deny that the theory of public goods has greatly improved our general understanding of the phenomenon. It nevertheless stretches credulity to believe that the concept 'explains' actual subsidy systems, unless we define public goods so embracingly, or tautologically, as to be useless. If this is the case, it is an abdication of responsibility for economists to confine their interest in subsidy policy to its compatibility with their traditional norms (with the implication that other subsidies 'ought not to exist'). The evidence about subsidy policies suggests that the objectives of government are not comprehended by the economists' logic of choice.[1] Whatever our own views of the good society, we should study the phenomenon as it exists: we need a model of group behaviour to do so.

The explanation and control of inflation   It is now fairly generally recognized that expectations are central to a satisfactory explanation of the inflationary process, and that the behaviour of trade unions is of great importance in this respect. But, while it has consequently become 'orthodox' to build 'trade union expectations' into econometric models of the inflationary process, it is much less usual to take account of the political power of trade unions (which varies between societies and is influenced by the behaviour of other social groups), and in particular of the relation between *experience* of inflation and the power and political attitudes of trade unions. We need to study the unions in terms of their own objectives.[2]

The family   The family is the basic 'social group' in many contexts, but its behaviour as a unit enters economics only through the economics of human resources, which is obliged to recognize the importance of the family unit to a series of decisions with fundamental economic implications – such as those about the education of children. While some aspects of these decisions can be 'explained' within the context of our 'orthodox' concepts (e.g. problems of financing education are related to the imperfection of the market for 'human capital'), it is also obvious that actual policies reflect not only the objectives and competences of the family unit as a decision-maker for its members but also the objectives of other social groups (e.g. there is a common view that 'society' – the largest 'social group' – benefits from the education of its members, and that the objectives of the family unit in this matter should therefore be 'corrected' or even over-ruled).

It is my belief that economics would benefit from a generalized model of group behaviour which brings out the common relevance of such groups to an understanding of a heterogeneous set of economic problems. At the same time, we do not wish to lose the undoubted value of the individualistic calculus in explaining important aspects of human behaviour. Economists are properly reluctant to abandon so useful a tool. I think they are right: the need is to extend the analysis rather than to replace it. That is, our interest is in the *generalization* of the group concept, implying the need for formal integration of a theory of group behaviour into the corpus of economic analysis. In this short paper, I can do no more than set out the essential logic, around which a general model might be developed.

Individual decisions and social groups
Given the initial postulate that all relevant values are those apprehended by individuals, the essential extension of the hedonistic calculus implied by the recognition of group activity is that participation in a group may be seen by individuals as a more efficient means of pursuing individual goals than would be direct transactions through a market. This suggests that we can 'explain' group membership, and thereby group behaviour, by extension of the concept of opportunity-cost to group situations. In principle, this requires no more than an extension of Coase's theory of the firm (1937), which explains the existence of multi-person firms by the superior efficiency in certain circumstances of direct negotiations and agreements between individuals over contract-type market transactions. It is important for us (though not central to the Coase thesis) that this explanation of the firm as a 'group' where members prefer direct coordination to the disciplines of the market permits the possibility that individual members of the group may have different objectives. They need not share the same goals: only the belief that, overall, group participation is a superior technique to arm's-length contracting for the achievement of their personal objectives.

The 'cost' of group membership, then, is the loss of individual freedom of action implied by commitment to the objectives of the group, the 'benefit' the expected differential gain from membership. The concepts are not unsubtle in application: e.g. as we have formulated the problem, a 'benefit' from trade union membership may be the expectation of loss of income and non-pecuniary benefits consequent upon exclusion from the relevant occupation which would result from failure to join.

There are some interesting inferences
1. Individuals will commonly belong to a multiplicity of groups: their 'society', their family, groups concerned with their direct economic interests (firms, trade unions), groups with 'social' objectives (but

economic implications), such as political parties, leagues against blood sports, churches.

2.   The opportunity-cost of participating in groups rather than pursuing objectives directly will be determined by the prevailing 'rules of the game' – primarily the laws and customs of the 'society' (the largest relevant group) with which we are concerned. Thus, *the relationships between groups*, discussed in the next section, are an essential component in determining individual behaviour.

3.   It follows from (1) and (2) that groups will evolve whose purpose it is to 'change the rules' (alter the opportunity-costs faced by individuals). The objectives of such groups may range from simple attempts to influence tastes and preferences to pressure, e.g. to change the law in ways that would further the interests of members of the relevant group. It is here that the notion of the freedom of the individual to choose, which underlies the classical position on economic policy, runs into difficulties.

A League Against Cruel Sports may campaign for laws that would prohibit the hunting of foxes. There are people who gain utility from fox-hunting. Is it really an adequate basis for policy to argue that those who object to fox-hunting are 'free' to bribe those who enjoy it to stop? (That is, we reach a Pareto-optimal outcome simply by allowing all concerned to include the welfare of foxes in their utility function.) If this is not adequate, then the freedom to try to change social rules by coercion (e.g. by promoting legislation making fox-hunting illegal) is a necessary part of the hedonistic paradigm but at the same time a negation of it. (This is of course no more than a reiteration of the conflict between the 'liberal paradox' – the need to 'force people to be free', and the (ethically neutral) prescriptions of welfare economics.)[3]

4.   Finally, the 'opportunity-cost' approach to group participation helps us to understand some superficially inconsistent patterns of individual behaviour. Simply, individuals as members (or putative members) of different groups face different opportunity-cost situations in ech group context: and there is no reason to expect their decisions over the set to be consistent with anything except their overall view of their own interest. The point is perhaps best amplified by an example. UK opinion poll evidence suggests that many trade union members think that the political powers of their unions should be curbed, and in particular that the laws concerning membership (supporting the creation of 'closed shops') are unsatisfactory. There is nothing paradoxical about this. It is perfectly reasonable for an individual to be a member of a union (because the

cost of non-membership may, e.g., be exclusion from the exercise of his labour skills), and also to participate in groups fulfilment of whose objectives would reduce that cost, but perhaps also his expected future money income by weakening the relevant authority of the union.

A generalized model of individual behaviour must thus incorporate the possibility of individual choice, not only between participation in groups and individual initiative, but also between membership of different groups. For the individual, the optimal outcome will be an individual action: group membership combination which for many people will involve membership of groups whose objectives may be in partial conflict. It is for this reason that we need a generalized logic of group behaviour and of inter-group as well as individual-group behaviour.

The relationships between groups
We have seen that an individual may belong to more than one group, as well as pursuing his objectives through markets, and his doing so is compatible with the fact that the objectives of the different groups he belongs to may be at least partly opposed.

The relationships between groups themselves is similarly complex. It is not uncommon to identify groups with particular single objectives, so that (e.g.) 'political' groups maximize their expected hold on 'power', somehow defined, 'economic' groups maximize expected 'profit', somehow defined, and 'bureaucracies' maximize 'security', somehow defined. But of course, all group activity is multi-objectived, and in at least two ways. First, we have already observed that individual members of a group need not share the same view of the relation between their own objectives and the objectives pursued by the group. For example, all the members of a firm may accept that their common objective is the maximization of expected profit, but the sales director may still believe that the maximization of the expected present value of his own future income requires that he maximize the expected value of the firm's future *sales*. How far the two are compatible, and what will be the results of divergence, are practical matters. Similarly (e.g.), the staff of a charity are not necessarily all committed to achievement of the objectives of the charity to the exclusion of consideration of (e.g.) the effects of alternative policies on their own expected income.

Second, it is inherent in the withdrawal of processes from the market that the group replacing market transactions is likely to be concerned with more than one objective. Put in its most generalized and simple form, the point is that groups, as well as pursuing the interests of their members within the existing politico-economic context, will *normally* also pursue policies which seek to alter the 'rules of the game' in favour of group members. Continuing an earlier example, a trade union must be expected not only to pursue the economic interests of its members within the existing social context, e.g. by representing them in wage negotiations (an activity which could – but need not – be interpreted as 'market perfecting'), but also to initiate and support policy measures which strengthen the bargaining power of the union, such as laws strengthening the union's control over entry into the relevant profession.

The multi-objectived character of groups is fundamental to an understanding of the relationships between them. At the one extreme, we can conceive of groups whose sole objective is the 'efficient' satisfaction of individual choices. Thus, the multi-person 'firm' existing in perfectly competitive market conditions can produce more efficiently than individual entrepreneurs relying solely on market transactions. The 'limiting case' that makes this possible also denies the possibility of independent utility-maximization by firm members that is incompatible with profit maximization by the group: sales maximization that is not profit maximizing must eliminate the firm.

At the other extreme, one can conceive of a 'government' elected by the individual members of a group (society) with the sole purpose of deciding the *rules* within which individuals and groups shall pursue their own objectives. But such a government can be thought of as single-objectived only in so far as it has no objectives of its own, as a government, which are different from those of the people who elect it.

Between the limiting cases, all groups must be expected to have objective functions concerned with changing the rules of the game as well as with operating in the interests of their members within the rules as they presently exist. Most important from the point of view of this section, group actions will affect the position of individuals not only directly, but also through the ways they affect the possibilities of other groups (and through this the expected costs and benefits attaching to group membership for individuals). Thus, e.g., the expected 'cost' to an individual of refusing to become a member of the trade union will include the consequent influence on his job opportunities. This in turn will be influenced by the laws concerning industrial relations etc., and by the actual behaviour of the unions (members and 'officials') towards non-members. These matters will themselves be affected by the view those concerned to control political power take of their own interest, which will include their view of the interpretation that individuals/social groups would place upon given changes in the law.

Clearly, these relationships would permit of considerable extension and complication: the illustrations are perhaps enough, in the context of this short note, to indicate that the relationships between non-market groups are at least as complex as the market relationships that economists have traditionally studied: we need to extend the individualistic model to comprehend them.

A general model of group behaviour

So far, we have defined the individual's opportunity-cost problem as being concerned with his choice between direct transactions and participation in social groups. It will, however, be evident from the preceding argument that this is itself too simple a distinction. Specifically, it ignores the question: how do groups take decisions?

A market transaction between two persons is conceptually the simplest relationship conceivable: A exchanges with B, and both value what they receive more than what they sacrifice. Participation in a group is inevitably more complex, in that it also implies an act of cooperation. In the case of a firm, the distinction is between a situation in which A pays B for a specific service, and one in which A and B cooperate directly in the exchange of goods and services with others, with some agreement with each other as to how the results of the exchanges shall be shared. The question thus arises: how do A and B in fact coordinate their affairs?

It is in this context that the notion of 'a set of processes withdrawn from the market' is an incomplete description of a group. It is also characteristic of group behaviour that *members delegate responsibilities to one another*, and in doing so establish a set of *authority relationships* within the group. In groups of any size, this process of delegation will be unilateral, in that the group gives particular members (sub-groups) authority to act on behalf of all, within limits and for purposes which are defined by the group's 'rules' (laws or 'custom' (entitlement)).[4] It is of interest, by way of illustration, to apply this extended concept to the firm.

At its simplest, the 'firm' is a 'partnership' whose members collaborate with 'equal entitlements' in decision-making and to the proceeds of the firm's activities, and whose decisions are taken according to agreed 'rules'. If such a 'partnership' employed 'workers', they could, as in orthodox economic analysis, be treated as 'factors of production' without a decision-making role. But if, as is realistic, we recognize that *all* 'human resources' are decision-makers, then the difference between 'the partners' and 'the workers' becomes one of degree, concerned with the differences in their roles and entitlements. In so far as the workers are members of trade unions, the firm is also involved in transactions with other groups to which its members also belong. Similar extensions would recognize the existence of distinct 'owning' (shareholding) and 'operating' (management) groups, which may also overlap, and of a 'client group' (actual and potential customers).

Perhaps the most interesting outcome of this formulation is the observation that groups of all kinds are likely to delegate authority, and so have a 'management' (bureaucracy). Given that individuals pursue their own ends, and that managements may therefore pursue objectives different from 'the memberships', an appreciation of the role of bureaucracies is thus necessary to an understanding of the behaviour of *all* social groups: the questions of interest concern the potential for, constraints upon, and consequences of bureaucratic behaviour in different 'group situations'. (Examples are the relations between voters, governments, and governmental agencies; between the shareholders, management and workers of joint stock companies; between the members elected delegates and 'officials' of trades unions; between the parents and other members of the family; between the donors, officers and beneficiaries of a charity.)

Again, it is not suggested that the notion of a generalized system of bureaucracy will come as a blinding revelation. But the notion that bureaucratic behaviour should be treated as part of *all* group behaviour, rather than as a distinct 'form', perhaps runs somewhat counter to current fashion. A generalized model of the resource-allocation process incorporating group behaviour needs to run, not in terms of 'organizations' of different kinds maximizing different objectives (e.g. governments maximizing 'power', firms maximizing 'profit', bureaucrats maximizing 'security'), but in terms of different groups with different objective functions, but *all* characterized by the problems of 'internalized' decision-making and potential conflict that the above argument has identified. Similarly, all groups must be expected to be interested in changing the 'rules of the game' (constraints on their own behaviour) as well as in pursuing the interests of members within the existent rules, all groups must be expected to have internal conflicts of interest between the objectives of at least three participant 'sets' (the members of the group as a 'constituency', the 'bureaucracy', and individual members pursuing their own interests), and all groups must be expected to have members who are also members of other groups with potentially conflicting objectives.

It remains to consider the 'external' relations of socio-economic groups, and in particular the relationships between characteristic types. Two characteristics would seem to be paramount. First, there are two groups that differ from others in that their members do not normally 'join' but can decide whether to 'resign'. These are the family and the political society. It will be observed that the two stand at opposite ends of a spectrum, as the largest and smallest 'group decision units'. Whether the difference between these and other groups is of more than formal interest merits more consideration than it can be given here. 'Membership' is not by deliberate decision but members can opt to leave, within limits, and the costs and benefits of doing so are determined, as with other social groups, by the extant 'rules of the game', e.g. the costs and benefits associated with the decision of a UK citizen to emigrate to Canada differ in significant respects from the costs and benefits needing to be weighed by a citizen of USSR wishing to emigrate to Israel.

Second, while all groups must be expected to be concerned in some degree with at least three objectives (maximization of the welfare of members from the direct benefits of group action, 'taste changing' (promoting the welfare of members by changing the preferences of others) and 'rule changing' (altering the structure of property rights (entitlements) within which the system currently operates)), the balance between objectives differs markedly from one type of group to another. Firms, e.g., may be conceived of as *primarily* concerned with the promotion of the economic well-being of their owners within the existing rules (though with strong 'secondary' motives in the case of limited liability enterprises), pressure groups with changing the rules of the game.

Some positive and normative implications

This paper is no more than a *jeu d'esprit*, and in conclusion we can only point to the kind of implications the suggested generalization of economists' formal models to incorporate group activities might have for positive and normative study.

So far as positive economics is concerned, the suggested formulation invites examination of the *consequences of institutional change*. Following the examples given above, it should be possible e.g. to test predictions of the consequences of changes in the position of trade unions in the community (and of the consequent changes in their bargaining behaviour) for changes in the size and character of government expenditures through time.[5]

At the normative level, the immediate conclusions would seem to be negative, though not therefore uninteresting. If it is accepted that the existence of groups whose objectives include the changing of tastes and/or of entitlements is an intrinsic part of a society which itself accepts the freedom of individuals to pursue their own goals as an objective, then the 'efficiency' of group (and therefore of all) behaviour cannot usefully be appraised solely by its contribution to the achievement of the 'static choice' objectives of a Pareto-type model. Somehow, we need also to devise 'optimal' rules for 'taste changing', and for 'entitlements', and embracing both 'group' and 'direct transaction' behaviour. There is growing interest in the development of such models: meanwhile, it will do no harm to recognize the serious practical limitations of any policy prescriptions that assume that group behaviour can be comprehended within the limitations of orthodox welfare economics.

Notes
1. Comprehensive supporting evidence for this view in the case of one country is to be found in Whiting (ed.) (1975).
2. On this question, see Olson (1965). Phelps Brown (1975) has provided a most perceptive review of the historical evolution of the behaviour of UK trade unions which is sympathetic to the position taken here.
3. This relationship is explored in detail in Rowley and Peacock (1975).
4. The term is used to describe the 'rights' that individuals behave 'as though' they possess. It is more embracing and less emotive than property rights as traditionally defined. The usage derives from Alchian (1961).
5. Phelps Brown (1975) provides much of the initial historical material needed for such a study.

References
Alchian, A. A., 'Some Economics of Property' (1961) *Rand Corporation Paper* P-2316.
Brennan, G. and Buchanan, J. M. (1985) *The Reason of Rules – Constitutional Political Economy*, Cambridge, Cambridge University Press.
Coase, R. H. (1937) 'The Nature of the Firm', *Economica*, n. s. IV.
Olsen, Jr, Mancur (1965) *The Logic of Collective Action*, Harvard.
Phelps Brown, Henry (1975) 'A Non-Monetarist View of the Pay Explosion', *The Three Banks Review*, (March).
Rowley, Charles K. and Peacock, Alan T. (1975) *Welfare Economics: A Liberal Restatement*, York Studies in Economics, Martin Robertson.
Vanberg, V. (1986) 'Individual Choice and Constitutional Constraints – the Normative Element in Classical and Contractarian Liberalism', *Analyse and Kritik*, Vol. 8.
Whiting, A. (ed.) (1975) *The Economics of Industrial Subsidies*, HMSO (Department of Industry).
Wiseman, J. and Peacock, Alan T., (1979) 'Approaches to the Analysis of Public Expenditure Growth', *Public Finance Quarterly*, Vol. 7, no. 1.

6 The Political Economy of Nationalized Industry*

Foreword

In his interesting discussion of the LSE tradition in cost theory, Professor Buchanan makes a perceptive distinction between the practical concerns of its members and the more general preoccupations of the Austrian School, and argues the need for the two somehow to be brought together if the mutually sympathetic ideas were to attract the attention they deserved (Buchanan, 1969). The papers in this volume reflect that distinction. I am the product of my background and training, in the sense that my ultimate concern has always been with the contribution of economics to the resolution of practical problems. But this concern regularly drives me back upon theoretical enquiry, because the tools I find available are inadequate for the job.

The present essay was concerned with a very practical issue: the economic characteristics and efficiency problems of nationalized industries, which then accounted for an important part of UK industrial production. It builds upon the logical foundations of the previous two papers, and identifies major differences between the way these industries were commonly described and studied within the neo-classical framework, and the behavioural characteristics that typified this form of organization in fact. The central problems are not those of pricing and investment *per se*, but rather the operational difficulties created by the fundamental changes in property rights, and hence in decision-making behaviour, that result from the nationalization of hitherto private activities.

The argument leads to the enunciation of a set of propositions describing the inherent characteristics of nationalized enterprise that crucially differentiate it from private production as a decision-making process.

If the form of organization is to be retained, it follows that reform needs to be sought not by way of supervisory committees or watchdogs, but in the improvement of the relevant decision-relationships (property rights) in fashions that change the (opportunity-cost) behaviour of the relevant decision-makers. But while I perceived the potential import-

* *The Economics of Politics*, (1978), Readings No. 18, London, Institute of Economic Affairs.

ance of comparative study of public and private enterprises to this end, it was less easy to identify actual enterprises that would be practically appropriate for such an enquiry. (Independently, John Heath (1980) put forward the decision-processes of a private conglomerate as a possible model. But I am not aware of any empirical investigation.) Attention shifted towards privatization, an outcome which I would have expected such a study to support.

When the paper was written, privatization was not on the political agenda in UK, and there was little appreciation that 'de-nationalization' would involve anything very different from the reversal of previous nationalization policies. The nature of some of the problems that have since emerged is anticipated in the argument of the paper.

Introduction

Nationalization in the UK provides a useful test-bed for ideas concerning the relations between economics, politics, government and bureaucracy, because of the manifest gaps between reality and belief observable in the debate about nationalization policy: because, that is, of the strength of myth in this area of public debate. Myth significantly affects the behaviour of nationalized corporations, the rules by which the behaviour is supposed to be governed, the interpretation of the outcome of that behaviour, and the consequent political attitudes to the corporations and their future governance.

It may seem strange to hear an economist talking about myths. But we are concerned to explain human behaviour, and if the way the community's resources are allocated between uses is significantly affected by myths, then myths are what we need to talk about: the more so if the relevant mythology is at least partly shared by all political parties, although some politicians do not know, or act as though they do not know, that the mythology exists.

I do not claim that the concepts I use are novel, but I think that perhaps their application to nationalization may give some of you a rather different view of the relevant policy problems, which is my prime purpose. Also, I shall concentrate my illustrative material on the situation before Cmnd. 7131, *The Nationalized Industries* (March 1978). This new policy document was published when my paper was almost completed. Its contents in fact fit well with my general theme, as I shall try to show in a Postscript.

The economic efficiency myth

The most pervasive, and probaby the most damaging, myth is that industries are nationalized in the interests of economic efficiency, to overcome the defects or incompetences of provision of the goods concerned through private markets. Since the diversity of products and historical circumstances within the existing nationalized sector makes this notion difficult to swallow save for the truly credulous or blinkered, the same notion also appears in a rather more sophisticated form: whatever the 'special circumstances' that in practice lead to a set of activities being nationalized, the *result* of nationalization will be an improvement in 'economic efficiency'.

Economic efficiency and nationalized industry
Economic efficiency is not a simple notion. It is indeed difficult in a paper as short as this to give a summary exposition of the debate on this question during the post-1945 era of nationalization. In the early part of this period the debate about the organization of nationalized industries was dominated by specialists in public administration, mostly sympathetic, and by politicians of left-wing views. The interests of consumers did not figure prominently in these debates: they could be left to well-meaning administrators, provided that suitable organizational arrangements had been created.[1] Nevertheless, the underlying, if implicit, notions of efficiency were essentially those of the competitive market economy – what economists like to call the 'Pareto-optimal' conditions, or, in everyday language, the direction of resources towards the uses in which consumers most want them. The most formal espousal of this perception of efficiency is to be found in the 1967 White Paper, Cmnd. 3437, *Nationalized Industries: a review of economic and financial objectives*, which effectively required that nationalized industry products should be sold at prices equal to their long-run marginal cost. I have argued elsewhere (1967, 1975) that the practical relevance of this prescription is of the same order as would be an injunction to price according to the principle that God is Love: the sentiment is difficult to deny, the practical consequences of conformity unidentifiable.

Events since the publication of the 1967 White Paper have given me no reason to change my views. But my immediate preoccupation is different. Without bothering you with an undue amount of technical exposition, I shall simply assert that the essential reason for promulgation of the long-run marginal cost 'rule' was that its use was expected to lead to the same (resource-allocation) outcome as would an efficiently functioning system of competitive markets. That the underlying economic analysis is wrong, or, rather, irrelevant to the real-world situation, is not immediately to the point. What matters to me here is that the policy-makers' notion of economic efficiency for the nationalized sector was essentially the same as the efficiency notion customarily applied to the private market economy.

Three arguments for nationalization

In this scenario, nationalization is simply a device, to be judged by its results. It is needed because provision through private markets fails to 'deliver the goods', and it is to be judged by its success in remedying the relevant defects. Thus, arguments for nationalization concern, for example, the need to deal with the problems of 'natural monopoly' to provide 'public goods', or to give the government authority over the 'commanding heights' of the economy.

Natural monopoly   None of these arguments emerges particularly well from a confrontation with the facts. The 'natural monopoly' argument derives from the proposition that atomistic competition is not possible in the industry concerned because of the existence of economies of scale: competition is destroyed by technology. But in which UK nationalized industry is the minimum size of a technically efficient *plant* so large that competitive production is impossible *for this reason*? The relevant consideration is clearly not the minimum size of the necessary investment, but the relation between the output appropriate to that size and the size of market demand. Would the coal industry, for example, qualify on these terms? Surely not. At best, there is the possibility that, for some goods (such as electricity), the relevant indivisibility lies in *distribution* rather than in production arrangements. But this is essentially a matter of property rights (of which more later). If the contractual relationships between the 'grid' and the 'producers' is appropriately specified, there is no *technical* reason why the generation of electricity, for example, should not be competitive.

'Public goods'   The essence of the 'public goods' argument is that certain goods will be under-supplied if provision is left to market forces, because their consumption is 'non-excludable': we all 'share' the same level of defence expenditure. For the UK, the argument has two major deficiencies. First, a problem of principle: it is very difficult to imagine a good whose consumption could not be 'rationed' by price if the community chose to pass appropriate laws and require producers and consumers to carry the appropriate costs. Again, the problem is ultimately one of defining property rights in such a fashion that the relevant exchange transactions become possible. Nationalization *per se* does not solve this kind of problem: the criteria determining how much of the good concerned should be produced and the price at which it should

be sold remain to be specified. (The provision of lighthouses, often cited as an example of a public good, provides a useful exemplar. Devices exist by which the receipt of warning signals could be restricted to vessels which have paid for and installed appropriate equipment. That such devices are not used is attributable not to any *inherent* peculiarity in the nature of the product, but *either* to the costs of creating the necessary market *or* to the concern of the community for the welfare of sea-going travellers (i.e. to interpersonal utility relationships).)

'Commanding heights'   The 'commanding heights' argument is even more nebulous. Its essence is the proposition that, through nationaliz-ation, the government acquires economic policy 'tools' that it would not otherwise have. But this suggests that industries can be classified as 'appropriate' for nationalization, or not, by reference to the 'com-manding heights' notion. However, no useful taxonomy has ever been proposed, and it would defy reason to suggest that the industries actu-ally nationalized in the UK enjoy this status because of their role as part of the 'commanding heights'. Many of them are more clearly part of the abysmal depths of UK economic performance than of the commanding heights of UK economic policy.

Nationalized industry decisions in practice
Whatever the plausibility of these technical arguments for nationaliz-ation, it is clear that they are of secondary relevance for the way decisions on the allocation of resources are taken in practice.[2] Conform-ity with the long-run marginal cost 'rule' does not seem ever to have been more than a formal matter: how to present 'commercial' plans in an 'acceptable' fashion. Levels of subsidization have been historically determined, and have not generally been related to notions of 'public-ness', or to identifiable community benefits not reflected in costs and prices. The industries have been protected from private competition, which would seem to be in contradiction of the efficiency concept concerned, unwanted resources have not been made freely available to other potential users at 'scarcity' prices, and no 'liquidation' rules simi-lar to those of bankruptcy in the private sector have ever been promulgated.

Finally, even if planning by the nationalized industries themselves had been developed in consonance with some common notion of efficiency for private and public sectors, the actual outcome would have been changed by Ministerial interference, e.g. in such matters as pricing and wage-bargaining. By stretching a point, such interference might be argued to conduce to efficiency in our defined sense, as being governed by the 'commanding heights' approach to global economic policy. But there is no way of knowing, since inadequate information about ministerial intervention is made public, and practically no information is available on the predicted *consequences* for nationalized industries of ministerial changes in management policies.

The politics myths

My separation of economics and politics is no more than a taxonomic convenience: the politics myths, of course, march with the economics ones. There are two sets of politics myths that concern us.

First, the myths about property. One reason for nationalization would be a moral objection to private property in the means of production – 'property is theft'. It would be difficult to use this argument to explain the piecemeal nationalizations which have produced the UK mixed economy. If it is private property *per se* that is morally objectionable, why nationalize only this particular set? Perhaps this is the reason why the argument of principle has not been more prominent in public debate. The myth, established by default rather than positively asserted, is that 'property is neutral' – the political counterpart of the economic notion that 'efficiency is neutral'. But while official statements avoid attaching a value to nationalization *per se*, the enabling Acts clearly derive from such a notion: how else, for example, can the existence of monopoly power, regarded as socially damaging if deriving from private property, become a positive benefit if conferred by law upon a nationalized undertaking? Equally, if less obviously, how else can it be assumed that the managers of nationalized enterprises can be relied upon to concern themselves with 'the public interest' (and to know what it is), while private property owners cannot?

Alongside the myth that 'property is neutral', there is a further one: the myth that the 'technical' management of nationalized industries can in principle be divorced from political control. Thus, the 'problem' of ministerial (etc.) interference with managerial decisions is seen as a matter essentially of finding the 'right' organizational structure, so that the relationship between the 'commercial' decision-process of the enterprise and the (political) policy-making process is in principle no different from that of private industry, though of course the channels of policy communication may be different. This myth ignores the fact that nationalization of its very nature must imply that property in the relevant productive resources must inhere in Parliament and its institutions as agents of 'the community': there is no way in which ultimate political responsibilty for the actions of the nationalized sector can be sequestrated.

From myth to reality

Central reasons for the persistence of the myths I have described are, first, the absence of well-articulated logical constructs capable of distinguishing the nationalized corporation and the private enterprise as organizational forms, and, second, a continuing failure adequately to distinguish these organizational differences from differences in objectives (a major example, already cited, being the refusal, in a policy context, to admit to preferences between the organizational forms *per se*).[3]

So far as the first of these is concerned, the most promising approach in my view is one which uses methodological individualism and some concept of group behaviour in the context of a theory of property rights. That is quite a mouthful: I shall try to explain it in everyday terms. The aim is to bring out differences in the relationships between the various participants in the economic decision-process in the two organizational forms. On the basis of particular assumptions about motivation, and about the detailed 'rules of the game' (property laws, nationalization statutes, etc.), this should enable us to predict differences in the results of choosing one form of organization rather than another. In an ideal world, we could then deal with the second problem, by appraising these differences against any 'value' we cared to attach to particular organizational forms. In this short paper, I can hope to do no more than sketch out the fundamentals of the approach: I hope it will be enough to persuade you of its potential, and to indicate some of the questions towards which further inquiry might be directed.

Methodological individualism

The essential proposition of methodological individualism is that an adequate model of socio-economic behaviour must treat *all* individuals as decision-makers pursuing their own interests (which does not, of course, preclude concern for the welfare of others).[4] This may seem obvious enough. But it needs to be specified for two reasons.

First, it is not the postulate underlying a good deal of 'orthodox' economic analysis. 'The worker' is there treated as a factor of production, responding automatically to the decisions of 'the entrepreneur'. Where trade unions are recognized, as in labour market theory, individuals still do not become decision-makers. As individuals, they are passive factors of production. As bargainers, they are completely identified with the objectives and behaviour of 'the union'. There is scant recognition, e.g. of a possible conflict between individual and group objectives. This is too simplistic for our present purposes.

Second, the values I treat as relevant to decisions, and to public policy, are the values perceived by individuals. Other papers will have dealt more fully with the relevant philosophical issues. My sole purpose is to emphasize that methodological individualism implies a rejection of any kind of organic theory of the state which superimposes higher 'values' on those of individuals. The notion embraces *conflicts* of individual values, but not 'superior' or 'external' values. The direct relevance of this is, of course, that there are strong historic ties between 'organic' philosophies such as Marxism and support for nationalization. I do not propose to pursue this matter further. As I pointed out earlier, these philosophies lead to the rejection of private property *per se*, and are of little help in understanding the problems of the nationalized corporation in a mixed economy.

Group behaviour

Traditionally, economic analysis has concentrated on the exchange relationship (direct transactions between individuals), to the relative neglect of non-market and group-participative behaviour. I think it is fair to say that we still lack a satisfactory *comprehensive* model of group behaviour, embracing firms, bureaucracies, pressure-groups, families, state corporations, governments and trade unions. I do not intend to try to elaborate such a model here. I want only to propose that the notion of methodological individualism can be used to develop such a model, simply by extending the scope of individual decision to embrace participation in group activities as well as the making of individual transactions.[5]

We can apply this concept to the theory of the firm operating in a private market environment. Professor Ronald Coase has explained the existence of firms as a set of processes withdrawn from the market (1937). We can elaborate this notion by recognizing that there are various types of process, and various types of withdrawal, all depending upon the decisions of individuals and the environment in which they operate. Thus, in the case of a limited liability company there are the owners of the assets of the enterprise (who have chosen to hold rights in these assets rather than others), the management (whose members will have contractual rights and obligations with the company, chosen in preference to, for example, 'freelance' exchange transactions), and workers, also with continuing contractual relationships chosen in preference to 'casual' hiring.

Two things are noteworthy. First, the individuals concerned have chosen commitment to the firm in preference to a simple market (exch-ange) relationship. But it does not of course follow that their personal objectives must be identical with those of the firm: only that the individ-ual predicts that this form of participation will best serve his own interests. Second, individuals may (and often will) simultaneously belong to more than one group. Workers, for example, will commonly be members of a trade union. There is nothing unnatural about this: that in particular circumstances the objectives of firm and union might be opposed obviously does not mean that an individual acting in his own interest cannot rationally be a member of both; nor does it mean that the worker may not participate in other groups concerned to increase (or decrease) trade union power.

It is apparent that the notions of methodological individualism and of group behaviour provide a method of comparison of different organ-izational situations. Before attempting this, however, we need to intro-duce our third concept, of property rights, since this is essential to an understanding of how decisions will in practice be made.

Property rights
The relevance of property rights to our problem is that the specification of those rights effectively determines the costs and benefits that individ-uals will expect to result from particular decisions, and so must influence the decisions themselves. An interesting example which has been of practical interest in the UK in recent years is the law relating to employ-ment. The 'cost' to a worker of refusing to become a member of a trade union is determined by the consequences for his freedom to exercise his skill: the more the law supports the exclusion of non-members from employment, the higher union membership must be expected to be.

Interesting work on property rights, and on the application of the relevant concepts to our kind of problem, has been developing in the United States, and is associated particularly with the work of Alchian (1961) and Demsetz (1967). Property rights in the relevant sense are the product both of law and of custom: the two together constitute the rights that individuals behave 'as though' they possess. (Alchian uses the term 'entitlement', both to escape the emotional overtones that have come to be associated with 'property', and to underline the relevance of custom and consent.) The concept is clearly a sophisticated one. The law itself does not fully define property rights in an operational sense. For example, ministers have legal powers over local authorities; but there are established consultative procedures ('entitlements') which they are expected to follow. The same is true of the exercise of ministerial powers under the Nationalization Acts. Equally, legal sanction is not necessary for entitlements to exist. Formally, private property in the legal sense exists only minimally in communist countries. But no one familiar with such countries would believe that those with political power do not enjoy significant entitlements.

In so far as nationalization changes entitlements, it will also change individual decisions and hence economic outcomes, save if the changes in entitlements are offset by changes in what individuals choose to maximize. I entitled this section 'From Myth to Reality': let us see if the ideas I have outlined can help us develop a realistic exposition of the character and problems of nationalization.

The private firm and the nationalized corporation
This concluding section uses the argument of the preceding one to bring together, albeit very summarily, the essential differences in the situation of the individuals concerned in production and consumption in a firm in the private sector and in a nationalized corporation. Unavoidably in a short paper, what I offer must be something of a parody: but I think the essential points may emerge.

I earlier described the private firm, after Coase, as a set of processes withdrawn from the market, and identified three types of individual participants in its activities: 'owners' (the shareholders), 'management' (the directors), and 'workers'. In the private market environment, the firm can be seen as constrained on the one side by the capital market, and on the other by consumers and other (competing) firms. The capital market constraint results from the fact that owners are interested in the profitability of the firm, in so far as this is reflected in the capital value or yield of their property in it. The existence of a capital market ensures that they can reflect this interest either by action *within* the firm (e.g. by voting to change the management), or *outside* it (by selling their shares). The ease with which such changes can be made will be determined by the existing system of formal property rights (as reflected, e.g., in company law) and of less formal entitlements (such as the customary procedures for making management changes). The crucial point is that there exists a set of individuals with a direct interest in the profitable use of the firm's assets, and with institutional arrangements through which their emerging judgements can be reflected in new decisions.

Role of directorate in private firms
The directorate is responsible to the shareholders. As a group, the directorate must satisfy the shareholders. In doing so, it faces the

constraints imposed by consumers, who can spend their incomes on other things, and of competitors, who have an incentive (from their own shareholders) to encourage consumers to do so. The nature of these constraints will vary *inter alia* with the state of competition in the industry concerned. But even in the most monopolistic sector, there is a continuing incentive for firms and individuals to try to break in by innovation: private markets are characterized by the search for new products/processes, success in which both confers short-term monopoly and stimulates competitive change by others.[6]

Individual members of the management group will, of course, pursue their own ends, which may not be identical with the ends of the owners. There is indeed a considerable economics literature devoted to managerial theories of the firm, built around the notion that firms may seek objectives other than profit, such as the maximization of predicted sales or predicted growth. Much of this literature is unsatisfactory, however, in that it postulates these other objectives essentially as *alternatives* to the maximization of profit, while the actual situation is one of *resolution* of conflicting objectives within the firm. Put crudely, the sales manager may correlate his predicted future income with the volume of his firm's sales. But other members of his management group will have different notions, and the group as a whole will have to adapt their individual objectives to satisfy the (profitability) interests of asset owners. This is not, of course, to say that no divergence of objectives between owners and management can exist, but that for firms in the private sector there are constraints upon the extent of such divergences, the particular efficacy of which will depend upon the detailed institutional arrangements (and related entitlements) concerned.

Finally, the workers. Workers commonly belong to a trade union 'group' as well as to the firm 'group'. I have already observed that in some circumstances the objectives of the two groups may be in conflict. But in the case of the firm in the private sector there is again a constraint. In so far as workers claim higher incomes for themselves through participation in trade union action, they reduce the expected profitability of the firm, and hence, through the process already described, encourage the withdrawal or devaluation of the firm's capital and so jeopardize their own prospects of future employment or potential income from the firm.

Nationalized industry and private firm differences
In asking how the situation of a nationalized corporation differs, I shall again offer a 'thumbnail sketch' which largely ignores differences

between individual Nationalization Acts in order to bring out the essentials. The differences can be summarized in seven propositions:

1. There is no one who has a *direct* interest in the fruitful use of the assets of a nationalized corporation, in the sense that he identifies his personal well-being with changes in that use. In Hayek's illuminating phrase: if everyone owns it, no one owns it.

2. The responsibilities of ownership are decided by the political process, and, effectively, inhere in the minister identified in the enabling Act. But the minister does not have available to him the set of direct sanctions available to the private market asset-holder. He cannot buy and sell the relevant assets, and he can divest himself of responsibility only by de-nationalization – which is itself a piece of political rather than of economic behaviour.

3. The difficulties of deciding the capital requirements of nationalized corporations derive directly from (1) and (2): *there can be no efficient market for the relevant assets.* (This difficulty is exacerbated by others discussed below: specifically, the effect of monopoly on asset values.)

4. Management is not profit-responsible to the asset-owners in the fashion we identified for the private firm. On the one hand, this greatly widens the scope of managerial discretion, in that the checks on managerial efficiency are inevitably much more nebulous. On the other hand, the behaviour of ministers (the *de facto* replacement of shareholders) is also less directly constrained (since there is no functioning capital market and no alternative asset owners), and consequently less predictable. Thus, the management of the nationalized corporation finds itself with considerable discretion, but nevertheless frustrated by arbitrary intervention in the decision-process.

5. It is an implication of (4) that the scope for divergence between the objectives of the individual members of the management group, the group as a whole, and the responsible minister, is much wider than in the private firm.

6. In so far as the nationalized corporations are legally protected from competition, it appears likely that, within the range of possibilities at (5), managers will attach less significance to innovative activity than they would in the private market environment, since they have less to gain from it: there is an incentive to substitute bureaucratic for entrepreneurial behaviour.

7. Finally, the constraints imposed upon the behaviour of workers and trade unions by the need to consider profitability is removed

to the extent that ministers can seek approval for the recovery of losses from the public purse. Unions and workers must be expected to behave differently in consequence, to the extent that they consider this kind of obligation to meet losses as an 'entitlement' conferred by nationalization, and the predicted costs and benefits to themselves that they impute, e.g. to the disruption of production, are consequently changed.

None of these seven propositions is particularly novel. What is important is that we should recognize that *they are not the result of human fallibility or wickedness, but are inherent in the nationalized corporation as a form of economic organization*. Recognition of this is the necessary starting-point for any programme of reform. Specifically, if de-nationalization is thought to be 'politically impossible' (because the 'neutrality' myths are too powerful, and/or because of the very significant 'entitlements' that nationalization itself generates, e.g. for present and imaginable future ministers), then, apart from trying to dispel the myths, the questions to be asked should concern the possibility of improving the set of decision-relationships that I have specified.

My own preferred starting points for such an inquiry would be the possibilities of exposure to competition, on the one hand, and the clearer elaboration of decision responsibilities (including an obligation on ministers to make public not only their instructions but their prediction of the consequences), on the other. I have little faith in the creation of more committees: toothless watchdogs have little difficulty in eating, but cannot bite.

But reform is a subject of iself: I do not here pretend to have done more than offer a way of thinking about it.

Postscript on Cmnd. 7131: The Nationalized Industries

The White Paper was published in March 1978, and I did not see it in time to comment upon it in the main text. I hope to deal with it more fully elsewhere, and confine myself here to observations on its consonance with the thesis of this paper.

At first blush, the myths I have discussed might appear from the White Paper less pervasive. The practical irrelevance of the long-run marginal cost 'rule' has been recognized, and it is no longer to be used. That nationalization necessitates ministerial involvement in the decision-process is also recognized, and it is proposed that the predicted consequences of the changes made to nationalized industry plans on ministerial instructions should be quantified.

A more careful reading, however, suggests that changes are not being made because the myths have been dispelled and the true nature of the problems recognized, but rather that experience has brought dissatisfaction with some practices, so, pragmatically, we must try something different. There are important respects in which the true nature of the problem to be solved still goes unrecognized.

First, despite the abandonment of the marginal cost pricing 'rule', and some obscurity in the argument, the proposed pricing and investment rules are clearly related to private-sector concepts of economic efficiency. But a new confusion has entered, for it is also asserted that nationalized industries cannot become bankrupt, and no possible incompatibility between the two positions is recognized.

Second, the proposed changes in the behaviour of the minister do nothing to deal with the loss of the function of private asset-holder, and since the minister's 'social responsibilities' are also reasserted, it would be unwise to predict that the exercise of their scope for discretion by minister and managements, and the consequent confusion and uncertainty, is going to be much inhibited by the new arrangements.

Third, there is a piquant reference to the need, in the appraisal of individual investment projects, to allow for 'appraisal optimism'. But there is no discussion of why such optimism is believed to exist. Could it just possibly be because, following the lines of my argument, the managers making investment decisions find their opportunity-cost situation very different from the profit-responsible situation in private industry? The recent history of the British Steel Corporation suggests that the possibility is not entirely remote.

If so, can we really make much progress by subjecting the optimistic judgements of one unconstrained group (the managers) to the scrutiny of others (such as the Treasury) for whom profit responsibility is of even more remote personal concern?

Notes

1   A useful survey is in Chester (1975).
2   R. H. S. Crossman quotes Mr James Callaghan (then Chancellor of the Exchequer) as follows on the 1967 White Paper: 'You, Crossman, are a don who knows nothing about the subject. Personally as Chancellor I couldn't care less. I take no responsibility and I took no part in composing it.' See also Foster (1971).
3   Some of the arguments here presented are developed in an interesting paper, as yet unpublished, by Robert Millward (mimeo).
4   A valuable survey of the literature using this approach is to be found in Littlechild (1978).
5   A general model of this kind is developed in Chapter 5 'Some Reflections on the Economics of Group Behaviour'.
6   E.g. Kirzner (1973).

References

Alchian, A. A. (1961) *Some Economics of Property*, RAND Corporation Paper P-2316.

Buchanan, J. M. (1969) *Cost and Choice, op. cit.*

Chester, Sir Norman (1973) *The Nationalization of British Industry, 1945–51*, HMSO (1975).

Coase, R. H. (1937) 'The Nature of the Firm', *Economica*, n.s. IV.

Demsetz, H. (1967) 'Towards a Theory of Property Rights', *American Economic Review*, Papers and Proceedings, (May).

Foster, C. D. (1971) *Politics, Finance and the Role of Economics*, Allen and Unwin.

Heath, J. B. (1980) *Management in Nationalized Industries*, NICG Occasional Paper No. 2, London, Nationalized Industries Chairmen's Group.

Kirzner, I. M. (1973) *Competition and Entrepreneurship*, Chicago, University of Chicago Press.

Littlechild, S. C. (1978) *Change Rules, OK?*, Inaugural Lecture, University of Birmingham.

Millward, Robert, 'Public Ownership, The Theory of Property Rights and the Public Corporation in the UK' (mimeo).

Wiseman, J. (1975) 'The Theory of Public Utility Price – An Empty Box', *Oxford Economic Papers*, (February).

Wiseman, J. (1967) 'Growing without Nationalization', in *Growth Through Industry*, IEA Readings No. 2.

7 Costs and Decisions*

Foreword

In the same year that the Nationalized Industry paper was presented at a conference of the Institute of Economic Affairs, the UK Association of University Teachers of Economics held its Annual Conference in York. I was invited to give a guest lecture. In keeping with my twin interests in theoretical development and practical policy, I chose to use the occasion to state an intellectual position. The time was ripe in that I had been developing the structure of the paper for some time, but, partly because of the essentially destructive nature of the conclusions, had needed time to test the argument thoroughly in discussion before committing myself to print. One consequence of this I had greatly regretted. I had originally planned the paper as my contribution to a *Festschrift* for Lord Robbins, but had finally been obliged to write him to say that I did not feel ready to participate.

(This had a further interesting by-product. As he did not attend the AUTE Conference, I sent him a copy of the paper, together with an invitation to participate in the forthcoming British Association meeting (see Chapter 8). His reply was complimentary, but ended: 'You are the conscience of us all.' I interpreted this ambiguous phrase to mean that, while he could not fault the argument, he also did not think that I should overestimate its likely influence upon the thinking or future activities of my compatriots. In the same letter, he graciously refused my BA invitation, on the ground that he had 'nothing new to say' – in fact, he must have already been preparing the Ely lecture, which was an illuminating statement of his position on the subject-matter of Chapters 7 and 8 (Wiseman, 1985).)

The paper reflects the evolution of my dissatisfaction with the theory of costs into a wider discontent with neo-classical economic theory in general. The underlying assumptions about human knowledge, in both the naive model and its more sophisticated formulations, are not 'legitimate simplifications' but a gross perversion of the nature of the decision-problem faced by people living in the real world. The argument of the paper is concise; I shall not repeat it here.

In relation to the development of my own thinking, the paper shows

* Currie, D. A., and Peters, W. (1980) *Contemporary Economic Analysis*, Vol. 2, London, Croom Helm.

me as confident in my criticism, but exercised about what can positively be done. I recognize the contribution of the Austrian School. But it does not seem to me to be enough. We have to come to terms with George Shackle's world, in which surprise and mistake are not unexplained causes of 'temporary disequilibrium', but are at the core of the economic problem. Effectively, therefore, the paper concludes with a plea for help, an invitation to my sophisticated mathematician friends to stop wasting their time, and try to help me in the study of the real world.

(While one can never be sure where one's ideas take root, I need hardly say that I was not overwhelmed by offers of help – though a delegation of graduate students did ask why they were not being exposed to these ideas. But I know of one specialist in the mathematics of uncertainty whose perception of the problem has greatly changed, I believe at least partly because of this lecture.)

If the paper is considered together with the earlier ones, it would appear that at this time I had two major but inadequately integrated concerns: one with the need for a more embracing logic of choice, the other with the internal deficiencies of the neo-classical model.

Introduction

> God only knows: and He won't tell. (Anon)

> We are not omniscient, assured masters of known circumstances via reason, but the prisoners of time. (Shackle, 1973)

I was asked to give this lecture at short notice, and consequently chose a topic that has preoccupied me for years, and about which I have a debt of conscience towards the many colleagues with whom I have debated and disputed over the years, and whose expectations of a written record, based on my promises, have so often been disappointed. It will perhaps comfort them, though I doubt it, that their disappointment is much more satisfactorily explained by my own conception of the nature of uncertainty than by the currently fashionable probabilistic models.[1]

There is an obvious temptation, given the circumstances, to cast one's contribution in the mould of current fashion, as a commentary upon the way economists presently deal with decision processes. But, although I shall have plenty of criticism to offer, I have resisted that temptation. It seems to me that my own formulation of the economic problem belongs to a much older and intellectually respectable tradition, and that it is for those who would reject it to give their reasons. Questions like: what would happen to positive economics if your arguments are conceded?, are at best contingent: let us decide where reason lies, and deal with these minor matters afterwards.

With this in mind, I start from some general propositions about the nature of the universe and of the economic problem:

1. Time is a continuum, in which decisions made in the present can affect what happens in the future.
2. The future is imaginable, but is not knowable.
3. The past is apprehended from personal experience or from 'records'. The available information about the past is incomplete, being determined by the past decisions of people who themselves could not know what information would be useful or wanted in the future. In any case, such information cannot explain why past events happened: a record of historical facts, even if 'agreed' and complete, does not obviate disagreement about causal relationships. Also, the recorded facts are *outcomes* (results of earlier decisions), and at least some outcomes must be the result of (earlier) predictions which were not subsequently borne out by events. Consequently, the historical record is a record at least in part of outcomes that were *mistakes*.
4. Between the past and the future is Whitehead's 'continuous present' – what is happening 'now'. Our observations of the continuous present must be incomplete: no *actual* observer (as distinct from the economists' substitute for God – Mr Omniscient Observer or Sir Finite States of the World) can be aware of all *current* information that might bear on his decisions for future action. Conceptually, the characteristic of the continuous present is that, at the relevant point in time, resources are in fact in particular uses, an actual constellation of prices exists: and so on. This is the economists' counterpart of the (physical) notion of the continuous present that, at the moment of observation, all objects are stationary. It has the same negative characteristic. A motor car is where it is: but we do not know from our 'continuous present' observation whether it is parked or travelling at 100 m.p.h. Similarly, the 'continuous present' is the only 'equilibrium' concept susceptible of direct (but incomplete) observation. Resources are always somewhere, but if the nature of the universe is as I describe it, this observation, of itself, tells us nothing about the process of resource-allocation through time.
5. Individuals take decisions. These decisions are purposive, in the sense that what they decide to do is regarded by them as 'better'

than other courses of action available to them. This is a tautology (excuse me for whispering in church). There is no such thing as an 'economic' decision. But to help things along, I am willing to accept an intellectual framework in which some decision-makers (the ones we are interested in) compare plans in terms of their expected 'discounted present value' to the decision-maker. The formulation is not free from ambiguity. It will serve for the present, where our purpose is to link past, present, and future. Essentially, the individual uses information from the past (his own experience, other information which can be extended by the commitment of time and/or resources), together with an apprehension of the present, to make and act upon plans for the future. Again, we shall return later to the characteristics of this planning process.

6. Individuals are capable of learning: this distinguishes the behavioural from the physical sciences. There are two opposed (though not contradictory) corollaries.

First, the possibility of learning does not imply that through learning the future will become knowable, but only that experience will change behaviour. The relation between learning and behaviour is complex: from our present point of view, the essential proposition is that learning can never make the future 'predictable' from evaluation of the past. Some predictions from experience are more trustworthy than others. I can predict from experience and 'learning' that the sun will rise at a particular time tomorrow. I can predict with less confidence that I will see it rise (death, fog, eclipses). I can drive to the railway station to catch a train (learning tells me that trains are more likely to leave at timetable times than others: but not that much more likely?). But the weather may affect my driving time. Summarily, learning changes the way we plan for the future, but it cannot make the future predictable. The extent to which 'forecasting' based on 'learning' improves our capacity to predict the future depends upon the (permanently unknowable) relation between learning as the interpretation of past experience and the actual shape of future events. We have more confidence in some future outcomes (the sun rising) than in others (the trains leaving on time). Learning may alter our views. But it cannot make the future 'knowable': nor can it produce a situation in which we can know that a decision-maker (or *all* decision-makers) have thought of all possible future 'states of the world'.

Second, one way in which learning changes behaviour is to modify the response of individuals to given perceived situations, and through this the results (outcome) of particular courses of action. We have a striking current example. The simultaneous emergence of rising price levels and unemployment rates has led people to ask: 'was Keynes wrong?'. But is it not a more plausible possibility that he was right 'then' but is wrong 'now'? I do not claim to have a complete explanation for the recent behaviour of this or other economies. But I find it difficult to conceive of a satisfactory explanation that does not involve learning. Post-war policies based on the Keynesian logic have affected the position of social groups – for example, trade unions – in particular ways. In consequence, their behaviour has changed, with the implication that the same policies can no longer be expected to produce the same results. There has been 'learning': but has the future become more 'knowable'?[2]

In what follows, I shall comment upon the implications of this formulation for the nature of economic decisions (the concept of opportunity-cost), and against this background comment upon the 'orthodox' presentations of the economic problem in naive and in more sophisticated form. This leads to a critical evaluation of the 'state of the art', and some suggestions for future developments.

The economic problem and the nature of costs

Economics is concerned with scarcity, and the defining characteristic of scarcity is the implied need to choose. That is, an economic problem exists whenever the choice of a course of action is expected to involve a sacrificed alternative course. The necessarily sacrificed alternative is the 'opportunity cost' of the chosen course of action.

As it stands, this description would command widespread agreement among economists. Yet its interpretation and use have produced quite diverse explanations of 'economic' behaviour, including a dominant 'orthodoxy' which treats opportunity-costs as essentially objective and which, I shall argue, leads both to misunderstanding about the nature of the resource-allocation process and to inflated claims by economists as to their competence as 'advisers' ('social engineers').

I am told that I am one of the few (perhaps the only) surviving member of the LSE 'subjective cost' school not yet retired.[3] Let me begin by stating the essentials of my position:

1.   All valuations relevant to the opportunity-cost decisions just described are the valuations of individuals. Consequently, any 'explanation' of the decision process must be grounded in individual decisions: any common logic must be a logic of methodological individualism. All members of society take decisions, and our subject-matter is the way they behave in doing so.
2.   The 'costs' relevant to decisions affecting the allocation of physical

resources between uses through time are the (opportunity-) costs of those resources in other uses *as seen by the decision-maker at the point of decision.*

3. It follows that there are no 'objective' costs: the costs relevant to decisions committing resources to future uses, in the universe described in the Introduction, are the predicted losses of 'yield' (somehow defined) which the decision-maker would expect to result if, for his chosen decision, be substituted the 'next best' course of action he thinks it appropriate to consider and which he believes he could implement.

4. The process of resource-allocation through time takes place through individuals making plans, acting upon them, and replanning in the light of emerging outcomes and new information. Because the future is uncertain, the outcome of plans can be different from the plan forecast. But the 'cost' relevant to an explanation of how resources come to be allocated between uses is the cost to the decision-maker at the (continuous present) point of decision – that is, it is the best course of action the individual believes must necessarily be forgone in order to implement the selected ('best') plan.

5. It follows that opportunity-cost is a *rejected plan* – one that is never implemented at all. Thus, it cannot have 'objective' existence, it need not be written or articulated in any particular form by the decision-maker himself, and (for example) there is no reason why two individuals deciding upon the same ('best') course of action should have the same opportunity-costs.

6. The plans that individuals think worth considering will be determined by their objectives and by the terms and conditions upon which they can exercise claims over resources relevant to the achievement of those objectives. These terms and conditions will in turn be influenced by the social institutions (property and contract law, 'entitlements',[4] etc.) within which planning takes place. Plans may incorporate actions intended to improve the individual's 'environment' for future planning, for example by changing the property laws in his favour or by reducing uncertainty by eliminating or restraining competing decision-takers.

By now, the acquiescence of colleagues in my formulation of the economic problem may be somewhat less absolute. They would perhaps not actually reject my description of the nature of cost: it is not easy to do so. Rather, experience suggests a simple refusal to be impressed. Of course, the real world is complex. We have no choice but to simplify it. The only relevant consideration is whether the simplified models help us to understand the essential characteristics of our problem: are they 'useful paradigms'? The qualification for a 'useful paradigm' is presumably that the general formulation concerned can be adapted without major change in the intellectual construct to fit the needs of particular special situations. I would not be so foolish as to suggest that the development of economic analysis has not greatly enhanced our understanding of the way actual economies work. What I am willing to suggest, however, is that that development is beginning to impose increasing constraints upon our ability to improve our understanding of a growing set of important problems. In these areas, our paradigms are not useful but restrictive: they produce confusion, or we abandon (not adapt) them, without full acknowledgement that we are doing so. A return to consistent development of the subjective cost tradition would overcome these difficulties. It might require some intellectual obsolescence, not least in its rejection of the dominance of general equilibrium concepts, but it would make our subject richer both to teach and to use.

These are large claims: to try to substantiate them, I shall first develop and comment upon the relevant 'orthodox models' in the light of my own formulation of the problem, then comment upon some particular current questions in respect of which the two produce different answers.

The 'classroom model'
From Marshall on, there has developed a 'standardized' economic theory of the competitive economy which now dominates at least Anglo-American textbooks. The version given here is not derived from any one text, but is, I think, a not unjust summary of the typical presentation. Most texts contain qualifications inserted to demonstrate the author's awareness of the 'unreality' (but not irrelevance) of the model, much as earlier writers hedged their bets about the savings–investment–interest rate nexus in the era before Keynes.

The typical argument has the following steps:

1. An explanation of opportunity-cost. This follows the formulation given earlier, but without directing attention to the fact that the relevant forgone alternatives are those perceived by a decision-taker and have no 'objective' manifestation. The examples are frequently 'real': the opportunity-cost of the cricket bat I buy is the tennis racket I must go without.
2. A technological 'law' – variable proportions – which postulates a physical relationship between the amounts of physical and/or human 'resources' used in production, and the resultant output of

physical product. The relevant relationships are invariant: they are determined by the current 'state of the arts', which is known to all decision-makers.

3. These two propositions are then used to explain the process of resource-allocation if there is competition in factor and product markets. Resource-allocation decisions (plans) are made by 'entrepreneurs'. The competitive markets throw up factor and product prices which are known to all entrepreneurs but outside their control. Opportunity-costs are the known prices of factors and are the same for all decision-takers, and output prices are similarly known. It is thus possible for entrepreneurs to determine their most profitable type and level of output, for workers to decide what factor services to offer and for consumers to decide how to spend a given income.

This basic model can be extended, e.g. to consider different numbers of firms and the relationship between them (market morphology), different types of maximizing behaviour (managerial, etc., models): and so on. These extensions are developed within the same underlying postulates as the competitive model just described.

Although I do not suggest that this naive and unqualified model is a fair description of any particular textbook, it gives the essential ingredients, and is worth examining a little, first because some students may get little beyond the basic model and I am not sure that we fully appreciate what we have taught them, second because such an examination is a useful way of identifying the problems that a more sophisticated treatment will have to solve.

The crucial deficiency of the model is of course the absence of uncertainty. In its extreme form, with everyone assumed to have knowledge of future opportunity-costs and future prices, the construct cannot be interpreted as a decision model at all. For if all future prices, and hence all future resource-allocations, are known with certainty, then there is no way in which present decisions can alter future prices or resource-use. In so far as we can find a reason for entrepreneurs to exist at all, they are all faced with the same information (i.e. 'objective' money outlay and revenue figures) and must reach the same price and output conclusions. It is not clear what skill is needed: perhaps addition and subtraction, but not obviously multiplication and division since there are no returns to speed of computation? In respect of this kind of model at least, the 'useful paradigm' defence is clearly dubious. An analogy is sometimes drawn between the use of the concept of a perfect vacuum in physics as a starting point for the examination of other states, and the use of the concept of perfect competition as the starting-point for the explanation of the resource-allocation process in the real world. The analogy is a poor one, in that in the second case the relevant phenomenon – the decision process – cannot be studied because it cannot exist.

It is an implication of the way the model is set up that it does not explain the *process* by which resources are allocated between uses through time, but rather describes 'equilibrium states'. Alternative such states are compared (comparative statics) but the assumptions about knowledge preclude satisfactory study of adjustment processes: either the model is not claimed to deal with change (disequilibrium), or changes are assumed to be completely unexpected yet productive of instantaneous and complete reactions. Similarly, the model has difficulty in embracing small-group situations, since if all decision makers know the response all other decision-makers will make their own decisions, the outcome of their reactions one to another is already specified and cannot be studied as a process.[5]

The 'orthodox' treatment of uncertainty

The problems and inconsistencies of the naive perfectly competitive model are well enough known. I have paused to comment upon them because, in fact, some of the essential characteristics of that model persist in more sophisticated versions of the problem, and also underlie much received doctrine concerning economic policy. But in doing so, I would not wish to seem to deny the considerable development of the economics of uncertainty since the Second World War, using techniques from mathematical economics, econometrics, decision theory and operational research. This section provides an unreasonably succinct, but I hope not totally unfair, survey of these developments, aimed explicitly at the question: given my initial statement of the nature of the universe and of the economic problem, do these developments provide the paradigm of which we stand in need? If not, what are their shortcomings? I do not question that the developments here considered have led to valuable new insights. But I shall argue that the problem is so specified as to leave out fundamental aspects of economic reality, and that this must be acknowledged if the models are not to become an obstacle to better understanding.

Littlechild (1977) identifies three broad approaches to individual decision-making in conditions of uncertainty which are currently popular: these allow such possibilities as contingency planning, information search, and the revision of expectations in response to new information (using Bayesian methods). They permit the development of partial and general equilibrium models. The three approaches are:

1.   Search theory, focusing on wage and price distributions for a single type of worker or product.[6]
2.   The temporary general equilibrium literature originating in Hicks's *Value and Capital*, but developed in interesting ways in the last decade.[7]
3.   The 'new' new welfare economics based on information theory.[8]

Between them, these approaches satisfy many of the conditions required by my initial formulation. Decision-makers have expectations as well as preferences, plans may be incompatible, preferences and expectations may change as a result of new information: in this sense at least (but it is a restricted sense) decision-makers can 'learn'. These more sophisticated models of the universe are undoubtedly an advance upon the earlier competitive 'perfect knowledge' one, and in some directions they lead to useful insights. But in fact, in one way or another they follow that earlier model in their emasculation of the nature of our ignorance about the future. The future is no longer pre-ordained, but nor is it unknowable. Instead of the Walrasian god in the machine – the known general equilibrium conditions – we now have (e.g.) known probabilities and risk-attitudes, or equilibrium defined as conformity of individual 'theories' and policies with emerging outcomes.

In Littlechild's graphic phrase, the decision-makers are 'clockwork Bayesians' programmed to respond to changes in conditions, but in pre-ordained ways and within a totally defined system. To use Shackle's terminology, the decision-makers cannot experience surprise; nor can they perceive new opportunities not anticipated as possibilities in the model; and they can 'learn' only in the very restricted sense that they 'programme' new information in the fashion prescribed by the model. Consequently, these models typically settle down into a 'stable' situation as the decision makers 'process' new information, and a consistent set of expectations emerges.

The 'new' developments of the economics of uncertainty are thus more sophisticated in their treatment of knowledge than the earlier models. But the difference is one of degree rather than of kind. Essentially, we have substituted for a knowledge of future factor and product prices a knowledge of probability distributions, risk attitudes, and possible future 'states of the world'. In whose head does this last information rest? That we still need a 'god' (i.e. an assumption that the future is somehow 'knowable') can be illustrated by a typical quotation (there are others):

> If we were to ask the consumer how he would behave if he were faced with a set of prices that did not lie in the range of (his expectations), then he would not be able to give us an answer. . . . The preceding anomaly would cause unsurmountable troubles for our proof . . . (Stigum, 1969, p.549)

Why does it matter? some unsettled problems

At this juncture, it would still be reasonable for an adherent of one of the 'new uncertainty' schools to acknowledge the difficulties to which I have drawn attention, but still to ask: 'Can you do better?' The insights we get by using, e.g., Bayesian techniques to study behaviour in uncertainty may not solve all our problems, but they do appear to extend our understanding. Why not simply persist along the same paths? The response has to be that there is no argument of principle against such an evolution. But it requires that the model be developed to embrace presently *unimagined outcomes* (including unspecified reactions to evolving (continuous present) situations: and this in some more positive fashion than, e.g., the expression of unforeseen outcomes in some kind of 'error term' or 'black box'). Unanticipated outcomes are not an unfortunate accident making our 'solutions' somewhat less tidy: they are an essential ingredient of the resource-allocation process in a world in which the future is unknowable, and efficient decision-takers are trying to find ways to take advantage of opportunities others have not noticed, and of adjustment to events no one had foreseen. I have invited my mathematically sophisticated colleagues to consider this problem, but so far they have not been able to help.

If the current orthodoxy is evaluated against the description of the universe from which this article began, and in the light of a consistent interpretation of the decision process in terms of subjective opportunity-cost, two important distinguishable but related groups of questions emerge, concerned respectively with the technical constraints imposed by our present models and with the policy interpretation of the relevant models.

A useful starting point is perhaps the recognition of what happens to the notion of profit-maximization once uncertainty is present, even in the orthodox mechanistic/objective cost models. Suppose a set of decision-makers are faced with the same 'evidence' about the future, and place the same reliance upon it (itself something difficult to conceive). Suppose further that the decision-makers have the same 'profit-maximization' objective: to maximize the expected present value of the stream of net revenues, somehow defined, from the plan they implement. If they have different probability distributions and/or risk-attitudes, they may still choose to implement different plans from the same available set. As the 'new economics' would recognize, the proposition that they are maximizing expected profit does not imply that they will choose the same plan. How much more difficult the situation becomes if we limit ourselves to the knowledge we can actually have about decision-making behaviour. We do not know what plans entrepreneurs consider, though we do know that competition will lead them to seek opportunities others have not thought of. We therefore do not know the opportunity-costs of implemented plans. We do not know their attitudes to risk. We know only what they made public about their plans, what they actually did, and, in course of time, what information becomes available about the results. Worse, we may not know from the latter information ('the account') whether the outcome of plans was the predicted outcome, though there is ample evidence that frequently it is not. Consequently, the 'success' of outcomes (achieved net revenues) is at least in part the result of accident, and, therefore, cannot be an unambiguous guide to the likely future 'efficiency' of decision-takers as forecasters. Clearly, a stream of inferences flows from this observation about the actual nature of decision-making under uncertainty. I shall content myself with two by way of illustration, one positive, one negative. The positive one is that 'higgledy-piggledy growth' is a natural consequence. The past (recorded) performance of decision-makers does not provide a simple guide to their likely future performance, and, for reasons argued earlier, 'learning' can never provide a more sophisticated, fully trustworthy 'investment rule'. The negative proposition is perhaps more disturbing: what becomes of positive economics once it is recognized that the basic econometric data (recorded prices, etc.) is, and is always going to be, the outcome of mistaken predictions?

These observations lead naturally to a consideration of the role of equilibrium. The concept has been central to the development of economists' understanding of their universe. Its appeal is easy to appreciate: it generates harmonious outcomes, and facilitates the manipulation of problems by mathematical techniques. But, in the present state of our technical (mathematical) competence, it also restricts our field of enquiry to problems with a 'known' (i.e. predetermined, pre-programmed) set of possible outcomes, and encourages the elevation of compatibility with consistency conditions over relevance to the real world in the specification of problems for study. This view does not go unrecognized, in quotes such as the one given earlier, and (at least in my own case) in discussion with colleagues. It leads most commonly to the view put forward in Hahn's well-argued defence (1973). This acknowledges that we have no theory of learning in its *entrepreneurial* sense of identifying and acting upon new opportunities: much less a formal analysis embodying the unexpected. In these circumstances, Hahn argues, formal general equilibrium models embodying only *routine* learning behaviour are the best we can hope to do – and of course such models are rich in technical interest and potential diversity. This seems to me to value formal elegance more than relevance. It will do if we see ourselves as 'schoolmen manqué', debating the niceties of pinpoint dancing. If we want better to explain the world we actually live in, it leaves too many problems unexplored.[9]

There is now a good deal of work on the theory of the market process emanating from the Austrian School: this places entrepreneurship and uncertainty in its true sense at the centre of the problem.[10] The need as I see it is to find ways to adapt our orthodox models in the same direction. I do not pretend to have a simple solution. But it seems clear that we shall need either to extend or to abandon our present general equilibrium concepts. Apart from 'continuous present' equilibrium any 'tendency towards harmony' in the system must come from the access of individuals to the decision (planning) process: that is, from the ability of one decision-maker to benefit from the oversights of others. But it must be a restricted tendency, in a world in which the future is unknowable and the greatest (only?) certainty is that what happens will not be what was expected, or even conceived. As fast as we get the boat on course, an unanticipated wind blows it off again. The gear keeps going wrong, people invent better boats, and the passengers keep changing their minds about where they want to go. A maddening and disorderly world, which we invent institutions like markets to cope with. It would be fascinating to study it as it is, rather than emasculate it to make it intellectually manageable. The world we study should be the world we live in.

Finally, some policy implications of subjectivism and uncertainty. These can be stated summarily: readers seeking further assurance that the issues are not trivial should refer to the several publications cited.[11] The central problem, of course, is that the confusion of subjective and objective cost and demand concepts, to which I drew attention in the discussion of the 'classroom model', in fact continues to permeate the thinking (and teaching and policy argument) of many economists. An illustration is provided by demand: not only is 'the market demand curve' treated as objective (although only the 'continuous present' price can ever be known), but its shape is used as the starting point for policy prescriptions (by way of consumers' surplus). In the world we live in, 'demand curves' are predictions, existing only in people's heads.

This confusion, together with the derivation of conclusions and prescriptions from models from which the basic essential of economic reality – adaptation to an unknowable future – is missing, generates fundamental misconceptions at the policy level. Social welfare functions may be mathematically convenient, but for the world I have described, they are practically meaningless. Paretian welfare economics provides too narrow a base: we need a model in which, e.g., all the participants are decision-makers, innovation and learning are incorporated, and plans can include actions intended to change the 'rules of the game' in the planner's favour. Pricing rules, offered as substitutes for entrepreneurial decisions, generate only confusion until it is recognized that they can be interpreted only subjectively, after which their actual meaning is decided by the planning procedures used – whose forecasts are accepted, what property rights all concerned have (e.g. what rewards and penalties attach to 'plan failure'): and so on. To prescribe that the products of nationalized industries should be priced at long run marginal cost is, of itself, of little more practical help than to prescribe that they be priced on the principle that God is Love. All the practical problems are interpretative. Whose forecasts are to be relevant (the 'manager', the minister?) What projected revenue and outlay information is to be provided? (Who decides which – rejected – plan is the opportunity-cost, and what records should be provided of it?) What 'property' do the various actors have in the outcome? (What incentive do they have to 'learn' or to seek out new opportunities – that is, to behave entrepreneurially?). The same reasons account for the disagreements surrounding the policy role of cost-benefit analysis: the underlying cause for discomfort is the (often implicit) claim that the 'values' of the analyst are 'objective' in some sense in which the 'valuations' upon which private citizens act are not.

I hope that I have persuaded you that there is here something more than a straw man: those of us who are interested in the study of a truly uncertain world could do with some help.

Notes

1 The record of my indebtedness is a long one. In general, it includes many of my colleagues at LSE and at York. In particular, I was stimulated in the pursuit of subjectivist ideas by George Thirlby and Lord Robbins. More recently, I have been indebted particularly to Jim Buchanan, Alan Coddington, and Brian Loasby: though in these cases I am not sure who has been most stimulated by whom (but I must say that the examination by Loasby (1976) of the general issues discussed in this paper is the best exposition known to me). I owe a special debt to Ronald Coase, who first aroused my interest in these questions as my tutor long ago, and Steve Little-

child, who in recent years has displayed a patience beyond reason in awaiting my contribution to our nominally joint ventures. The form and content of the present paper has evolved from our discussions together.

2 With the kind of boldness that invades me only on after-dinner occasions, I would claim Milton Friedman's Nobel Prize lecture (Friedman, 1977) as evidence of his conversion to this general view of the nature of the universe and of the economic problem: his exposition builds upon individualism and subjectivism, allows learning, and depends upon mistakes and 'unanticipated changes'. I am less sure that he has yet recognized the consequences of his argument for Chicago-style positivism (see also Littlechild (1977) and Loasby (1976)).

3 See Buchanan (1969) and Buchanan and Thirlby (1973).

4 The term is from Alchian (1961): roughly it extends the traditional concept of property to embrace the 'rights' that individuals act 'as though' they possessed.

5 Cf. Hutchison (1938), Ch. IV.

6 See e.g. Stigler (1961), Alchian (1969), Rothschild (1973), Lippman and McCall (1976).

7 Cf. Hicks (1946), Stigum (1969), Hahn (1973), Radner (1974), Grandmont (1977).

8 Cf. Reiter (1977).

9 On all this, see also Hutchison (1973).

10 See Kirzner (1973) for an excellent example. The literature is surveyed in Dolan (1973), Littlechild (1977) and Littlechild (1978).

11 See, for example, Littlechild (1977) on social welfare functions, social costs, etc., Wiseman (1978) on a broader decision model, Wiseman and Thirlby (reprinted in Buchanan and Thirlby (1973) on pricing rules), Littlechild (1978, AUTE Proceedings forthcoming) on cost-benefit analysis, and Littlechild (IEA 1978) on general public policy implications.

References

Alchian, A. A. (1961) *Some Economics of Property*. RAND Corporation Paper P-2316.

Alchian, A. A. (1969) 'Information Costs, Pricing and Resource Unemployment', *Western Economic Journal* 7.

Alchian, A. A. and Allen, W. R. (1974) *University Economics*, Prentice-Hall, 3rd edn.

Buchanan, James M. (1969) *Cost and Choice*, Markham.

Buchanan, James M. and Thirlby, G. F. (1973) *LSE Essays on Cost*, LSE and Weidenfeld and Nicolson.

Demsetz, H. (1969) 'Information and Efficiency: Another Viewpoint', *Journal of Law and Economics*, **12**, 1, (April).

Dolan, E. G. (ed) (1976) *The Foundations of Modern Austrian Economics*, Sheed and Ward.

Friedman, Milton. (1977) *Inflation and Unemployment: The New Dimensions of Politics*, IEA Occasional Paper 51.

Grandmont, J. M. (1977) 'Temporary General Equilibrium Theory', *Econometrica* **45**, 3, (April).

Hahn, F. H. (1973) *On the Notion of Equilibrium in Economics*. Cambridge University Press.

Hicks, J. R. (1939) (2nd edn 1946) *Value and Capital*, Clarendon Press.

Hutchison, T. W. (1938) *The Significance and Basic Postulates of Economic Theory*, Macmillan.

Hutchison, T. W. (1977) *Knowledge and Ignorance in Economics*, Chapter 4, Basil Blackwell.

Kirzner, I. M. (1973) *Competition and Entrepreneurship*, University of Chicago Press.

Lippman, S. A. and McCall, J. J. (1960) 'The Economics of Job Search: A Survey. Parts I and II', *Economic Inquiry* Vol. XII Nos 2 and 3, (June and September).

Littlechild, S. C. (1977) *Change Rules OK?* Inaugural Lecture, University of
  Birmingham.
Littlechild, S. C. (1978) *Government and Industry: an Austrian Approach*, IEA Hobart
  Paper.
Littlechild, S. C. (1978) 'The Use of Cost-Benefit Analysis: A Re-Appraisal',
  Proceedings of 1977 AUTE Meeting.
Loasby, Brian J. (1976) *Choice, Complexity and Ignorance*, Cambridge University
  Press.
Radner, R. (1974) 'Market Equilibrium and Uncertainty: Concepts and Problems',
  1972 lecture; reprinted as Chapter 2 of Intriligator, M. D. and Kendrick, D. A.
  (eds) *Frontiers of Quantitative Economics*, Vol. II, North-Holland.
Reiter, S. (1977) 'Information and Performance in the (New)^2 Welfare Economics',
  American Economic Review, **67**, 1.
Rothschild, M. (1973) 'Models of market organization with imperfect information: a
  survey', *Journal of Political Economy*, **81**, 6.
Shackle, G. L. S. (1973) *Journal of Economic Literature*, (June).
Stigler, G. J. (1961) 'The Economics of Information', *Journal of Political Economy*,
  LXIX, 3.
Stigum, B. (1969) 'Competitive Equilibrium Under Uncertainty', *Quarterly Journal of
  Economics*, **83**, 83.
Wiseman, J. (1978) 'Some Reflections on the Economics of Group Behaviour,
  Festschrift for Professor Biucchi. Nur Oekonomie ist Keine Oekonomie (ed. Caroni,
  Dafflon and Enderle) (Haupt – Bern and Stuttgart).
Wiseman, J. (1985) 'Lionel Robbins, the Austrian School, and the LSE Tradition', *loc.
  cit.*

8 Beyond Positive Economics – Dream and Reality*

Foreword

I spent ten weeks of the summer of 1980 at the Center for the Study of Public Choice, then at Virginia Polytechnic Institute, Blacksburg, Virginia. Prodded by Stephen Littlechild, I had embarked upon a joint enterprise whose end-product was to be a student textbook of subjectivist economics, and Jim Buchanan had kindly provided us with both research facilities and a panel of critics. We were ultimately to abandon the textbook plan, though the episode did provide us with an interesting long article (see Chapters 1 and 13). But that summer, I had a firm forward programme. My academic output has always been influenced by the kind of uncertainty I perceive in other human activities: I have always tacked around my chosen programme under the influence of unpredicted but tempting random invitations and opportunities. But this time there was to be no such vacillation: the book must be written, and all else refused.

Shortly after my return to York, my opportunity-cost situation changed. It was a striking illustration of the importance of the emergence of new choice-influencing information. I was invited to be President of Section F (Economics) of the British Association in 1981. This was not an invitation likely to be repeated, nor a compliment easily turned away. More, it was a wonderful opportunity to further my ideas. So my earlier resolution went for nothing: other schemes went on the back burner, and I set about arranging a series of *Proceedings* lectures which could be edited as a book (Wiseman (ed.), 1983). The title of the volume reflects the way I had come to see the economic problem. The dominant theme is radical subjectivism, in the sense that participants were concerned in one way or another to come to terms with the problems created by the unknowability of the future. The essays are in my view penetrating in their collective insight. One reviewer, commenting that 'Instead of . . . ' would have been a more appropriate title than 'Beyond . . . ' Positive Economics, continued: 'the stated intention is not to overthrow positive economics but to inform it; in this task the

* Wiseman, J. (ed.) (1983), *Beyond Positive Economics*, London, Macmillan. (Proceedings of Section F of the British Association for the Advancement of Science, York, 1981.) Reprinted in: *Universities Quarterly* (1983), Vol. 37, No. 3.

book was very successful indeed in informing this rather orthodox reviewer' (Haddock, 1984).

My personal contribution consisted of an Introduction and an initial essay. The latter is essentially a development and extension of the arguments of the previous paper (Chapter 7), but with greater concern to find solutions, at least of principle, to the identified intellectual problems. There are some illustrative procedural suggestions (the need for 'possibility' formulations alternative to objective probability; the substitution of comparative-behavioural and case-study approaches to actual behaviour for 'rationality'-based approaches; more concern with the behavioural (decision-making) consequences of institutional changes). These alone signal a growing belief that there is need to 'change the questions' as well as seek new 'answers'.

Further, there is concern for the development of more relevant mathematical and econometric techniques; for an explanation of human decision-processes in time-as-a-continuum which incorporates imperfect 'learning' and accepts, not only the possibility of mistake, but also the incorporation of expected mistake into individual plans and decisions; and for a recognition of the inevitably transient nature of many so-called 'economic laws'.

Above and beyond this, the paper contains an explicit assertion of the inadequacy of an intellectual model restricted to the study of choice-through-markets, and the need to replace it by one in which 'non-market decision situations . . . ' are treated as 'integral parts of a complex decision-process'.

Introduction

What song the sirens sang or what name Achilles assumed when he hid himself among women, though puzzling questions are not beyond all conjecture. (Browne, Sir Thomas, *Urn Burial*, Chapter 5, 1658)

The purpose of the series of lectures of which this is the first is not to attempt to destroy or reject the notion of a positive economics, or to deny that important insights have emerged from the exposure of 'mainstream' (neo-classical) economics to positivist ideas. Rather, it is to argue that a new kind of positivism is now needed, if the subject is not to become increasingly sterile, and divided between ever more sophisticated but practically unhelpful mathematical modelling on the one hand, and an unsatisfying institutionalism or unsupported conceptualization on the other. The essential reason for this division lies in the growing importance of the inadequacies of the underlying behavioural model (the set of propositions concerning man acting in his 'economic environment') used by economists; and allied with this a natural reluctance to accept the obsolescence of a considerable stock of intellectual capital, particularly as the kind of new model that is needed lends itself easily neither to mathematical exposition nor to econometric sophistication. Its claims rest more upon relevance than upon formal beauty, at least for the present.

These are bold claims: but the British Association is the place for that. You will find them supported in particular contexts in other papers. In this general introduction, I shall try to summarize what I believe to be wrong, and then make some suggestions as to directions of development that seem to me to be desirable.

The dominant orthodoxy and its deficiencies

The core of the neo-classical explanation of 'economic' behaviour is the *exchange relationship*: humans transact one with another to their mutual benefit. The essential transaction is a two-person exchange. Money enters as a convenient *numéraire*: but the essence of the logic of choice is contained in Edgeworth's exposition of the transactions between peasant-with-corn and peasant-with-wine. Inevitably, other types of transactions have to be admitted: multi-person firms involve transactional relationships not easily comprehended by the Edgeworth direct exchange, as indeed do trade unions, families, governments and other social groups. But while these group-involvement activities are acknowledged and analysed in the specialist literatures, they are generally seen simply as extensions of the logic of choice developed around two-person exchange. This logic of choice is the basis for the accepted model of human 'economic' behaviour that I wish to examine. In its naive form, it treats the future as predictable, and has no place for group behaviour: 'firms' and other groups are simply combinations of human and non-human resources, coordinated by an entrepreneur who has perfect knowledge of all (future) factor and product prices, and whose choice of a 'best' plan of action never results in an unexpected outcome. As a description of the economic decision-process, this is not only naive but logically inconsistent. If the future is known, as it must be if future input and output prices are known, then in what meaningful sense can entrepreneurs make decisions (choose between alternative plans of action), since that choice must affect the prices concerned? The professional economist is well aware of the problem, and is normally cautious in the use of this naive model in his own work. But it is the general point of departure: and it is what thousands of students who study only a little economics are left thinking that the subject is about.

Also, there are whole specialist literatures that have been developed on the assumption that choosers are fully aware of, and certain about, the future implications of their present choices.

More sophisticated formulations admit that the future is uncertain. But they deal with the resultant difficulties by assuming that the number of possible futures is finite, and is in an operational sense 'known'. If the risk-attitudes of decision-makers are also known, then their choice between plans can be deduced from this knowledge, together with the assumed knowledge of the (objective) probability attached to each of the outcomes within the finite set of outcomes considered. This formulation lends itself to great technical sophistication: models can be developed which permit entrepreneurial predictions to be disappointed, and the resultant 'learning' used to modify subsequent decisions. But the 'learning' is written into the model in advance: the 'clockwork Bayesians' programme information in a specified fashion until the process has run down and no further 'improvements' can be made.

The greater sophistication of this formulation must not be allowed to conceal the fact that the model fails to deal with the fundamental problem. If the future is unknowable (as it is) then the assumption of a finite set of possible future outcomes, known to someone (who? how?), and of a predetermined re-planning process ('learning' can only change plans in the programmed direction) reduces to a mechanistic system a decision-process whose essence is that it is *subjective* and *ignorant* (in the sense of depending on judgements about matters concerning which the decision-maker can have only opinions based upon experience). The assumptions are necessary if objective probabilistic techniques are to be used: writers in this genre acknowledge that the model cannot cope with a non-finite set of outcomes. This severely curtails its ability to explain decision-processes in the real world.

Let me be clear. The implication of my argument is not that positivism is somehow 'wrong'. Nor is it that the received doctrine is wrong because the assumptions from which it proceeds are 'unrealistic'. Assumptions are necessarily unrealistic, both because simplifying and 'stylized', and because any 'new' assumption ('suppose the earth is round') contradicts 'received truth'.

The criticism is not general in this sense. It is the *nature* of the simplifying assumptions that is crucial. Can we really expect models that assume the future to be known, whether perfectly or in an objective-probabilistic fashion, to provide satisfactory explanations of human behaviour in a world in which the future is not knowable and people are not surprised when the outcome of their plans differs from their predictions?

It is because the model lacks relevance to decision-making in the real world that it is beginning more and more to restrict the contribution of the economist to the resolution of practical problems, and we need to 'break the mould' if we are to reverse this trend. The purpose is not to reject positivism, but to develop behavioural models that enable a more practically useful positivism to emerge.

This invites the question: How can we do better? It is not an easy question to answer. Intellectually satisfying models which embrace an unknowable future and are compatible with some form of positivism are not easily constructed: which undoubtedly helps explain the reluctance of economists to stray outside the neo-classical paradigms. But we are obliged to try (which is why this series is titled *beyond* rather than *in place of* positive economics). We must try to create a 'better positivism', which is not content with the *a priorism* of the more extreme proponents of the Austrian School, but also recognizes the deficiencies of received positivism. The task is difficult but not impossible. It is also likely to be considered unrewarding by those for whom formal symmetry is of itself an appealing goal: we are attempting to understand human phenomena which are neither simple nor by their nature explicable by continuously reliable 'laws'. In the space available to me, I can do no more than indicate the major changes in the specification of 'the economic problem' that seem to me to be called for (these of course follow from the earlier argument), and suggest some examples of ways in which a new (or 'better') positive economics might emerge.

The way ahead
The essential need is for a positivism that relates the 'facts' more satisfactorily to the conditions and decision-processes of a world characterized by an unknowable future. 'Learning' from historical facts and the results of past decisions cannot make the future 'knowable', since there is no permanent nexus between past, continuous present (what is happening 'now'), and the future. Indeed, it is not easily demonstrable that learning improves the quality of decision-making (since we cannot know what decisions individuals would have taken had they not 'learned', much less what the outcome of those decisions would have been). Nor is it obvious that the universe of economic phenomena is becoming more predictable. In this single lecture, I can do no more than list some of the important specific problems and suggest ways in which progress might be made. I do not claim originality for the arguments: there are many economists who would agree with some or all of them, and most will be dealt with more thoroughly in one or other

of the papers to be presented here. But they may have value considered as an agenda for future development.

The use and development of mathematics and quantitative techniques
This may seem a strange choice of first topic. But there is an urgent need to reconcile the mathematical and conceptual development of the subject if a more policy-relevant positivism is to evolve. Mathematics as a system of formal logic has made and should continue to make an undeniable contribution to the advancement of our understanding, and it would be stupid to deny its potential. But it is not unfair to describe the present state of the art as one in which the economic problem has come to be specified in ways that make it susceptible to mathematical formulation, rather than the mathematics being developed to deal with the important practical problems that need to be solved. The underlying reason is simple: we do not have the mathematical techniques to deal with a non-finite set of future outcomes, or with relationships between past, continuous present and future that are not subject to continuously reliable 'laws'. Professor Shackle has made the point more elegantly than I could hope to:

> The mathematicians were incisive and efficient. The formal authority and finality of their results, the swift economy with which their answers were attained, seem sometimes to deride the labours of the conceptualists. . . . The mathematicians incline to regard economics as the study of mechanism, and with mechanism we are able, sometimes in practice, always in abstract argument, to abolish the distinction between past and future, to design a system where 'ignorance' can no more affect outcomes than it can affect the operation of gravity. . . . But the rich and fruitful theory is a structure, not of nameless quantities existing only in relation to each other, but of named concepts, images, enjoying an almost personal life in our minds. That is why neither the mathematicians nor the conceptualists can be allowed to bear the palm alone.

Shackle was writing of the development of economics between the wars: since then the problem has become more severe. More and more mathematical constructs are concerned with mathematical (mechanistic) rather than with behavioural developments or sophistications: we need to persuade the mathematicians to attempt formulations more closely relevant to the economic problem as I have been describing it in this paper.

In respect of quantitative techniques, there is a similar phenomenon to be observed. The development of econometrics is a natural offshoot of the commitment to positivism. There is nothing wrong with this in principle: practically, it has tended to shift the commitment of economists away from concern with the formal properties and relevance of models (in relation to real-world decision-making) and towards sophistication in quantitative techniques.

Professor L. R. Klein, himself no mean exponent of quantitative techniques, has put the matter thus:

> [Quantitative analysis] is becoming an end in itself, and abstruse mathematical models for models' sake are substituted for reflective thought . . . Regression analysis is the new Hyperion.

He gives illustrations, such as a study of economic influences on marital separation, which concluded that the sophisticated economic model supported 'the inclusion of women as active participants in the process of marital separation'.

The illustration is no doubt extreme, but the general point is well taken. It is also worth pointing out that much of this work uses data often collected for other purposes by means that are not themselves the subject of enquiry ('secondary sources'), and treats the data as the outcome of successfully implemented plans. But if the future is unknowable, men must make mistakes, and the historical record is a (partial and inaccurate) record of those mistakes. How can we make propositions about causal relationships based on econometric models that do not take account of the fact that the historical record is a record of disappointed expectations?

The decision-process

The standard short- and long-period distinction by which time is incorporated into economics becomes inadequate as soon as it is recognized that decisions take place in time-as-a-continuum. Once this is so, decision-makers have to be seen as making present plans for implementation over different future time-periods, and those plans will be mutually interdependent. If in addition the plans are made in the light of an unknowable future, then we have to conceive of decision-makers considering and choosing between plans they believe possible of implementation in the light of their possible 'outcomes' (expected benefits and disbenefits). They will choose the plan they believe to be 'best', at the (opportunity-) cost of rejecting the next most favoured plan. Cost in its decision sense is subjective, and in an uncertain world it has no objective counterpart.

Through this process of planning and replanning, decision-makers 'learn' from the results of past plans, and this learning will influence their choice between future plans. As already explained, the future does not thus become knowable. But this is not to say that learning is irrelevant to the explanation of decision behaviour. Decisions are not taken at random, nor do decision-makers believe the future to be beyond conjecture. But equally they do not believe it to be predictable with certainty. They plan on the basis of a set of beliefs, modifiable by experience, but not explicable by devices such as objective probability. A simple illustration may help. People do not go to railway stations at times chosen randomly. They consult timetables. But they treat the timetable as a forecast, not as 'certain knowledge': they do not assume that the trains will always run at the advertised times. The possibility of error is built into their plans, and has a cost attached to it (a woman will take an earlier train to avoid the possibility of being late for her wedding, but not to avoid the possibility of being late for a visit to her mother-in-law). Learning may modify planning (e.g. the discovery that in Britain the trains do not run at advertised times on Sunday), but will not change the fundamental propositions: there is no foundation for the proposition that 'learning' must always lead to 'better' decisions, and individuals do plan their behaviour on the basis that their decisions may be mistaken.

Of course, we can use historical information to establish the probability that trains will run on time, or within different divergences from predicted times. But planning concerns *the future*, and past probabilities can give only partial information about the possibility of any train tomorrow being on time.

In sum, learning helps (we rely on the sun rising) but can never make the economic problem predictable (fog may still stop us getting to the railway station) in a sense that 'explains' how individuals make decisions. People take decisions in the expectation of error, and 'planning error' is not of itself evidence of incompetence. Individuals will incorporate it into their planning process, and not mechanistically, but as part of the ongoing process of plan-revision (learning).

An amplification of this reformulation of the economic decision-process concerns the role of competition and innovation. The neo-classical model has no satisfactory explanation of innovation (since it is developed within the assumption of a given 'state of the arts'), and competition is seen as a coordinating mechanism (since plans always adjust in the 'right' direction to changes, e.g. in preferences or relative prices). The Austrian School, in contrast, places emphasis on the role of innovation – 'taking advantage of unforeseen opportunities'. What receives inadequate recognition is the likelihood that the innovation of one decision-maker will result in the disappointment (in terms of expected outcome) of the plans of other decision-makers. By, for example, inducing a shift in demand, innovation and competition have as their incidental objective the frustration of the plans of others.

The logic of choice and the exchange relationship

The concentration of mainstream economics on two-person transactional exchange has already been pointed out. In addition, the standard formulation distinguishes decision-makers who are 'resource-allocators' (entrepreneurs) from other decision-makers who are allowed to take decisions only in restricted contexts and about specific matters – for example, as demanders or as factors of production (wage-earners). This formulation is incompatible with the decision-process I am here proposing, and, I would suggest, with the reality of the decision-processes relevant to an understanding of the real world. All individuals in a position to choose between alternative plans for the future are decision-makers. At least equally important, all decision contexts, and not only two-person exchange transactions, are relevant. (Indeed, the latter are probably not a very large proportion of all significant decisions.) Particularly, the centrality of participative behaviour needs to be recognized. Men choose to participate in collaborative groups (firms, trade unions, political parties, and so on), even though they frequently sacrifice freedom of future action to do so. In so choosing, they are not ceasing to maximize their own expected well-being: they are simply predicting that a plan involving membership of the chosen cooperating group will result in a better personal outcome than would direct exchange or participation in some other group. Their behaviour is still explicable in terms of choice between plans and personal opportunity-cost. But the decision context is greatly broadened.

This argument is well recognized in some specialized branches of the literature, such as the advanced theory of the firm, in which group-participative behaviour involving non-market transactions between members of the firm is integrated with market exchange behaviour involving the products, shares, etc. of the firm. It is less satisfactorily developed elsewhere, as for example in the economics of the family or the use of rational expectations to explain trade union behaviour. What is as yet lacking is general recognition of the need for an unified and comprehensive model embracing *all* the decision-situations relevant to resource-allocation outcomes – not only market exchange, but also the decision-processes of government and constitution-making, participation in relevant social groups (firms, families, unions, political parties, pressure groups), and so on.

Such a recognition is not needed to stimulate the specialist study of particular decision-situations. But it is needed for there to be acceptance of the view that the facts and predictions relevant to a more relevant positive economics need to be more broadly conceived than they now are. Non-market decision-situations are not simply extensions of the two-person exchange model, but integral parts of a complex decision-process.

Economic 'laws' and economic efficiency

Efficiency is of course a normative concept. It is proper to introduce it here, however, since there must necessarily be a relationship between the notions of efficiency that are thought interesting, and the positive predictions that economists set out to test.

First, a comment on the nature of economic 'laws'. It is dangerous to place too much faith in the notion that positive economics is likely to produce many 'laws' which are ineluctable and timeless. This does not mean that we should abandon hope, but that we should not expect too much, and should interpret our results with great caution. Physical 'laws' are predictions which are expected to be fulfilled only in carefully specified and controlled conditions: a physicist asked to predict what would happen to the next leaf to fall from a tree in my garden would not be willing to say much more than it would probably fall towards the ground. The subject-matter of economics is difficult because it is concerned with human behaviour: the potential for controlled experiment is very severely restricted. Further, the fact that humans exercise free will (could slaves be trusted to produce precision machinery?) and learn from experience restricts the possibilities of continuously-reliable prediction. The most significant current example is the changing influence of Keynesian policies on employment levels. Economists may disagree about monetarist and Keynesian interpretations of what has been happening. But how many would deny that the changing relationship between deficit financing and unemployment has been fundamentally influenced by learning-induced behaviour changes?

These problems become more severe if the description I have given of the real-world economic problem is persuasive. Within the current orthodoxy, one might try to save the situation by building learning into the specification of the 'laws'. But this would imply some discoverable ongoing and reliable nexus between learning and individual plan-revision. This is hardly conceivable in a world in which individuals must appraise information for themselves and relate it to a truly uncertain (that is, unknowable) future. Further, the difficulties of interpreting the results of empirical testing become more severe (or, rather, become more obvious, since they are there anyway). How to distinguish, when interpreting results, between inadequacy of data, results imputable to failed plans, statistical correlations and genuinely causal relationships? Frequently, this seems to lead to positive economics becoming a search for the 'best' correlations which are then treated as causal without much concern for their behavioural implications. Of course, causality can never be 'proved'. But the 'credibility gaps' are greater in economics than in the physical sciences. Publication of the falsification of predictions of articulated behavioural assumptions is relatively rare.

Second, the notion of an efficiency yardstick related to the optimum conditions of choice becomes much less helpful in the much broader choice-situation now being proposed, the more so in that all choices are subjective and do not have outcomes known with certainty. In this new context, freedom of choice cannot be concerned simply with mechanistic problems of resource-allocation through markets. In so far as it is not treated as an end in itself, irrespective of its consequences for economic efficiency, it is as much concerned with questions of constitutions, trade union law and so on, as with the behaviour of markets treating other decision-situations as 'inputs'. The implication of this is the need for a major shift in emphasis from general 'efficiency' concepts towards, for example, the positive study of the consequences of institutional change, without too much concern with prescription, of which economists have no monopoly. This would not reduce their influence on policy. Currently, an important reason why their policy proposals are ignored or questioned is that their normative origins are remote from those of policy-makers. (Consider this: a policy derived from the static logic of choice will legislate against all forms of monopoly. But the value of the freedom to innovate depends upon the existence of some form of property right in the results of invention. Thus, innovation and monopoly are part of a common problem. A useful positive approach to the problem thus needs to incorporate predictions about both monopoly laws and patent laws, etc., as well as about the consequences of inhibition of choice for current consumption and economic change.)

Finally, a word about equilibrium. The mathematical modelling of the orthodox logic of choice has led economists to concern themselves increasingly with the question of whether a postulated situation is 'consistent with equilibrium' – that is, will produce an eventual outcome in which all plans are fulfilled and outcomes consistent, so that there is no further 'tendency to change'. This 'consistency with equilibrium' is commonly treated, implicitly or explicitly, as an efficiency concept. But in a truly uncertain world, in which plans are subject to continuous revision as new information emerges, the consistency of a given present set of plans with an eventual equilibrium outcome is no doubt intellectually interesting but of little practical utility. Attempts have been made to overcome this problem by programming 'learning' into the model, so that the eventual consistency situation emerges from plan-revision. But the attempts fail, as the authors themselves acknowledge, if there is no unique relationship between learning and plan-revision, and if the future is unknowable and cannot be restricted to a finite set of possibilities. Equilibrium is a fascinating intellectual toy. But it is irrelevant to the real problems of economics, and should be dropped from our vocabulary.

Some specific suggestions

To conclude, I shall comment on a few possibilities that seem to me potentially fruitful. The list is suggestive rather than exhaustive, and in part reflects a few interests of my own. I expect some of the suggestions to be examined more thoroughly in other papers.

Probability and possibility
There is room for more exhaustive consideration of the possibility of replacing objective probability, whose use in positive economics I have criticized, by Shackle's notion of bounded possibility. This sees decision-makers as choosing between a set of plans that they conceive to be possible of implementation and which may produce a desired outcome. The reformulation, which is to be found in Shackle's earlier work and will be discussed in his lecture, offers the potential for fusion of the notions that decision-makers do not believe the future to be beyond conjecture, but are also not surprised by unforeseen outcomes. It could therefore contribute to the reintegration of mathematical and conceptual approaches to the economic problem, the need for which I have earlier emphasized.

A more direct approach to the study of 'economic' behaviour
This has several facets:

The rejection of 'mechanistic' formulations of the economic problem and their substitution by comparative-behavioural ones For example, rules for pricing-by-cost treat costs as objective – that is, as existing 'outside' the subjective judgements of decision-makers. They are irrelevant in a world of which this is not true, as has been demonstrated by their practical irrelevance to the decision-problems of nationalized industries and public enterprises. (The multi-part pricing public utility literature is a calculation of relative prices on the basis of restrictive assumptions about technology and demand. It is really an engineering-type input to the actual decision-process through time which is concerned with the planning and replanning of investment, prices, etc., through time in the face of an unpredictable future. To appreciate this point, consider what would happen to all the multi-part electricity tariffs if someone invented an effective generator small enough to be purchased and operated by individual households. The instruction to UK nationalized industries to price their products at marginal cost proved unworkable (uninterpretable?), and, practically, has been abandoned.)

An alternative and more useful approach is to attempt to predict changes in the behaviour of enterprises when institutional conditions change. Thus, nationalization changes the decision authority, property rights, rewards and penalties, of the various 'actors' contributing to production, as well as changing the cast of actors itself. By comparing the (formal) situation before and after nationalization, it is possible, at least conceptually, to develop hypotheses about the consequent changes in decision-processes and outcomes. The collection and interpretation of evidence will be neither easy nor tidy: but the results are potentially more policy-relevant than anything we have now.

The direct study of human behaviour   Economists are rightly suspicious of attempts to turn them into applied psychologists. But the time has come to broaden our subject from the study of the implications of 'rational' behaviour, as economists choose to define rationality, to the study of *actual* behaviour in so far as we can observe and interpret it.

Demand theory illustrates the point. It uses a concept of rational choice to demonstrate why and when more of a good will be purchased when price falls, but with some exceptions is not concerned with *why* people choose as they do, or with the fact that their predicted behaviour is one aspect of the kind of subjective planning with which this paper is concerned. In this regard, it is noteworthy that the notion of 'the' market demand curve is part of the *lingua franca* of economics. If challenged, economists will acknowledge that market demand curves are graphic presentations of forecasts, although few seem to think this worth more than a passing comment. But if the future is unknown, there are as many demand curves (forecasts) as there are individuals with an interest in the product. If demand theory were about what actually determines the demand for products, one would expect producers to make use of it in their planning. The fact that they turn elsewhere is evidence of the inadequacy of the subjective postulates and the lack of concern of 'economic rationality' with the unpredictability of outcomes.

It is interesting to observe that economists have begun trying to test the predictions of demand theory by conducting controlled experiments using rats and other species. These experiments appear to confirm the laws of demand derived from 'mainstream' economics almost too well for someone who adheres to the arguments I have made in this paper. But the preference set of the rats is severely constrained by the experimental conditions, and uncertainty is restricted to the periods of 'learning', outside of which plan predictions are not disappointed. The practically interesting results will emerge if and when these conditions are relaxed. Pavlov's experiments indicated that complete uncertainty produces madness or apathy: the interesting results will be those in which plans are sometimes fulfilled, but sometimes disappointed, and this in a non-systematic fashion.

Other papers will I hope have more to say on this subject. I will say only that economics as a behavioural science can no longer stand aloof from psychology.

Business decision-making Linking this topic with the previous one, there is room for development of the study of the ways business decision-makers actually acquire and process information. An interesting development in this regard has evolved from the disciplines of artificial intelligence and cognitive psychology. This is the *production systems* approach. The production system provides a framework for the development of rule-based systems for modelling economic behaviour. A production system model has three elements: a data or information base, a set of production rules and an interpreter. The production rules are decision rules, indicating how the information in the data base provides the basis for decision-making. The interpreter provides the underlying control structure of economic behaviour (loosely, the firm's corporate plan). The appealing feature of this approach is that, while it is behavioural in character and can embrace the conceptualization of uncertainty and non-market decision-processes advocated in this paper, it also lends itself to computer simulation and hence has the potential to contribute to the intellectual reintegration of the subject.

This development in turn would overlap naturally with another one: the need for a more direct concern with the way business decisions are reached. We shall be hearing something about this from someone actually involved in the process. I myself find fascinating the relation between identification of possible plans (e.g. the use of 'scenarios' to evaluate the consequence of conceived future events); and the choice between the plans which remain worth considering after the first step has been taken. This procedure is intellectually consonant with both the notion of bounded possibility and with the production systems approach. But it is not the only way the decision-problem can be approached: where better to learn more than from those who take the decisions?

In this regard, the alienation of 'business studies' using a 'case study' approach from economics as a study of 'rational' economic behaviour seems to me another limitation of our present positivism: the two should surely belong within a common intellectual construct, and that necessarily a subjective one?

The study of comparative economic systems

I have chosen this final example because it provides support for a proposition made earlier that, while the kind of 'new' positivism that I am advocating is likely to be less intellectually or empirically 'tidy' than what we have now, it has the potential to be more relevant to the world we live in.

With a few notable exceptions, the literature concerned with the comparative performance of different systems is singularly unsatisfying, commonly degenerating into a combination of description and advocacy.

It seems to me that the formulation of the economic problem here proposed has the capacity to generate many more interesting testable propositions than now emerge. The general approach I have in mind is the one already described in relation to the study of nationalized industries, and I shall not develop it further. Essentially, it calls for the systematic study of the behavioural (decision-making) consequences of specified changes in the property rights, benefits, penalties, etc. of the relevant economic 'actors' within their *total* (not just market) decision-environment. (To take one simple example, there are good grounds for hypothesizing that there will be less innovation (in the sense of the emergence of new products) in the USSR than in the USA: and it should not be impossible to collect evidence bearing upon this.)

References
Haddock, D. (1984) *Journal of Economic Literature*, Vol. XXII.

9 Economic Efficiency and Efficient Public Policy*

Foreword

Before publication, I sent the manuscript of this paper to an intellectually sympathetic colleague. While he personally found it interesting and useful, he warned me to expect our more orthodox colleagues to be puzzled and perhaps disturbed by it, as it demanded a considerable departure from established modes of thought. The paper was another contribution to a *Festschrift*, and has not yet been widely enough disseminated for the accuracy of this prediction to be judged.

The chapter constitutes – at last – a formal extension of the radical-subjectivist insight to embrace the general decision-processes of a society. The stated aim is to explore 'the relation between "economic efficiency" as this is commonly conceived by economists, and "social efficiency" in the general sense of the efficiency of the policy processes of a society and their outcome'.

Mainstream and Austrian economics differ in their treatment of the future and hence in their interpretation of 'efficiency', which is primarily an outcome concept to the former and a process notion for the latter. But the two schools are united in giving central importance to choice-through-markets. But whatever the technical virtues of the social invention we call the market, it is surely mistaken to treat that or any other social invention/institution as superior *in principle* to other institutions which create, direct or facilitate individual choice. 'Social' efficiency must necessarily be concerned with the whole system of social institutions through which individual choices are implemented. A Wicksellian concept of efficiency (compatibility with an unanimity voting rule) is argued to be more appropriate to this reformulation than a (market-related) Paretian one. Put directly, choices made through markets can usefully be evaluated only in the context of the totality of institutions that provide the market with its social setting. 'Choice between choice-processes' and 'choice-through-markets (or other particular institutions)' are different aspects of a common efficiency concept.

This formulation is compatible with the notion of libertarian individual choice, with efficiency concerned with process rather than outcome

* Hanusch, H., Roskamp, K. and Wiseman, J. (eds.) (1985), *Public Sector and Political Economy To-day*, Stuttgart and New York, Fischer-Verlag.

(a wider interpretation of the role of choice simply extends the importance of the unknowability of the future and its corollary of mistake),
and with the existence of cooperative (group-participative) as well as
competitive behaviour. The unifying element in the choice-process
remains the idea of opportunity-cost, but now interpreted to embrace
the whole complex of choices faced by the individual-in-society.
Efficiency relates to the absence of unacceptable coercion rather than
Paretian optimum resource-allocation. The former is a complex notion,
requiring a sophisticated interpretation of the Wicksellian rule (particularly, citizens must be willing to accept policies expected to be to their
direct disadvantage, if by doing so they anticipate compensating indirect
benefits). But what the concept loses in comparative simplicity is more
than compensated by the gain in practical relevance (the paper gives
some illustrations).

A final note points out the great influence on the argument of concepts of public choice. Indeed, the message of the paper might with
hindsight have been clearer had it been explicitly stated to be concerned
to bridge the intellectual gap between 'orthodox' economics in its neo-
classical and Austrian formulations, and the more embracing concepts
of choice-in-society which are the core of the public choice approach.

Introduction

This paper explores the relation between 'economic efficiency' as this
is commonly conceived by economists, and 'social efficiency' in the
general sense of the efficiency of the policy processes of a society and
their outcome. The concepts and ideas discussed are not unfamiliar,
but it is my view, reinforced by my observations of the activities and
observations of my compatriots, that their implications are inadequately
recognized or acted upon. This is not surprising, since the consequence
of their acceptance must be to diminish the confidence of economists
in their ability to contribute to policy formation, at least in a specific
and prescriptive way, as the price of making a less dogmatic but ultimately more useful contribution to the policy problems that are of
practical concern to others. But while this is at present an obstacle, I
do not regard it as an insuperable one, since the price will have to be
paid sooner or later. Scepticism among policy-makers about the so-
called 'hard', but often contradictory, advice that they are given by
economists is considerable and growing. It will continue so to grow
until we recognize its underlying cause. I hope to move us a little
towards a situation in which our policy advice is less 'authoritative'
(since the 'authority' has no sound foundation), but more worthy of

attention. The potential loss is of dogmatism (and a contradictory dogmatism at that), the gain practical relevance.

Inevitably, I must deal in generalities. I do not suggest that the 'orthodoxies' I describe so summarily would be held without qualification by anyone. But they are not 'straw men': they state the essence of some currently dominant intellectual positions, and are to be so interpreted.

Economic efficiency and the market

Mainstream economics, and consequently economic efficiency, are concerned with choice. For the neo-classical economists, the *outcome* of uninhibited choices is of central concern: efficiency in its Paretian sense is identified as the 'optimum conditions of choice' – an outcome such that no individual can improve his choice-situation without worsening that of others. It is recognized that efficiency in this sense will imply a different outcome with differences in the *power* of individuals to choose. A notion of *equity* is consequently admitted to consideration. But it is not generally speaking itself an ongoing topic of analysis: simply, for any postulated equity situation it is possible to specify an 'efficient' choice-outcome.

Another view sees efficiency as concerned rather with the *processes* from which choice-outcomes emerge. Simplifying drastically, if the future is uncertain in the sense of being unforeseeable, then efficient choice-behaviour must relate to the *procedures* through which decisions are reached rather than only to the actual *outcome* of those decisions (since if the future is unknowable, unanticipated outcomes cannot of themselves be regarded as 'inefficient').

The latter seems to me to be a more plausible formulation of the problem that individuals actually have to deal with. But that is not the crucial issue here, and (as I warned) these summary descriptions are in any case something of a parody.

For our purposes, it is enough that both focus on the act of choice as the key concept: economic efficiency is about choice, whether in the outcome or in the process sense. Further, both schools would claim that the relevant notion of choice is an embracing one. For the Paretian, efficiency is about the uses to which resources are put rather than the means by which they arrived in those uses. For the 'Austrian', choice is an embracing concept (in principle, 'economic' choices are not distinguishable from 'other' choices) and 'process efficiency' is similarly embracing.

But the practical situation is different. Neo-classical economics examines the characteristics of the optimum conditions of choice by way of the behaviour of markets, while insisting that the end-conditions (i.e. 'efficiency') may of course be attainable by other means. The enormous preponderance of neoclassical writing takes market transactions as a datum, and analyses the outcome of specified market situations/conditions. Similarly, within the postulated unity of individual choice, choice-through-markets is *de facto* the 'specialist' concern of the Austrian school economist.

These are admittedly stereotypes. The point to be made, and the point of departure for what follows, is that 'economic efficiency' as currently interpreted is about choice-through-markets, whether in its 'outcome' or in its 'process' sense.

The market in its social setting
It is far from my intention to dispute the importance of the social invention called the market. I am of an academic generation that matured, at least in the UK, in an environment in which the value of the market as an institution was widely discounted or misunderstood. If the heretics of that time have become priests, I suppose I could now be called a dissident churchman: I have lost none of my respect for the market, but do not therefore think it necessary completely to identify market efficiency with the efficiency of social institutions as a whole. Acceptance of the value of the market should not lead us to ignore other social institutions, or to interpret these solely by reference to their contribution to 'market efficiency'. Unless other institutions which create choice – i.e. opportunity-cost – situations are subjected to common scrutiny along with market institutions (to which they may provide an alternative or a necessary input), the treatment of the market as in some ways the 'paramount' social institution must rest either on the assumption that what is good for 'market' efficiency (in the narrow sense we have defined this) must be good for 'social' efficiency, or on the view that other social institutions are of secondary importance relative to the market and its efficiency. Neither position is easily supported.

But before pursuing this question further, two possible ways of dealing with the problem must be mentioned. It has not of course escaped the attention of economists that the individual members of society may have personal goals not encompassed by the narrow interpretation of the Pareto-optimum. This can be dealt with by postulating that 'society' has goals, and embracing these in a 'social welfare function' which relates choice to a set of goals which may be competitive with one another. This has produced valuable insights concerning problems such as the consistency of policy choices. But in general it has developed as a study of the symbolic logic of multiple choice-situations, rather than of the character or outcome of particular choice-processes. Its contribution to an understanding of the efficiency of the choice-processes of actual societies is consequently restricted, even leaving aside the difficulties inherent in the notion that 'societies' can have 'goals' that are not the choices of individuals expressed through the institutions they have themselves created.

The other development is of greater actual and potential interest. If choice is interpreted in its Wicksellian sense ('efficiency' being concerned with compatibility with an unanimity 'voting rule') rather than (or as well as) in its Paretian one, then *all* choices can be seen as subject to a common efficiency criterion, and the problem I have postulated disappears. This solution is the more appealing if, as has been argued, the Wicksellian formulation of the choice-problem can be interpreted to embrace the Paretian one. I have no intellectual quarrel with this position, but would claim that its acceptance supports my own argument: that any policy-relevant efficiency concept must embrace all the institutional arrangements that influence the outcome of individual choices in either (or both) a Wicksellian and a Paretian sense.

To put the matter directly, a comprehensive interpretation of the choice-problem, and hence of the nature of efficiency, requires that choices made through markets must be evaluated in the context of the institutions that provide its social setting, these other institutions being seen not simply as 'contributors' to the functioning of the market, but as alternative or complementary procedures for the achievement of particular objectives. The market, that is, is one institution among many others that may be utilized to facilitate the making and implementing of individual choices in the face of uncertainty. It is to be evaluated by its contribution to end-achievement. The 'choice between choice-processes' is itself an important opportunity-cost problem for decision-makers; the choice of a procedure for making or changing a constitution and the (market) choice between apples and oranges offered for sale are equally parts of an integrated total process whose overall efficiency is our proper concern.

Before developing the argument further, a few amplifications and clarifications may be helpful:

1 Nothing in the argument so far requires abandonment of the notion of individualism: the end-purpose of the system remains the fulfilment of individual human desires.
2 It is accepted that individuals will have different goals, or attach

different weights to similar goals. 'Efficiency' cannot ignore this, but must be related to the successful reconciliation of the differences.

3   The notion of opportunity-cost (that courses of action are chosen at the 'cost' of the necessary sacrifice of the best alternative course conceived by the chooser) continues to be the guiding principle of human action.

4   'Policy efficiency' must have a 'process' component. This is so because, while decisions may be taken with an 'ideal-result' in mind, failure to achieve this outcome in conditions of 'future unknowability' can be interpreted as 'inefficient' only if no other decision-process could imaginably have produced a 'superior' outcome (which itself can only ever be a matter of *ex post* judgement).

5   Choices are exercised through co-operative as well as through competitive activity. Many social institutions which are substitutable for or complementary to market institutions emerge because individuals choose membership of cooperating groups over direct (competitive) action. An understanding of group behaviour is thus integral to an understanding of 'social efficiency'.

Choice in a complex society

In pursuing their objectives, individuals may find it necessary to compete with others; they may alternatively see benefit (for the achievement of their own ends) in cooperation. Typically, they will indulge in both, the decision depending upon their preferences, goals, and their appraisal of each decision situation in which they are involved. Cooperation is in no way a denial or rejection of individualism: it is simply a particular means for the pursuit of individual ends.

In this situation, choice still manifests itself as an individual opportunity-cost problem. The individual considers alternative possible (but mutually exclusive) courses of action which he considers feasible for the attainment of his objectives, and implements the chosen plan at the cost of rejecting the next best envisaged alternative, which consequently never becomes objective reality. There is no point in trying somehow to disaggregate this subjective-choice process into sets of 'two-person' direct exchanges. The content of (subjective) plans can be known only to the individual, in so far as it can be known at all, but the opportunity-costs of chosen plans will clearly contain anything that the individual chooser considers to be relevant. A person deciding whether to join a trade union, or how to vote, is in a choice-situation just as much as one deciding to exchange an orange for an apple. Obviously, not all these choices are about two-person relationships or the simple exchange of goods: they are about different procedures, different institutional involvements, different social rules: in sum, about all human action to which individuals see a possible alternative.

As a result of the dominance accorded to market transactions, competitive behaviour has received much more examination and analysis than cooperative or participative behaviour, though the latter has attracted increasing attention in recent years with growing interest in public choice and in the behaviour of particular institutions such as firms. But a satisfactorily integrated exposition of the choice-process as a whole, unifying the diverse choice-situations that individuals face in a complex society, remains to be developed.

Individuals start life as members of two groups: a family and a society. As no alternative is possible, no opportunity-costs are involved in joining these groups, which may be labelled 'obligatory'. But, though initial membership is inescapable, withdrawal from membership is possible. In the case of the family, withdrawal from the original decision-unit (group) is indeed normal. An individual who finds the rules of his society oppressive or unacceptable may also choose to join a society whose rules he expects to prefer, by emigrating. There are costs involved, some broadly common to all such decisions, such as the need to leave family and friends, others related to the rules, procedures and institutions of the societies involved. The opportunity-costs of a Russian Jew considering emigration to Israel will be very different from those of a British citizen considering emigration to Canada. This example brings out an important practical refinement of the concept of efficiency here being developed. A citizen who is dissatisfied with the institutions and decision procedures of his society can properly try to get them changed. If he does not believe the procedures available to him to do this to be themselves unsatisfactory, then his current dissatisfaction need not be evidence that the system is inefficient overall: individuals will expect to have to accept situations of this kind that they do not believe are in their own best interest, in return for the larger benefits obtained because others do the same. Nevertheless, the fact that citizens accept the procedures is not itself unambiguous evidence of efficiency. The anticipated cost of rejection (implying some form of withdrawal from society or breaking of its rules) may be higher than that of unwilling acquiescence. In the case of our example, the Russian Jew may believe the obstacles placed in the way of his emigration unjustifiable, but be unwilling to bear the cost of rejecting the institutional arrangements which produced them. Absence of emigration is clearly not an indicator of social efficiency, nor is armed insurrection necessary evidence of social inefficiency in my sense of the term, since insurrection may be intended to inhibit the individual's freedom to choose as well as to extend or preserve it.

Other groups come into existence because individuals expect voluntary cooperation to serve their own ends better than would direct action. Groups proliferate in complex societies: firms, churches, charities, pressure groups, trade unions, clubs, choirs. There must be few persons who are members of no voluntary group.

Economists are not unaware of the existence of groups, and there is an extensive literature concerned with the behaviour of particular groups – firms, families, charities, trade unions, and so on. There is also a specialist literature concerned with group behaviour, and the public choice and politico-economic literature concerning political parties, governments and pressure groups. But save for some aspects of the study of public choice, these 'specialist studies' are not seen as part of a cohesive whole, but either develop a specific logic to fit the group problem concerned, or (as in the case of the economics of the family) try to extend the neo-classical formulation of the choice-problem to include authoritarian and coercive situations which that formulation is singularly ill-adapted to explain. Summarily, there is no *embracing* general analytics of groups, applying a common basic logic to a series of group situations.

The unifying element needed for this, as I have already hinted, is the extension of the concept of opportunity-cost. An individual joins a group to further his own ends: he expects the consequences of joining to be preferable to those that he would expect to follow from acting alone or participating in some other group. As with all opportunity-cost decisions, these expected costs cannot be known to an outside observer, though introspection and indirect observation may provide insights into their likely *character* – it will be expected that there will be less applications for exit visas from Russian citizens if an observed consequence is loss of employment. The costs are subjective, and will be capable of more or less clear articulation only by the individual himself. But it is possible to outline the broad considerations involved, and from this (e.g.) to evaluate the likely outcome of specific policy changes. Groups are associations of individuals who come together in the pursuit of particular objectives. There is a 'group objective' which may be more or less clearly articulated, and a set of 'rules' to which members are expected to conform in the pursuit of that objective. There will commonly be penalties for breaking the rules which may be fines, withdrawal of membership, or whatever. In groups of any size, a formal hierarchy will develop, with certain powers delegated to a sub-group ('bureaucracy' or 'management') who can be elected or deposed, again by agreed rules and procedures. Thus, voluntary groups existing within the embracing obligatory group called society will manifest within themselves, in varying degrees of sophistication, the same problems and institutional 'solutions' as we find in the obligatory body (to which the notion of 'social efficiency' has been postulated to refer). An individual considering whether to participate in a group will see as negative consequences the need to subordinate himself to constraints (rules) designed to achieve an objective which may not be identical with his own aims, and the possibility that the group's institutional arrangements may be inefficient (in relation to goal-achievement). On the positive side, the group may be able to develop strategies superior to those available to the individual. He may thus see his choice as lying between the expected more successful achievement of an objective that is sympathetic with but not identical to his own, and the less successful attainment of his specific goal by direct action. We would thus expect to find human action comprehending a diverse pattern of individual behaviour, some activities involving group participation, others direct market transactions, and the whole producing a set of decision-processes that delineate the implementation of individual plans through time.

At the formal level, this can be seen simply as complicating the time-process of individual planning and plan-revision. In the simpler 'economic' models, individual decision-makers in a society see themselves as constrained by the activities of other individuals who are implementing their own plans and objectives: now, they see themselves as constrained also by the potential activities of groups, and also as having as part of their own 'opportunity set' the possibility of participation in such groups: even of groups whose objectives are at least partially in conflict (as when a worker participates in both a firm and a trade union).

Complex choice and social efficiency
The argument can usefully be pulled together by listing the characteristics of the individual decision-process that have emerged as relevant to the notion of efficiency:

1. Individuals pursuing their own goals may do so by direct participation in markets, by direct (i.e. non-cooperative) action of other kinds, or by participation with others in groups whose objectives are seen as sympathetic to those of the individual. Typically, actual behaviour will comprise a mixture of direct action and group participation. The decision to participate in a group does not depend upon identity between the goals of the group and the individual:

all that is needed is that the individual should believe that the curtailment of freedom implied by membership of the group will be more than compensated by the widened opportunities that group participation is expected to bring.

2. The various groups that individuals join need not themselves have compatible objectives. This is best seen as a problem of decision-making (individual planning) through time. A hairdresser may not buy the extra chairs he believes he could fill (so improving his expected net revenues), if his lease is due to expire and his longer-term plan does not include its renewal. Similarly, an individual may join a trade union, if the predicted opportunity-cost of failing to do so is the need to work outside his vocation. But the same individual may also participate in groups (political parties, etc.) whose aim is to reduce the power of trade unions.

3. Individual action utilizing different 'types' of individual action or group participation need to be seen as mutually supportive, and this in two general ways. First, the 'mix' of plans selected will be those considered best for the achievement of individual goals. To use a labour market example, an individual may act cooperatively by joining a union, but seek also to improve his income prospects by adopting courses of action that are expected to improve his chances of promotion. Second, coterminously with planning to 'do the best he can' in the short-term context in which he finds himself, the individual will also be adopting courses of action planned to improve his situation in the longer term. He may, for example, campaign on his own account, through his union, or by joining other groups such as political parties, for the nationalization of the industry in which he works. In doing so, his aim may be to change the political characteristics/institutions of his society ('promote socialism') as an end in itself. Or he may see his own self-interest as served by the change in the system of property rights and entitlements which, as we explained earlier, nationalization would bring. Simply, nationalization may be expected to permit real wages in the industry to rise faster than could be the case in an unsubsidized competitive situation.

4. Efficiency, then, is multifaceted. It concerns the ability of existing institutions to facilitate the implementation of the immediate wishes of citizens, and to adapt to changes in those wishes, in technology, and so on. It concerns efficiency in the procedures through which institutions can be directed to change the environment – e.g. in the procedures by which laws are adumbrated and property rights invented or destroyed. Finally, it comprehends efficiency in the

reconciliation of differences in individual conceptions of their rights in society – that is, in the procedures through which the freedom of individuals are reconciled one with another.

Finally, but crucially, efficiency is concerned with *purpose*. Specifically, social efficiency can fruitfully be discussed only in so far as the individual members of a society are in broad agreement concerning their rights in relation one to another. If a society of slave owners see slaves as chattels without rights (that is, simply as 'resources') then social efficiency can have meaning for that society (it could, e.g., have an 'efficient' contract law facilitating market transactions, including those involving slaves). But a slave believing himself to have rights would not see such a society as efficient, or indeed consider social efficiency worth discussing in any context that continued to deny those rights.

This paper follows an established tradition, in beginning from concepts of choice and unanimity, of treating individual freedom from unacceptable constraint as a common purpose: inhibition of freedom is 'efficient' only if it is the outcome of institutions and processes that are not improperly coercive (that is, do not violate the principle of unanimity).

But if this position is rejected, so will any notions of social efficiency that follow from it be rejected (but so will the conclusions of a narrower logic of choice). There are two broad reasons for rejection. One is quite general: it can be summarily described as the organic theory of the state, and the central proposition is that there is a 'social welfare' (general will) that transcends individual welfare as perceived by individuals themselves, and that this justifies coercion of the individual if there is conflict between the two. I have no space to examine this at length, but will say only that I cannot personally take it seriously in the absence of persuasive evidence from those who claim the right to coerce that they have special access to the content of the general will.

A less extreme version of the same argument is one form of other of 'social paternalism'. This is the proposition that our choices are 'imperfect' because conditioned by background, family, class, lack of expertise, or whatever. Again, we must ask: how do those who use these arguments to inhibit the choices of others justify their own special position? If they can persuade others that it is in their interest to cede authority in particular matters, subject to constraints decided by those others, then no insurmountable difficulty arises. If not, my own view would be that it is for those who make such claims to substantiate them to the satisfaction of those who would be coerced by them.

Relevance to practical policy

At this point, it is tempting to conclude that the outcome of this attempt to understand social efficiency has been to replace some relatively simple but comprehensible concepts by a global interpretation that is practically unhelpful. If in fact the narrower concepts of efficiency were no more than simplifications, and hence capable of refinement for use in practical situations, this would be a powerful criticism. But this is not the situation. The original criticism: that the concepts we seek to replace miss out the essential elements of the decision process, remains valid. We must consider what can be done to relate our broader construction to the practical needs of the policy makers. Certainly, our conclusions will lack the neat conclusions of the narrower concept of 'economic efficiency' it is proposed to replace. But a sundial tells the time better than a high-precision watch without any hands. The problem is perhaps less difficult than it might seem. Certainly, social efficiency has become too complex a notion for us to translate it into a simple set of rules or characteristics (similar to those of welfare economics) save at the most abstract and formal level. It may plausibly be argued that 'whole system' efficiency relates to *breakdown*: that is, to the conditions needed if the social order is not to be rejected by citizens (e.g. by revolution). There are important questions here, which with a few notable exceptions have been neglected. But there are also useful things to be said while taking the 'global situation' as given: there is benefit in cleaning the plugs of an automobile without also reconditioning the engine. There are two practical 'lower levels' at which issues of social efficiency can usefully be examined. At the one extreme, there is the examination of the *objectives* of the process, which must be enunciated if efficiency is to have meaning. We have rejected the notion that there can be a 'social objective' that is not the reflection of the objectives of individuals. This facet of efficiency is thus concerned with the procedures by which individuals can choose the constraints that are used to reconcile their objectives with the objectives of others, and behind this, with the procedures by which individuals choose the arrangements (political institutions, governments) through which these specific choices are presented.

This second 'lower level' might be called 'marginal'. It seeks to answer the question: within the existent general framework (of laws, institutions, etc.), are there changes that would make the system 'work better'? This may simply involve laws changing individual property rights, changes in the institutional arrangements through which rights (and bids) are channelled, and so on. These changes will encourage or discourage the emergence or disappearance of new group activities, markets, etc. because the opportunity-costs of participation have been changed. Of course, the predicted results of changes of this kind are not easily translated into normative form. In so far as individuals have different objectives, they must be expected to differ about the desirability ('efficiency') of particular proposals. Commonly, therefore, the two aspects of what might be called 'internal social efficiency' need to be considered together. An individual who accepts that the decision framework is satisfactory may accept a specific change as 'socially efficient' even though he himself may see the measures as antipathetic to the achievement of his own specific objectives. (This may be recognized as an unfamiliar way of restating, e.g. the practical issues involved in the implementation of a unanimity rule. If a citizen is not to dissent from specific proposals he sees as inimical to his interests, it has to be because his acquiescence is expected to cause others to accept other measures *he* sees as desirable that *they* would otherwise reject.)

Summary illustrations

Were space available, the last section would clearly justify considerable expansion: but in a limited contribution of this kind it must be left as a statement of general principles, which the reader must himself relate to policy issues of interest. The two concluding short illustrations may encourage this, if only by their suggestion of a unity of intellectual approach to a wide range of policy problems.

Commonly, dissident groups emerge within societies of any size, and seek to detach themselves from the community of which they are formally a part. In extreme situations (such as the situation in Northern Ireland), the prime objectives of such groups will be the rejection of the rules and procedures of their present society, to be replaced by others acceptable to the (then separated) members of the group concerned. In such a situation, notions of 'social efficiency' of the kind here being adumbrated may seem to be irrelevant. Certainly, they do not point to any particular 'procedure', or 'solution'. But it is observable that where extreme disagreement causes violence to replace negotiation, means of reconciliation are commonly sought by way of *the invention of new institutions/procedures* that will enable peaceful transactional relationships to emerge – that is, for those involved to accept that the arrangements proposed could shift them towards faith in the emergence of a society with some hope of satisfying the specified efficiency conditions. There can, of course, be no expectation that the necessary arrangements will in fact be discovered: there may be no 'solution' better than separation. But explanation in the language of 'social efficiency' is something more than a re-statement of the obvious, in that it draws attention to the fact that the processes described are simply an extreme form of those that are continuously to be found even in the most settled of societies.

At a more mundane, but by no means trivial, level, the concept can be applied to the current debate about policy towards the restriction or prevention of smoking. Again, my comments can only be summary: I have developed the argument at greater length elsewhere.

The debate about what restrictions, if any, should be placed on the freedom of individuals to smoke appears first of all to illustrate the postulated inadequacy of mainstream interpretations of economic efficiency. These concern efficiency in the responsiveness of the system to individual ('economic') choices, or in the process of choice through time. *What* is chosen is not a relevant problem. But this question is at the core of the smoking debate.

The anti-smoking lobby advances a battery of arguments for control or prohibition. Some of these are concerned with what we commonly call 'market imperfection': consumer ignorance, externalities of various kinds, misleading advertising, and so on. In so far as these arguments are well taken (and by no means all of them are), the first question to be answered concerns the possibility of dealing with them simply by institutional, etc., change. My own judgement would be that there is little of significance that could not be (and indeed in many countries is not being) appropriately dealt with.

But the anti-smoking lobby is not, or is not solely, interested in market imperfection. It has other arguments for rejecting the libertarian position; i.e. the position that subject to the corrections referred to, smokers should be left free to decide their own trade-offs between life and health-expectancy and smoking. I do not find these other arguments convincing. But I cannot pursue this question here. The aim is to look rather at the ability of our social institutions to adapt to needs of smokers or non-smokers alike. The aim has to be to improve the procedures by which decisions are reached, rather than to claim to know what those decisions should be.

It transpires that, while there is no objectively correct framework from which an 'efficient solution' must emerge, it is possible to identify institutions and procedures that may be expected to produce acceptable compromises (i.e. compromises that obviate the possibility of societal breakdown (inefficiency)). Within this framework, it is further possible to discover reasons to expect that, failing countervailing influences, 'negative' pressure groups (aimed at restricting the choices of others) will be disproportionately powerful, so that social efficiency will be promoted 'at the margin' by measures restraining the power of pressure groups or strengthening countervailing powers.

To go further requires more detailed specification of existing arrangements. In the case of UK, with which I am most familiar, the indicated measures would include scrutiny of the special privileges enjoyed by pressure groups, particularly those with charitable status, measures to facilitate open discussion in the media, use of devices such as opinion polls to discover especially the views of those who would be adversely affected by restrictive or prohibitory legislation, and, perhaps, consideration of politico-constitutional reform (choice of constraints) by requiring 'special majorities' for laws/procedures to curtail rights, or more deeply, dual representative assemblies (concerned with legislation and with 'government' respectively).

It would be naive to expect that this argument would be accepted as convincing in countries in which the anti-smoking pressure groups are particularly fanatical. But it will be helpful if it directs their attention to a particular characteristic of the social efficiency discussed in this paper. That is the fact that, if the social institutions of a community produce a policy outcome seen by a substantial minority as a breakdown of the principle of unanimity, the result will not be conformity, but rejection, social unrest and pressure for institutional reform. The experience of prohibition in USA is a sufficient example. Such a result may produce more efficient institutions in the long term. But it is hardly the outcome such pressure groups envisage (nor would it stop citizens from smoking).

Notes

This paper brings together some general thoughts that have been influenced by many colleagues over the years. I have made no specific references: those same colleagues will no doubt recognize their own 'mark' with greater or lesser pleasure.

The influence of public choice concepts will be obvious, and I am indebted to my colleagues at George Mason University (Center for the Study of Public Choice), both generally and for useful discussion at a Seminar at the Center for the Study of Market Processes. I also benefitted from seminars/discussions at New York University (Austrian Economics Colloquium), Rensselaer Polytechnic Institute (Vollmer Fries Lecture and seminar), University of Arizona, Tucson, Hellenic Republic Centre of Planning and Economic Research, and from comments from Professor A. J. Culyer.

10 The Political Economy of Restriction of Choice*
(With S. C. Littlechild)

Foreword

One of the illustrations used in the last chapter concerned public policy towards smoking. The present paper takes up this issue in more detail. We are thus once again concerned with a live issue of practical policy, but one to which mainstream economics has little to contribute. The question to be addressed is: What can economists say about the *restriction* of individual choice? The orthodox logic of choice treats any inhibition of the freedom of individuals to choose as wrong in principle: the sole reason for interference being the failure of markets to function 'correctly'. Nor does the social choice literature deal adequately with this problem.

The argument of the paper develops by identifying and examining alternative intellectual frameworks that might be used to handle the problem. There is the market failure framework, the paternalist framework in its different versions; and the libertarian framework. These differ in their underlying value judgements about the 'good society'. But the distinction between them is argued often to be a fine one, as is illustrated by the examples of merit goods, of the proposals for intervention to 'break the pattern' of consumption, and of externalities (the term being shown to embrace a host of different interpersonal relationships with varying implications for policy).

The reconciliation of these approaches is argued to be found, for anyone accepting the insights of methodological individualism, in the libertarian framework in its contractarian formulation. This kind of public choice approach can reconcile all the different formulations save those (such as the extreme authoritarian form of the paternalist position) which find unacceptable the initial value judgement that 'within the law, all members of the polity have equal access to decision-making

* Littlechild, S. C. and Wiseman, J. (1986) *Public Choice*, **51**.

We should like to acknowledge helpful comments on an earlier draft by E. Marshall, W. S. Siebert, B. Simpson and G. Studdert-Kennedy; contributions from participants in a seminar at the Center for the Study of Public Choice, George Mason University; and support from the International Tobacco Information Center.

structures, and all have equal weights in the determination of collective decisions'.

The paper is a practical illustration of the conviction which has begun to emerge in earlier chapters; that progress has to be concerned not only to seek new answers to old questions, but also to find ways to answer important questions that currently it is difficult to ask.

Introduction

There are many goods whose consumption has, or is believed to have, adverse effects on the health of the consumer, and perhaps on the health of others. It is frequently asserted that government has a duty to impose restrictions on the sale or consumption of these goods. What do economists reared on the logic of choice have to say about such *restrictions* on choice?

Economists typically approach the question 'which is the best public policy?' by postulating the analytic framework of 'market failure' within which to appraise alternative policies. Yet, as we argue below, this framework has significant ambiguities and weaknesses in its application to goods with possible adverse health effects. Non-economists commonly employ other frameworks, such as paternalism or libertarianism, which may have quite different policy implications. The question therefore arises: 'Which is the best framework for appraising public policies?' But there is no universally acceptable 'meta-framework' within which such a question may be answered.

Our conclusion is that the problem has to be resolved by changing the question and refocusing the analysis. The logic of choice provides little guidance where the problem is to design rules by which it is decided whether or not people should be allowed to exercise such choice. It is more helpful to examine the process by which people living in societies can or do make such decisions.

An important contribution which the economist can make is to trace the relationships between institutional arrangements and the types of policies which emerge from them. One may thereby characterize those processes of social decision-making which the majority of people are likely to find acceptable. The normative social choice literature does not adequately focus on such processes. To understand and evaluate how social decision-making actually works inevitably takes economists into the realms of public choice.

The arguments of the paper will sometimes be illustrated with reference to tobacco, which raises all the issues we wish to discuss, and with which we are familiar from previous research (Littlechild and Wiseman, 1984). The goods we have in mind include alcohol, 'soft' drugs and certain foodstuffs, though problems and principles under discussion are relevant to a much wider range of goods and activities where government intervention is often urged. We exclude from consideration hard drugs, which raise additional and different problems spilling over into the area of policy towards mental illness. There are difficult borderline cases, which will need to be taken into account in any practical situation, but they are not our concern here.

The market failure framework

Economists typically assume a unified framework within which available policy alternatives can be evaluated against a set of policy objectives. The concept of market failure, coupled nowadays with that of government failure, provides one such framework. The fundamental theorem of welfare economics asserts that rational choice as expressed in properly functioning markets will lead to an efficient (Pareto-optimal) allocation of resources. Government intervention in the economy is justified if and only if it can improve the functioning of the market or more effectively substitute for it. The criterion for assessing the relative performance of government and the market is the efficiency with which resources are allocated to meet consumer preferences.

In this framework, individual preferences are taken as given (along with abilities, technology and initial endowments of resources). It is acknowledged that choices may be misinformed, and there has been discussion of how far lack of information constitutes a market failure which could and should be remedied by government action. But the notion that preferences might simply be 'wrong' (as opposed to misinformed) is outside the market failure framework as normally conceived.

Similarly, the market failure framework takes as given individual rights. There is discussion of how externalities and transactions costs might be reduced by clarification or reallocation of property rights, and of whether government can more cheaply substitute for the market. However, transactions costs aside, the question of what rights each individual ought to have (and, hence, what one can legitimately call on the government to enforce) also lies beyond the scope of the market failure framework.

We discuss these two points at greater length later. For the present, we merely note that the market failure framework of analysis is clearly inadequate in the present context, where public policy is concerned not with the implementation of individual choice but with its inhibition. The question at issue is not how the desires of individuals to smoke, drink, take drugs or drive without seat belts can efficiently be met, but rather whether these desires should be controlled or frustrated, and if so for what reasons and by what means.

At the heart of the debate on public policy towards smoking are the questions of whether an individual smoker is the best judge of his own welfare, and whether and how preference should be given to the rights and concerns of smokers or of non-smokers. The market failure approach can shed only limited light on these two questions.

The paternalist framework

The paternalist framework postulates that certain groups of citizens (notably the young, the senile and the mentally subnormal but also, in some circumstances and to some people, the less educated or less affluent?) are insufficiently well informed or competent to make adequate judgements about the consumption of certain goods or services. Where people are not in a position to make decisions which will be in their own interest (properly understood), it is argued that government has a duty to take these decisions out of their hands and entrust the decisions to others held to be better informed or more competent. The paternalist view is sometimes (but by no means always) associated with the view that human life is beyond price, and that individuals should not be forced into the position of having to trade-off their health and safety against other material goods.

A far-reaching variant of the paternalistic framework emphasizes that individual behaviour, including consumption behaviour based on personal tastes and preferences, is conditioned by history as well as by experience. Children are born into a family and a society. Both are authoritarian groups (although differences of style and degree can and do occur), and the growing child is both constrained and influenced by the group. If this conditioning process is 'wrong', it is argued, individual preferences will also be 'wrong'. Society must prefer policies that, at the very least, take this imperfection into account, and preferably attempt to remedy it. This view is succinctly expressed by Room (1983: 264).

> . . . the individual preferences and behaviours one observes at any moment are not simply the result of a constantly updated Benthamite calculus carried out by the individual in isolation. The preferences and behaviours reflect the existing structuring of the market and, more generally, a wide range of cultural and historical influences. In modern society, most commodities are subject to habit formation in a technical sense, which is indeed a legitimate object of collective concern. To cry that this is 'paternalism' is to ignore the non-Benthamite functioning of preferences and purchases and to lend de

facto support to existing conditions in the system's structuring of consumer behaviour.

This argument might be used to restrict (e.g.) smoking, drinking or drug-taking, on the assumption that younger generations, if less exposed to such activities by their elders, will develop preferences in which such activities figure less highly or not at all. By analogy with the term 'market failure', we might describe the standard paternalist framework as based on 'individual failure', and its more extreme variant as based on 'societal failure'.

The libertarian framework

A third framework may be termed libertarian. Its guiding principle is the preservation of individual liberty in a free society. This is argued to imply the right of the individual to pursue his own interest, subject to not infringing upon the rights of other individuals to do likewise.

In this simple form, the libertarian framework would seem to preclude the possibility of policies inhibiting, say, the use of tobacco or alcohol. Like the market failure model, it seemingly excludes consideration of precisely those concerns and policies which are of interest in the present context.

However, the libertarian framework does not rule out government action altogether. Indeed, the question of what rights should be assigned to individuals (and, by implication, to the government) is quite central (Buchanan, 1975). Suppose public policy is based on conformity with a *unanimity rule*: that no policy should be implemented from which any citizen witholds consent. This limits government to those policies (and those institutional arrangements for the introduction of policies) that all citizens will accept. It does not follow that no policy is possible that any citizen considers to be against his direct or immediate interest. There is scope for compromise, with citizens willingly accepting constraints they do not like in return for reciprocal behaviour on the part of others. But the rule clearly sets limits to the role of government, and provides a principle by which to judge its institutional arrangements.

Interrelationships between constructs

In the summary form presented above, the three frameworks differ in their underlying value-judgements about the nature of the 'good society', in their identification and perception of the policy problem, and even in their view of human characteristics and behaviour. Yet in particular cases it may be a fine distinction as to which framework is being invoked. As noted earlier, the market failure framework is more ambiguous than at first appears. Three examples will illustrate this point.

Merit goods

Economists are familiar with the proposition that there exists a class of 'merit goods' whose benefits are likely to be underestimated by consumers. The merit goods argument is used to argue for the provision of more education (or housing or health care) than some citizens would voluntarily pay for. By analogy, a parallel class of 'demerit goods' might be identified which would justify the restriction of access to other goods and activities. For example, it might be decided to prohibit the sale of certain products, to supply them only upon the recommendation of some authorized person (e.g. a doctor), to limit their production or hours of sale, to prohibit their advertising, or to increase taxes on them.

The merit goods argument may be analysed within the market failure framework. One market failure argument for encouraging education and health care is based on the notion of externalities: people suffer if their fellow-citizens are ill-educated or unhealthy, hence the social benefits of these goods exceed the private benefits. Alternatively, it may be argued that the market fails to provide consumers with adequate information on which to base their decisions; as a result, some citizens may be, or are claimed by others to be, insufficiently well informed about the advantageous or deleterious consequences of particular forms of consumption, such as education or smoking. The government should therefore try to ensure the provision of relevant information, but where this is not possible should directly influence or constrain the decisions taken by consumers.

Suppose it is argued, however, that people do not always appreciate the 'true significance' of 'objective information'. Do data on the improved job prospects of university graduates adequately convey what it is like to receive a university education? Do data on illnesses statistically associated with smoking adequately convey the pain and suffering likely to accompany these illnesses? Is it possible, then, to draw a clear distinction between the market failure argument for 'merit' or 'demerit' goods, and the paternalist argument that, even if adequate information is available, some consumers simply are unwilling or unable to decide 'correctly'?

Breaking the pattern

A recent argument is that an individual may wish to change his consumption habits, but does not do so, not because the habit is physically addictive, but because he lacks the will to 'break the pattern' (Schelling,

1978). Public policy designed to make the particular form of consumption more difficult or impossible would thus help the individual attain his own desired objectives which would otherwise be beyond his reach.

Is this a market failure or a paternalist argument? In so far as all citizens were of this state of mind, and would voluntarily accept or even support policy restrictions on their freedom, government intervention seems consistent with the elimination of market failure (and indeed, with the libertarian principle of unanimity). But if these conditions do not hold, so that some people are helping others to help themselves against the wishes of the latter, then the argument is a special form of paternalism.

Externalities
The market failure framework provides for public policy to deal with externalities. The operational value of this concept depends upon the ability to identify the existence of an externality. In welfare economics, this would be the identification of a disutility imposed on some individuals by the behaviour of others. However, the simplicity of this notion disappears once we enquire into the nature of utility and disutility.

Consider some of the various ways in which smoking by one person A might be argued adversely to affect a non-smoker B:

a. B's health may be adversely affected, in ways that can be verified by persuasive empirical evidence.
b. Even without such evidence, B may *believe* that his health is adversely affected.
c. B may be simply annoyed by tobacco smoke.
d. B may be concerned about the effect of smoking on A's health.
e. B may be concerned about the effect of A's smoking on the happiness of third party C, who is exposed to A's smoke, or on third party D, who is a concerned friend or relative of A.
f. B may be annoyed at what he believes is A's lack of awareness of the suffering he is causing.

These different effects are not mutually exclusive; an individual's (subjective) evaluations will commonly be influenced by any or all of them. Since they together amount essentially to a state of mind, or subjective assessment, there is no way to distinguish them objectively one from the other. They are all aspects of externality. However, there is a diminution of credibility in the market failure argument for policy intervention as one moves from the first situation (where there is an identifiable loss that could in principle be internalized or compensated), through less explicit situations, to the final ones in which the 'failure' amounts only to the acts of one person making another feel less happy.

To be practically helpful, the market failure-externality argument must provide a rule to decide what kinds of externality are to be treated as policy-relevant, since without such a rule few human actions can be excluded. But the search for such rules inevitably leads outside the boundaries of the welfare economics framework from which the market failure model derives. The question can be answered only by specifying the *rights* of the individuals concerned. These rights are assumed given in the market failure framework, but are of course of fundamental relevance to the paternalistic and libertarian ones. It does not follow that the insights of the market failure model become irrelevant, but they need to be translated into the idiom of the other approaches.

Conflicts and complementarities

There are clearly potential conflicts between the various frameworks, especially between the libertarian and the other two. The libertarian framework does not accept the duty, much less the right, of government to influence an individual's pattern of consumption, provided that the individual does not arbitrarily infringe the rights of others. It does not accept that the possibility or even likelihood of resources being misallocated, or of individuals making what others consider to be wrong decisions, is of itself justification for government intervention. A greater value is placed on freedom from coercion than on remedying market, personal or societal 'failures'.

Conflict is not inevitable, however, and there may be scope for compromise. Some of the frameworks imply rather similar policies, albeit for different reasons. Thus, taxation of tobacco and alcohol has been advocated as a means of remedying alleged market failures (lack of information and/or externalities) as well as on paternalist and societal failure grounds. Or again, the strengthening of property rights to deal with externalities could both reduce market failure and promote individual liberty. It is therefore possible for an individual, or indeed a group of individuals, to agree on specific policy measures without necessarily agreeing on the underlying rationales for these measures.

There may also be situations where one framework implies a range of equally acceptable alternative policies, so that the choice within this range may be made in the light of a second framework. Thus, if market failure considerations call for policy to deal with externalities, the libertarian framework favours the establishment and enforcement of private property rights rather than banning, taxing or arbitrarily restricting the activity in question. Individuals can thereby resolve the externality problem between themselves, acting freely within a framework of laws and conventions. (As a corollary, the libertarian framework suggests giving precedence to 'positive' rights (the right to be free of constraint by others) over 'negative' rights (the right to constrain the behaviour of others). This puts the onus on those who press for constraints to persuade their fellow citizens to accept the implied coercion.)

Where there is more direct conflict between policies implied by different frameworks, this is not necessarily absolute, in the sense that commitment to one objective requires rejection of all others. In many circumstances a trade-off may be possible, whereby a little more of one objective may be secured by giving up a little of another one. Applying automobile seat-belt legislation to front-seat passengers only might be viewed as a compromise between the libertarian preference for no restrictions and a paternalist preference for restrictions on all passengers.

An individual may well believe that all the frameworks have some merit; he will typically attach some positive value to several objectives, rather than adopt one to the total exclusion of all others. He may, for example, believe in liberty for adults and paternalism for children. Each individual will seek, within his own mind, a form of policy which takes into account all the objectives and frameworks according to the relative weights he attaches to them.

Finally, because each person can sympathize with the views of others, even though he may not share them fully, and because each person is aware that he lives in a society of others, compromise solutions are possible and sought for. Debate is typically not between extreme solutions (e.g. complete prohibition versus complete freedom) but 'at the margin' of current policy (e.g. whether and how to increase or decrease government intervention slightly). This suggests that it will be fruitful to focus attention on the analysis of the processes most likely satisfactorily to achieve such social compromises.

From policies to processes

To summarize, the argument that there is no 'best' policy towards inhibition of choice because there is no 'best' framework within which alternative policies can be evaluated does not mean that nothing useful can be said. Since there is no right answer to the question initially posed, it is more fruitful to change the question. The analysis suggests that it will be more useful to consider the acceptability of the *processes* from which policies emerge than to attempt to evaluate the *outcomes* (i.e. the actual policies) of these processes.

Such a change of emphasis can be observed in other areas of public

policy analysis. The pricing and investment policies of UK public enterprises are a prime example. From the 1930s to the early 1970s there
was great interest among economists in deriving optimal policies (e.g.
marginal cost pricing) within a market failure framework. The guidelines in the 1967 White Paper, nominally reaffirmed in the 1978 White
Paper, mark the highpoint of this approach. But there was never complete agreement among economists as to the validity of this framework,
let alone among ministers, managers, employees and consumers. In
practice, nationalized industries and government sponsor departments
largely ignored the guidelines. By the end of the 1970s attention had
shifted to alternative administrative and political structures, and by
the early 1980s to ownership, competition and alternative forms of
regulation. In short, the question 'what is the right pricing and investment policy?' has been abandoned, and the focus of interest is now on
the broader characteristics of the policies emerging from different
decision processes associated with alternative institutional environments
(see Alchian, 1967; Wiseman, 1978; Heath, 1980; Littlechild, 1981;
Beesley and Littlechild, 1983).

Acceptable decision processes

What can be said about the acceptability of social decision-making
processes? By what criterion is acceptability to be judged? We noted
earlier that both the market failure framework and the libertarian
framework identify the fulfilment of the wishes of the individual as the
central purpose of public policy. Both frameworks imply the need for
agreement about rights and rules. But can this also be said of the
paternalist framework?

There would certainly be a conflict with an 'extreme' paternalist,
defined as one who rejects the libertarian position completely, and
attaches no importance to the preferences of others. His ideal policy is
one which requires the behaviour of others to conform to his own value
system. For such a paternalist, the ideal policy outcome is completely
specified by his own value-system, and coercion of others is an acceptable (perhaps a necessary?) characteristic of the social order. He has
no interest in decision *processes*, save that the achievement of the
specified outcome should not be inhibited by them.

But this is not the common paternalist position. If, as is more usual,
the paternalist accepts the right of others to resist his attempts to change
their behaviour, then he will accept the need for a social process through
which his paternalist wishes can seek and perhaps achieve credibility.
Put differently, he will recognize the difficulty of deciding *who* is to be
father, and will consequently accept the need to *persuade* others that

his paternalist policies are acceptable, with its corollary that he himself will not necessarily reject social processes that negate them.

It follows that an acceptable social decision-process must meet an 'equal access' condition such as the following:

> Within the law, all members of the polity have equal access to decision-making structures, and all have equal weights in the determination of collective decisions. (Buchanan, 1984)

This equal access condition alone provides a fruitful way to develop and evaluate policy towards choice-inhibition. It does not rule out the correction of market failure, but does require, for example, that the decision processes used to identify the externalities that are to be treated as policy-relevant are themselves acceptable. The public smoking debate illustrates this point. Smokers might well accept inhibitions on smoking in circumstances in which significant adverse effects for the health of others had been established. But they would not be equally willing to accept such a limitation of their freedom if the only predicted consequence for others were a reduction in psychic well-being.

The equal access condition directs attention towards the rules and procedures affecting the behaviour of pressure groups. Persuasive paternalistic behaviour is not improper in principle, but society's decision processes must not abrogate the equal access condition, e.g. by conferring undue influence on pressure groups via tax privileges.

More broadly, this specification of the problem emphasizes the importance of *moderation*. The emphasis on social processes rather than outcomes reflects the need to translate the libertarian principle of unanimity into operating principles that do not unduly stultify cooperative action. If citizens accept that the social decision processes from which policies emerge are themselves fair, then they will be willing to accept the possibility that at least some policies which emerge will be contrary to their best interests, since this is the price they must pay to obtain agreement from others to the policies they themselves want.

It is a corollary of this that efficient procedures will produce outcomes that inhibit individual freedom no more than is necessary (and hence acceptable) for the designated purpose. It is not difficult to find practical illustrations of the importance of this proposition (notably the history of prohibition in the USA).

The contractarian approach

The initial specification of our problem (policy towards the inhibition of choice) acquires interest only if the general preservation of individual freedom of choice is itself believed to be of interest. Given this value-judgement, the intellectual framework that emerges from our survey and analysis as deserving further investigation is the libertarian framework in its contractarian formulation (e.g. Buchanan, 1975). Starting from the libertarian framework, as described above, the contractarian uses the insights of methodological individualism to elucidate the procedures by which individuals may agree on rules (contracts, agreements), adherence to which will best achieve individual goals as constrained by the need to respect the rights of others. This will generate acceptable decision processes embracing all the viewpoints we have considered (save those that reject the initial value judgement, as with the extreme form of the paternalist position).

The approach also points towards some larger questions that demand our attention, and that the narrower perspectives tend to pass over. To follow Buchanan's specification once again, behind the guiding equal access principle quoted above there lie two others that are necessary to give it substance. First, there must be satisfactory processes not only for action taken within the law but also for the creation and changing of law. Second, there need to be constitutional procedures that create, specify, and change the constitutional arrangements within which individuals (as choosers and as policy agents) are empowered to act in the implementation of social rules and procedures. For if these larger rules are wrong, then the policies emerging within the law can hardly be expected to be efficient in the larger sense, however effective the procedures at this level. This is no trivial comment: as Buchanan argues, there are serious problems in devising practically efficient higher level constraints on the behaviour of policy-makers.

This is a much larger question than we set ourselves. But its recognition prompts the final observation that, since arbitrary authority is more likely to be exercised in the inhibition than in the promotion of individual choice, there is here an important reason for treating policy proposals for choice-inhibition with cautious suspicion.

References

Alchian, A. A. (1957) 'How should prices be set?' *Il Politico* 32(2).

Beesley, M. E. and Littlechild, S. C. (1983) 'Privatization: Principles, problems and priorities', *Lloyds Bank Review* (July).

Buchanan, J. M. (1967) *Public Finance in Democratic Process*. Chapel Hill: University of North Carolina Press.

Buchanan, J. M. (1972) 'Towards analysis of closed behavioral systems'. In J. M. Buchanan and R. D. Tollison (eds.) *Theory of Public Choice: Political applications of economics*. University of Michigan Press. Ann Arbor.

Buchanan, J. M. (1975) *The Limits of Liberty: Between anarchy and Leviathan*. Chicago: University of Chicago Press.

Buchanan, J. M. (1984) *Can Democracy be Tamed?* Paper presented at General Meeting of Mont Pelerin Society, Cambridge, September (see also comments on this paper by H. Demsetz).

Coase, R. H. (1970) 'The theory of public utility pricing and its application', *Bell Journal of Economics and Management Science* 1 (1) (Spring): 113–28.

Heath, J. B. (1980) 'Management in nationalized industries', Nationalized Industries Chairman's Group, *Occasional Papers* No. 2, (March).

Littlechild, S. C. (1981) 'Ten steps to denationalization', *Journal of Economic Affairs*, 2 (1) (October).

Littlechild, S. C. and Wiseman, J. (1984). 'Principles of public policy relevant to smoking', *Policy Studies* (January).

Room, R. (1983) 'Paternalism, rationality and the special status of alcohol'. In M. Grant et al. (eds), *Economics and Alcohol* Ch. 19, London and Canberra: Croom Helm.

Schelling, T. C. (1978) 'Ergonomics, or the art of self-management', *American Economic Review, Papers and Proceedings* (May): 290–94.

Wiseman, J. (1978) 'The political economy of nationalized industry'. In *The economics of politics*. London: Institute of Economic Affairs, *Readings*, No. 18, (reprinted as chapter 6).

11 The Political Economy of Government Revenues*

Foreword

This chapter was an invited lecture presented to the Athens Congress of the International Institute of Public Finance. It takes up a different aspect of my evolving general model of social behaviour, in that it is the first paper in the collection to bring together my direct concern with the problems of the public sector and my abiding interest in costs and decisions.

The paper questions the actual or potential value of the kind of empirical studies of the growth of government that I had earlier pioneered with Alan Peacock. The major deficiency of these studies is their lack of behavioural content. They need to be replaced by a 'new' political economy, capable of integrating the insights of economics (in its public choice – voter-behaviour manifestation) and a sympathetic political science. Such a model would have the general characteristics indicated by the argument of earlier chapters. That is, it would be concerned with decision-making as a process conditioned by the unknowability of the future (and hence by an interest among individuals in the responsiveness of their institutions to unexpected outcomes). The relevant choice-concept would be 'sophisticated Wicksell' rather than Pareto, and government would be seen as Leviathan in need of restraint rather than as the passive servant of a median voter, much less as the omnicompetent authoritarian ringmaster of the neo-classical model of the so-called liberal market economy.

It follows from this formulation that there is no 'right' size or pattern of government spending and taxing, save the level, whatever it might be, that would emerge from the 'free' (not improperly coerced) choices of citizens, whatever those choices might be.

The argument is applied by way of illustration to the areas of emigration policy and fiscal federalism. In the latter case, it is standard form to use a criterion of efficiency couched in terms of the allocation of governmental functions to the levels at which resources are best 'economized'. The broader model suggests that this criterion is seriously

* Chiancone, A. (ed.) (1989) *Changes in Revenue Structures*. Detroit, Mich., Wayne State University Press (Proceedings of 42nd Congress of International Institute of Public Finance, 1986).

deficient; there is no reason why citizens should not prefer functions to rest at other levels, if for example they value the anticipated improvement in protection from coercive behaviour by government more highly than the expected loss through additional resource-use. This argument will come as no surprise to political scientists, since they commonly cite diffusion of power *per se* as a positive attribute of the federal arrangement.

(There is also a much broader implication. For similar reasons, the very existence of government cannot satisfactorily be explained by the recognition by citizens that it brings advantages of scale economies. Perhaps it does. But how can we be sure that citizens must always value these more highly than the potential for coercion that Leviathan also brings?)

Introduction
Subject to minor clarifications, concerning the treatment of such categories as payments for publicly provided services, we know what we mean by government revenues. But what do we mean by political economy? We have travelled a long and tortuous path from the certainties that could lead Mrs Besant to write of children learning the principles of political economy at their mother's knee. But without such 'principles', what can economists say about government revenues?

Clearly, nothing normative. The temptation is therefore to turn to positive enquiry, and seek evidence concerning the 'determinants' of the size and character of government revenues. I became involved in this search for determinants, with Alan Peacock, when 'positivism' was the new buzzword rather than the industry it has since become. Our concern was public expenditures rather than revenues. But the experience has relevance, in that the intellectual issues that have to be confronted have common roots. Our initial interest was sparked by the observation that the extant theories of government behaviour did not appear to be consistent with the available evidence concerning the historical development of public expenditures in the UK. This led us to speculate about alternative explanations, and to suggest as possibilities the displacement effect and the (local–central) concentration process. We did not see these as much more than speculations (hypotheses) about government behaviour: their 'scientific' foundation was essentially observation of the general behaviour of time-series of public expenditures in relation to series of other economic magnitudes.

Subsequent discussion of these ideas has thus been coterminous with the evolution of econometrics and positive economics, and it has become standard form (and somewhat monotonous, in so far as writers have a propensity to copy one another's footnotes, not forgetting the errors) for specialists in the area to introduce their own contribution by criticizing the lack of formal scientific rigour of our original contribution. When we came to reappraise our work, we took these strictures seriously, hoping that the subsequent literature would guide us as to how to do better. It would be both untrue and churlish to claim that we learned nothing new: the literature concerned offers many valuable new insights and speculations. Nevertheless, I do not think it unreasonable to suggest that the central problem remains unresolved: the literature is rich in alternative hypotheses and speculations, but grossly deficient in developing plausible techniques for discriminating between them – that is, in propounding econometric techniques the use of which would convincingly identify any one 'explanation' of the growth of public expenditures as 'better' than any others. This disappointment led us in two closely related directions: to try to devise a satisfactory methodology of our own, and to identify the precise reasons for the intractability of the problem.

We were disappointed in the first of these enterprises, to such an extent that, while we have published an explanation of the methodology we chose and our reasons for choosing it, we have refrained from publishing the empirical findings because of our own misgivings as to how they should be interpreted. Summarily, we used spectral analysis to attempt to establish significant relationships between the growth of sub-categories of public expenditures. When we tried to interpret the results, however, we faced two insuperable difficulties. The first of these is simple to explain but impossible to avoid: the relationships that are thrown up are decided by the choice of expenditure categories into which the expenditure data are initially divided. The results can thus provide a trustworthy 'behavioural' explanation of the time-pattern of expenditure change only in so far as the categories selected are the effective 'decision-categories' for the society and the time-period being reviewed. A different classification must be expected to produce different relationships/explanations, and failing some procedure for the selection of categories (break-down of expenditures) that can itself be recognized as 'scientific', there can be no confidence that 'explanations' derived from one breakdown by techniques such as spectral analysis are more satisfactory than the possible alternatives.

The second difficulty is closely related. The expenditure categories available for study are determined by the accessibility of data. The relevant data are in fact the records of the spending departments of government. The spending responsibilities of departments derive from their legal obligations which in turn emerge from the political process.

There is no simple or obvious relation between the responsibilities of departments and the kinds of behavioural categories commonly used to describe or 'explain' economic behaviour. It is tempting to treat this as an operational rather than an intellectual or conceptual problem, soluble in principle by the detailed reclassification of departmental expenditures. But I shall argue below that this view is mistaken: in so far as departments, and their bureaucrats and political heads, are the relevant *actors* in the decision process from which public expenditures (or any other category such as taxes) emerge, then the need is not to reclassify the data to fit the economists' behavioural model, but to change the models used by economists to fit the behavioural situations that we wish to explain. If departments take spending decisions, then departments must have a place in a plausible behavioural model. But how to reconcile this with the behaviour of the customary economic categories is one of the great problems that remains unresolved.

This last observation bears directly on the second question: why has methodological dissatisfaction produced so little satisfying technical development? The essential reason seems to be this. For econometric techniques to be operationally useful, certain preconditions must be fulfilled. For our present purposes, two are important. First, the set of possible 'explanations' must be agreed to be reasonably exhaustive, in that there is no major disagreement that the set to be studied excludes no potentially important possibilities. Second, the different explanations must be capable of statement in a form that permits empirical investigation of a kind that enables selection between the alternative available explanations. Put differently, it must be possible to distinguish the explanations by reference to data which enables some to be rejected in favour of others. Neither of these conditions is satisfactorily met by studies of public expenditures or of government behaviour generally. A welter of explanations of the secular growth of public expenditures alone has been offered, and it would be difficult to produce an agreed comprehensive list that was not too extensive for practical study. Also, the 'explanations' take such a variety of political, economic, politico-economic, and technological forms, that it is difficult to conceive of tests that would permit a clear identification of what has been excluded and what not.

What emerges as missing is an agreed intellectual construct for the study of such problems: that is, a 'new' set of principles of political economy. This is what I wish to attempt to create, though in one short essay I can hope to do no more than erect the signposts to the country I suggest we need to explore, to identify, that is, the intellectual framework I believe to be needed, and which I am already developing at greater length elsewhere.

Also, while most of what I have written so far describes a joint. voyage of intellectual exploration with my respected colleague, Alan Peacock, the journey from here onward I am undertaking alone. I do not believe that he will find the journey uninteresting, but he must not be held responsible in the not unlikely event that I end up in danger of shipwreck.

The nature and purpose of a new political economy

My dissatisfaction with neo-classical economics is not of recent origin, and has been recorded elsewhere. The present topic offers an opportunity to try to respond to the frequent reaction to such criticism: tell us how to do better. The introductory observations point the way towards an answer, since to find a way through the difficulties I have identified requires both the development of new intellectual constructs and an examination of their (normative and positive) implications. In this short paper, I can offer only a thumbnail sketch. Particularly, I can do no more than suggest lines of empirical (positive) research that the argument of principle suggest might be fruitful. I am myself attempting to apply the ideas in the context of fiscal federalism, but beyond this I hope only to persuade others of the emerging research potential.

The preceding paragraphs have suggested a useful prescription from which to begin: to understand/predict the behaviour of such magnitudes as government revenues of public expenditures, we need an intellectual construct that embraces the behaviour of all the 'actors' whose decisions bear upon the magnitudes (revenue or expenditure) categories concerned. The total cast of actors comprises all the individual members of society. But we need to take account of them in all relevant decision roles – that is, in all choice-situations that bear upon the questions of interest. Clearly, all the decisions (choice-situations) embraced by this are not captured by the study of individual choice-through-markets that is the central preoccupation of economics. Other choices, and particularly those commonly called 'political', or 'administrative/ bureaucratic', also influence the relevant outcomes. Indeed, these other influences are in a sense primary, in that revenue and expenditure decisions emerge directly from the politico-bureaucratic process, with 'economic' behaviour as normally construed influencing outcomes less directly. This identifies the nature of the 'new' political economy that I argue to be needed. It must embrace *all* choice-situations within a common intellectual construct, choice-through-markets, choices of and through political institutions, social groups, etc., being studied as part of a common process to be evaluated by its results. The *normative* characteristics of such a political economy would be concerned with the consonance between specified social arrangements/institutions and identified social goals. Two kinds of *positive* question then arise: what behavioural relationships can be identified between particular political, institutional and economic arrangements and the behaviour of particular economic magnitudes (such as the evolving size and structure of the tax 'take')?: and what are the causal relations ('determinants') of the behaviour of identified magnitudes within a specified (political economy) setting?

It might appear that this is no more than a re-statement of the problem I began with. Our own (the original Peacock/Wiseman) expenditure study, for example, could be argued to have been a search for 'determinants': and we did not need a 'new' political economy to recognise the potential value of comparative studies of other politico-economic situations; indeed we quickly set out to stimulate the study of countries other than UK. But the results of this initiative identify the ongoing need. Summarily, the many 'country' studies now available identify 'determinants' that appear to have been important in individual cases: but considered as a set these do not invite any striking new generalizations. This is not attributable to any lack of subtlety or ingenuity on the part of the many authors, but rather to the lack of the embracing intellectual construct needed to give the studies common form. Failing this, we are left with a shopping list of influences that have been important somewhere. This list grows along two axes, one conceptual (producing the variety of political, technological and economic models/hypotheses to which I referred earlier), the other concerned with specific characteristics that seem to have been important somewhere at some time (external debt, dependent-economy status, colonialism, federal character, or whatever). What is lacking is any means to place these diverse studies in a common intellectual context from which fruitful generalizations might emerge. It is that common context that the 'new' political economy is intended to provide.

What is needed, then, is an intellectual construct that integrates the insights of economics and of political science. The integrating device is an expanded concept of individual choice. Mainstream economics is dominated by choice-through-markets, and tends to appraise choices in other (non-market settings) by their impact on choices-through-markets which are the central concern of 'efficient' economic (and by implication, social) organization. Political scientists, in contrast, would claim that they are concerned with *all* aspects of human behaviour, so that 'economic' behaviour is subsumed in their formulation. But in fact they usually concern themselves directly with choice only in the context of 'voter-behaviour', and tend to eschew technical notions of 'efficiency' in favour of philosophical speculation.

The description is to some extent unjust and inaccurate, in so far as members of both groups are aware of the problem concerned, and there is an identifiable school of thought concerned to find solutions, whether through the evolving study of public choice or through the development of normative/philosophical models that incorporate a concept of individual choice. It is not my intention to ignore or belittle the importance of this work, and I shall discuss it in more detail later. But the dichotomy I describe remains a fair description of the dominant position of scholars in the two fields: it is the burden of my argument that this is likely to persist pending the emergence and acceptance of the kind of integrated political economy whose features I am attempting to describe.

The economics of government revenues

'Orthodox' tax analysis develops within the logical framework of mainstream economics, and so must share any deficiencies of that construct. These are not trivial. Apart from the limitation of the choice-context to market or market-related choices, the *conditions* of the choice-situation are severely limited. Although choice is defined in very general (opportunity-cost decisions in conditions of scarcity) terms, the alternatives in relation to which choice is exercised are assumed either to be known with certainty or capable of reduction to 'knowability' by the assumptions made about knowledge of objective probability. As I have argued elsewhere, this severely limits the ability of the analysis to contribute to an understanding of real-world choice-behaviour characterized by 'unknowability', in which learning is important, but the outcome of choices is often going to be different from that predicted by the choosers, in ways not capable of objective-probabilistic explanation. This is a fact of common experience (a product of learning): choosers are not completely *surprised* that their predictions are from time to time falsified by events. This is a large topic which I cannot here pursue. I want only to offer a conclusion: not only is there need for a drastic reconstruction of economic models to take account of these arguments, with the implication (among others) that efficiency in choosing has to be concerned with *choice-processes* rather than with *outcomes*; but the same will remain true in any useful expanded formulation of the choice-problem: citizens choosing, e.g., about laws, governments and institutions will do so in the expectation that their predictions concerning the outcome of their choices may be falsified in unpredictable ways. The broader model must therefore also be concerned with efficiency as process, and must take account of the fact that citizens may attach weight (e.g. in appraising alternative political or administrative organizations) to their ability to 're-contract' in the event of their expectations being disappointed.

Within this inadequate context, orthodox tax analysis examines the economic implications of government revenue-raising policies, and uses the conclusions to offer policy advice. The policy problem may be formulated in a number of different ways (familiar examples being the social welfare function, the theory of the public household, optimal taxation models, and input-output 'ends-means' models) which share the common characteristic of having no *political* input. The normative policy framework is essentially a set of ethical norms imposed by an implied 'benevolent despot'. More accurately these models allow choice only *within* the specification of a previously postulated set of goals that are not themselves the subject of choice. Paradoxically, the advice which emerges is being offered to a government that within the confines of the underlying model does not exist, or exists only as the costless instrument of policy implementation. There is no political *process* (since the process has nothing to decide), and the politicians/bureaucrats are not only obliged to accept the ethical norms pre-imposed by the model, but also have the power unambiguously to determine policy outcomes through unexplained political/bureaucratic processes that require no resource-use. No mistakes are made, and decisions as to what is 'fair' or 'best' do not emerge from the choice-process but are imposed upon it.

It was recognition of the shortcomings of mainstream economics that led to the development of theories of public choice. Essentially, public choice emerged as a reaction to the notion of 'perfect' government, which became the practical implication of the use of models that effectively required no government, and hence had no means to study the possibility that government action could be mistaken or inefficient. In principle, therefore, public choice has to be seen as the kind of development of an expanded choice-framework that I have argued to be needed. But while there can be no question as to the importance of the initial insight, the kind of new political economy that is needed has not yet emerged from the development of public choice, for reasons that it is illuminating to explore. A simplified, but not grossly misleading description of the changed policy construct that has so far emerged would be this:

The 'public choice orthodoxy' does not postulate a 'perfect' government, but treats the government as a politician/bureaucrat, fully constrained by the voting system. The political mechanism is not argued to be an efficient means of making collective decisions. But it is the controlling mechanism: if there is a 'mainstream' public choice model, it is one in which the median voter controls the system. Politicians obtain power (from government) by offering policies that attract the support of the median voter, who is seen as reflecting the wishes of the electorate. But in getting power, the politician is seen as being *committed* to carry out the policies that gained the support of the median voter. Since there is no question of governments reneging on their promises, the median voter in fact determines public policy, including tax policy.

The essential change is this: in orthodox tax analysis, the government is essentially a benevolent despot guided by tax advisers whose ethical norms he shares, and which are imposed on citizens and uninfluenced by their individual choices. In the orthodox public choice model, there is no benevolent despot, but the 'government' is effectively a bureaucracy implementing the wishes of the median voter. Neither formulation has any room for mistake, in the sense of unforeseen policy outcomes that the decision-maker would be concerned to correct.

From public choice to political economy
While it might have been expected that public choice would have evolved into the kind of unified choice model that is needed, it has not yet succeeded in doing so. This is because thought has developed primarily in two directions, neither conducive to the necessary evolution. Indeed, one line of development is essentially a diversion of interest from the questions of major importance, and relevant to our discussion only because it threatens to stultify the necessary evolution of the study of public choice. I have in mind the treatment of public choice as essentially an extension of the logic of choice-through-markets to be found in mainstream economics. This is the school of thought that proceeds by the specification of public choice 'situations' in a fashion appropriate for formal (mathematical) modelling sympathetic in character to the evolving models used in 'mainstream' economic analysis, and extends the related econometric techniques (with all the problems that follow from the inadequacies of the underlying behavioural model, described above) to the 'empirical' investigation of so-called public choice problems. The end-consequence of this approach is the introduction of a chapter or two concerned with public choice concepts (and perhaps bearing a title like *The Role of Government*) as extensions of the content of textbooks of economic analysis. This 'absorption'

leaves the central problem unresolved: the desirable goal must be the creation of an intellectual context in which 'market choice' can be treated as one element in an integrated public (non-market) and private (market) choice-model.

The second broad direction of development is the one I have already referred to, and is concerned with voter-behaviour. This meets the requirement of concern with non-market choices, the more so in that it is compatible in principle with the evolution of (choice-related) general models of group behaviour and of bureaucracy. For a satisfactorily integrated intellectual construct to emerge, however, two further things are needed: median-voter type models need to be replaced by a more sophisticated and satisfying model of political behaviour, and a more relevant positivism needs to displace the fruitless attempt to apply the logic and methods of orthodox econometrics in increasingly implausible contexts. In some degree, progress in dealing with the second of these must wait upon success in dealing with the first: that is, upon the enunciation of a set of 'principles' of political economy. How public choice will need to evolve to this end, and what sort of related positive research might thereby be generated, is examined in the concluding section which follows.

The way ahead: an outline political economy

I do not of course claim that I am alone in finding median voter type models inadequate, and indeed there have been developments in the field of public choice that are sympathetic to my general approach. Two such developments demand specific recognition. The first is a response to the need for an interpretation of the concept of choice which is more embracing than the market-related choice of mainstream economics. Broadly the Paretian (welfare economics) interpretation of choice is replaced by a Wicksellian one. That is, the Paretian criterion for 'desirable' change: that some are made better off and none worse off, is displaced by a Wicksellian 'rule' that no change is desirable to which any citizen objects. The latter is clearly a broader rule in that choice is interpreted to carry a right of veto (though it must be pointed out that this is a much less restrictive rule than might appear, in that citizens in a 'process' situation must think reciprocally): the consequences of exercising a veto in respect of a current policy proposal may be to provoke the future veto of policies they desire. From the point of view of the development of a relevant political economy, the importance of substitution is that the Wicksellian interpretation can be argued to embrace both 'economic' and 'other' (political, etc.) choice-situations.

(I leave aside, as irrelevant in the present context, the question of whether 'Paretian' and 'Wicksellian' choice are formally compatible.)

The Wicksellian formulation rests of course upon an ethical proposition: the 'libertarian' position that the preferences of all members of society have equal status. It is important that the implications of this be recognized, since many who would accept it in principle, would also support policies of an essentially 'paternalist' character, because some citizens have special knowledge of what is good for others. The Wicksellian principle does not require outright rejection of this kind of paternalism, but rather would admit it only in so far as A's claim of superior insight is recognized by B's willingness to cede decision-authority to A in an institutional situation that he (B) does not regard as itself improperly coercive. For A to go further than this requires the emasculation of B's right of (Wicksellian) veto. Thus, a 'Wicksellian political economy' is clearly normative in character, and policy recommendations deriving from it will be relevant to actual societies only in so far as the underlying ethical position is accepted. It is simply a means of ordering our policy ideas, as are all such models, but is nevertheless a significant improvement upon what happens now, to the extent that the ethical implications of the model are explicit, and have relevance to the actual goals of many societies.

Second, it is increasingly coming to be recognized that the notion of government as the passive servant of voter intentions is quite unrealistic. While the voter may have reserve powers that influence (coerce) politicians, those powers are exercised indirectly and through necessarily imperfect institutional arrangements for the expression of individual policy, etc., preferences. Consequently, governments do have residual powers of independent decision: in the classic description of two of the innovatory authors in this field, the policy problem is how to curb the Leviathan of government, rather than how the voters instruct their government servant.

It is the further development of these insights, together with the recognition of the need to re-define the choice-environment to take account of the deficiencies I have identified in mainstream economics (and particularly to recognize the unknowability of the future and its implication of 'expected error' in the outcome of human plans), that provides the foundation for a new political economy.

Summarily, *all* social arrangements, in this formulation, are to be judged by the extent to which they are responsive to the wishes (choices) of the citizens. The implications of this apparently simple notion are a great deal more complex than might first appear. I have already pointed out that the Wicksellian interpretation of the choice-situation does not imply that citizens would reject all policy proposals whose direct consequences they expected to be unfavourable to them: the decision-situation (opportunity-cost problem) they face must involve the predicted further consequences for rejection, so that, effectively, the 'cost of lost indirect benefits' enters into the individual cost-benefit appraisal of any policy proposal. From the point of view of the individual, then, an efficient set of social institutions will not be one in which no policies are implemented that he thinks undesirable of themselves, but rather one in which he does not feel that his right of veto is being unacceptably constrained – that is, one in which he is being improperly coerced.

Clearly, this formulation demands considerably more development than is possible here. I must be content to try to convey the flavour of the proposal by a couple of examples:

First, the efficiency of a system of social organization cannot be judged by any simple rules, analogous, e.g. to the net revenue 'rule' of mainstream economics. A decision taken in conformity with the existent constitutional and voting rules of a society may produce reactions that identify the situation as inefficient (unacceptable). For example, prohibition was introduced in USA by due process, but produced widespread illegal behaviour among a considerable minority who regarded themselves as being improperly coerced. Similarly, the magnitude of emigration cannot be treated as an indicator of satisfaction or dissatisfaction with a country's institutions, since the cost of attempting to emigrate itself varies from one country to another, and in ways that are themselves in large part a reflection of the institutions concerned. (This also underlines the importance of the ethical postulate underlying the model: the inhibition of emigration will not be regarded as inefficient if the citizens who support it reject the libertarian postulate upon which the model is founded.)

A more directly relevant illustration concerns fiscal federalism. The usual analysis uses (choice) efficiency-criteria of a Paretian kind, and even the most sophisticated studies in general treat 'efficiency' as being concerned with finding answers to such questions as: What is the technically efficient level of government for the performance of particular (taxing and spending) functions? But in terms of the expanded-individual choice model here being proposed, there is no reason to expect individual citizens not to prefer other 'technically-inferior' institutional arrangements for the performance of particular functions, because, e.g., they value the greater protection these provide against potential coercion. After all, the devolution of power *per se* is frequently put forward as a virtue of the federal constitutional arrangements. (It might be observed in passing that a similar deficiency is to be found in even the liberarian-philosophical 'justification' of the existence of government: the argument that citizens must recognize the 'scale economy' benefits of government action cannot be assumed inevitably to outweigh in importance their fear of coercion by 'Leviathan'.)

Finally, what are the positive implications of all this? To some extent, the arguments are already being reflected in empirical study. Particularly, there are studies that use the different conceptions of the state as passive servant and the state as independent decision-maker, and an interesting recent paper compares and contrasts such studies. To make further progress requires that we find means to integrate the two, so that revenue or expenditure data can be interpreted in relation to a *de facto* situation in which citizens can be coerced, because the (non-market and market) institutions through which they express their preferences give them less than complete control over the behaviour of government, but in which those same institutions constrain the importance and form of that coercion. In my judgement, this makes it questionable whether it is likely to be fruitful to continue to seek for cross-country generalizations about the behaviour of such magnitudes as government revenues. It follows from the argument of this paper that the situation at any point in time is the product of the preferences of citizens and the institutions through which they are reflected over the relevant preceding decision-period. A 'process' approach to such material requires the interpretation of this data behaviourally. But the behavioural change may be either adjustment within the existent institutional framework because of learning from emerging experience, attempts to change the framework because that same experience generates dissatisfaction with those institutions: or any combination of these things. (The Peacock-Wiseman original observation of the apparent importance of social disturbances fits such a framework, as does the subsequent response that it is unclear whether these represent anything more than departures from a trend. My present position is that there is no reason to expect a general answer to such questions.)

Rather than seeking broad universal generalizations, then, the expanded choice-model should be used to develop studies concerned with the relation between institutional structures and revenue patterns, and with the prediction of change in the behaviour of such magnitudes in relation to specified institutional changes. In time, such studies might begin to produce broader generalizations that we could trust (the behaviour of public debt is one area in which this could be true). But that is in the distant future.

References

Brennan, Geoffrey and Buchanan, James, *The Power to Tax*, Cambridge University Press, 1980.

Buchanan, James M. and Tullock, Gordon, *The Calculus of Consent*, Ann Arbor, University of Michigan Press, 1962.

Peacock, Alan T. and Wiseman, J., *The Growth of Public Expenditure in the United Kingdom*, London, Oxford University Press, 1961.

Peacock, Alan T. and Wiseman, J., 'Approaches to the Analysis of Public Expenditure Growth'. *Public Finance Quarterly*, Vol. 7, No. 1, January, 1979.

Wiseman J. 'Costs and Decisions' in *Contemporary Economic Analysis*, Vol. 2, (eds. Currie and Peters), London, Croom Helm, 1980, (reprinted as Chapter 7).

12 General Equilibrium or Market Process: An Evaluation*

Foreword

This essay returns to the critique of established theory which was the topic of Chapters 3, 7 and 8. It is concerned specifically with the question of equilibrium, but although the conference assignment for which it was prepared called for a comparison of neo-classical general equilibrium theory and Austrian market process, I interpreted my remit more ambitiously, to incorporate a criticism of both formulations from the point of view of a radical subjectivist, and to make some suggestions as to what is now needed.

The paper identifies six components of the neo-classical general equilibrium framework which are sources of difficulty: that the future is assumed in some sense already to exist; that in so far as it is not known, it is 'knowable' in an objective probability sense; that the notion of subjectivity is restricted to the existence of tastes and preferences; that the treatment of cost is ambiguous; that ignorance of the future is somehow 'inefficient'; and that the model has no formal role for innovation and imagination – that is, for the human mind. These problems cannot be reconciled with the proposition that neo-classical general equilibrium theory is 'fundamentally sound', but may need 'restructuring'. The difficulties derive from the initial (mis-) specification (it might be more precise to say emasculation) of the problem, and can consequently be remedied only by fundamental change.

The Austrian specification of the problem is more appealing, in that it recognizes many of the difficulties of the neo-classical model. But writers in this genre then generally fail to come to terms with the radical implications of their own insights, preferring rather to argue that there is nothing wrong with neo-classical economics that could not be remedied by a return to its earlier traditions. Austrians continue to be preoccupied with notions of consistency and harmony, to the comparative neglect of the powerful insights implied by the role in human decision of the 'filter of the human mind', radical uncertainty and spontaneous learning.

* Bosch, A., Koslowski, P. and Veit, R. (1989) *General Equilibrium or Market Process: Neoclassical and Austrian Theories of Economics*. Tübingen. J. C. B. Mohr (Paul Siebeck) (Proceedings of a Liberty Fund Conference organized by the Eucken Institute.)

The paper concludes by extending the discussion to incorporate the arguments of radical subjectivists such as Shackle, Littlechild, Lachmann and myself. This invites a rejection of much of both the earlier positions, the recognition of equilibrium as a pseudo-concept (it changes each time an economic agent changes his mind), and the need to incorporate the new insights and behavioural postulates into the kind of broader notion of choice as a social process which earlier chapters have elaborated.

Introduction

There are two other conference papers concerned respectively with the meaning of general equilibrium and the meaning of market process, and my own paper is to provide 'an evaluation'. I assume from this that the earlier papers will have dealt with the technical characteristics of the two concepts, and that my own task (since 'evaluation' must be in terms of some concept of *objective*) is to relate these characteristics to the purpose which the ideas of economists are expected to serve.

There is no 'right' set of such purposes that can be identified objectively; and different purposes may be better served by different intellectual constructs. There is consequently nothing inherently disturbing in the existence of different schools of thought: the problems arise when the schools offer conflicting answers to what appear to be common questions. Such a situation may be attributable to either or both of two causes: that the two schools each have limitations which affect their relative value in particular contexts, and that they share common deficiencies that can be resolved only by their integration into a broader common intellectual framework.

I shall argue, in the context of an examination of the rival core concepts of general equilibrium and market process, that both these causes are present. Examination of the ideas within their own intellectual contexts suggests that something can be said about the relative practical relevance of the different inferences to which they lead. But, and this is less generally recognized but certainly not less important, the two schools also share common deficiencies capable of remedy only by incorporation into an overarching intellectual framework capable of embracing the central ideas of both.

I take it as given that the two schools share a common 'general philosophy', of the kind encapsulated in two phrases in the Statement of Purpose of this Conference: '(We are concerned with) . . . the specific contribution each of them can make to the scientific foundation and political realization of a social order of freedom', and 'both schools are market oriented and ostensibly wedded to the concept of a free society'.

While there is undoubtedly room for debate about details, I believe this very general specification, of individual freedom as the objective (and hence the ultimate criterion of 'social efficiency'), and the market as the primary policy instrument, to be an adequate description of both schools.

I shall first examine the two ideas (general equilibrium and market process) within and in relation to their own chosen context (their 'scientific foundation'), before moving to the broader considerations ('political realization', and relevance to 'a social order of freedom'), and suggestions as to the way forward. To do this, I shall need to describe the approaches and concepts concerned, so that I must choose whether to provide a composite 'school' view, without claiming that it would have the total support of any individual school member, or offer the views of a 'representative' member. I have tried to have the best of both worlds. I shall rely heavily upon individual contributions (not least because an individualistic Austrian in particular might be uncomfortable with the idea of a 'school' view), but make use of general surveys written by recognized proponents of the views concerned. This reduces the scope for misunderstanding-through-misinterpretation.

Neo-classical general equilibrium
This section relies heavily upon the exposition of Professor Hahn (Hahn, 1980). It is a précis of and commentary on his own description and evaluation of general equilibrium theory in an article which encapsulates the views he has argued at greater length elsewhere. Professor Hahn is not only a distinguished proponent of the general equilibrium approach; he is also refreshingly open-minded about its shortcomings and difficulties. We thus have in one place the position of a respected and 'representative' advocate on the nature, problems and future potential of general equilibrium theory.

The theory
Hahn's 'simple account' of general equilibrium theory starts from individual agents, as firms choosing the most profitable from a set of alternative known output (production) sets, and as households choosing the 'best' among the bundles of goods that they can afford. *Equilibrium is a state in which the independently taken decisions of these agents are compatible.*

In this description, 'output' consists of 'goods', defined by their physical attributes, location, date of delivery and the state of nature. All such goods have markets, and therefore a price. *Consequently, the defined general equilibrium is a set of prices such that the maximizing*

decisions of firms and households would make the total demand for any
good equal to the amount of it initially available, plus the amount prod-
uced. It is further characteristic of this situation that any reallocation
away from the equilibrium must make some agent worse off.

Hahn draws critical attention to three aspects of this specification;

1. The assumption that there are current markets for all possible
    future goods (so that they have current prices) is intrinsically unre-
    alistic. Particularly, it implies that the 'profit-maximizing' and
    'affording' decisions of agents are unaffected by uncertainty about
    the future.
2. It is also necessary to postulate the absence of economies of scale.
3. Hahn (implicitly) imputes a *qualified* normative content to the gen-
    eral equilibrium conditions, by referring to them interchangeably
    as 'Pareto-optimal' and 'Pareto-efficient'. But he points out that
    'Pareto-efficient' may not be construed as 'just' or 'socially opti-
    mum', because there will be a competitive equilibrium for each
    'distribution of endowments', and the 'right' distribution is itself a
    moral question.

These caveats notwithstanding, Hahn argues that 'at least some of
the disorders of a capitalist society . . . can be traced to the absence of
some of these Arrow-Debreu (i.e. inter-temporal) markets' (p.124),
and that the equilibrium prices 'impose order on potential chaos' in a
decentralised economy.

Interpretation and difficulties

The list of questions and criticisms examined by Hahn is a lengthy one.
Some of these are not directly relevant to my present purpose (such
as his castigation of interpretative error by neo-classical economists
themselves, and his justified rejection of attempted criticisms founded
on Marxist-type theories of power and conflict). The others are of
diverse importance. I present them reclassified in a form that better fits
my own purposes, but without I hope any misinterpretation of Hahn's
own argument.

He perceives the need for the theory to deal with a larger range of
questions. But while some of the questions he raises might be thought
essentially technical, others clearly raise deeper conceptual issues. The
distinction is not a neat one, in that the technical questions are to a
greater or lesser extent the product of the underlying assumptions of
the model. But it is useful in identifying the conceptual questions upon
which I think it appropriate to concentrate. In the first (technical)

group Hahn identifies problems in explaining the role of money in Arrow–Debreu type models, the inability of the theory to explain the behaviour of share markets, the need to abstract from economies of scale (with the resultant difficulty of explaining why firms exist other than as sole proprietorships), oligopoly and imperfect competition, and the problems created by 'small' economies. Important and intellectually fascinating though these questions are, I think them secondary in importance to (and indeed they can be argued to derive from), the underlying questions concerning the nature of the environment within which the agent decision-takers are making their choices. In respect of this, Hahn makes a number of comments on the treatment of time and uncertainty which can be summarized as follows:

The assumptions about time effectively 'collapse the future into the present'. This requires that there be present markets in 'goods' that are unlikely to emerge in practice (Hahn gives the example that a man must be able to exchange labour today for orange juice tomorrow if he has a cold (but not if he does not)). For such markets to exist requires assumptions concerning agents' knowledge of the future that are inherently implausible. Specific problems of this kind identified by Hahn are the difficulty of developing the theory to take account of 'certain forms of uncertainty and market expectations', and of asymmetry of access to information between economic agents. He also comments that if exchange is costly certain markets will not open 'because it does not pay to do so'. This is an unusually revealing comment, and I shall return to it. What Hahn himself concludes from these observations is simply that the conditions needed for all Arrow–Debreu markets to exist are 'very restrictive', that once these markets are incomplete 'rather terrible things happen to the theory', and that attempts at 're-styling' to deal with the problems 'may have fateful consequences'. 'Incomplete markets' imply the need to study 'a sequence economy in which actions depend upon *beliefs* about the future'. But we have no theory of expectations like the theory of agent (household and firm) choice. More, says Hahn, we have no axiomatic foundations for such a theory, and 'scarcely have we a psychologically plausible account'.

The way forward

The sort of developments needed and envisaged centre on two general steps which can be taken. One is to 'take expectation formation as exogenous and restrict attention to short-period equilibria'. As Hahn acknowledges, this implies that expectations may be falsified in the next period, the economy 'staggers from one short period equilibrium to another' depending on 'unexplained expectations formation', and 'the price system can no longer ensure Pareto-efficiency'.

The other route is through Rational Expectations. This requires that 'rational agents will learn what is the case'. But he acknowledges that the theory 'has not shown how, starting from relative ignorance, everything that can be learned comes to be learned'.

Nevertheless, Hahn's view is that hope should not be abandoned. Specific studies concerned with 'neo-Walrasian' equilibrium concepts, and dealing with sequence, contingent market and information problems, are producing new and valuable insights. The result of these may be that in time the general equilibrium theory 'is likely to recede and be superseded'. But not because its deficiencies have caused it to be recognized as valueless. The route ahead will be 'straighter and clearer' for beginning from general equilibrium theory.

Market process
The essential differences in the approach of the Austrians is usefully presented by Kirzner in a paper published together with that of Hahn (Kirzner, 1980). For my purpose, this paper has the valuable quality that it explains the special Austrian insights by way of a reasoned critique of modern neo-classical economics, with general equilibrium as a central issue. Professor Hahn sees general equilibrium theory as suffering greatly from its friends, and I am sure Professor Kirzner would also not expect his views to be more than generally representative of those of other scholars *dit* Austrian. Indeed, given his bent of mind, I suspect that he might find too great a consonance disturbing. But his views would attract the same kind of respect within the Austrian school as do those of Professor Hahn with general equilibrium theorists. A juxtaposition of the two views is the most unprejudiced way I can think of to lay the cards on the table.

A critique of neo-classical economics
In contrast for example with Marxist economics, Kirzner believes neo-classical economics to start from foundations that are 'essentially sound'. It is not fundamental 'new insights' that are needed, but renewed recognition of the insights inherited from our intellectual forbears. The problem is how to bring about that recognition. The insights perceived as 'revolutionary' by Austrians are apt to be regarded by neo-classical theorists, at best as sympathetic but hardly fundamental, and at worst as a pointless attempt to persuade them of things they already accept. Those seeking an intellectual rapport thus face two tasks: the identification of the different insights deriving from the

Austrian perspective, and the demonstration that those differences are of more than trivial importance.

Kirzner identifies what he regards as 'the essential difference' as emerging post-1870. Until then, economists were all concerned with the role of the consumer, marginal utility, and the demand side of the market. Subsequently, the dominant neo-classical paradigm subordinated this to concern with the conditions of market equilibrium, with the subjectivity of choice reduced to the specification of given consumer tastes and preferences as an input to the equilibrium construct. This had three very damaging consequences: the role of the entrepreneur was emasculated, the dynamics of the market process were ignored or misunderstood, and the nature and role of competition was changed into something very different, and less useful, from its earlier meaning. The shift did not occur of conscious decision. I have myself elsewhere (Wiseman, 1985) drawn attention to the ambivalence to which Kirzner refers, typified by the fact that Robbins' *Nature and Significance of Economic Science*, which 'helped crystallize the new direction taken by neo-classical thought' was not believed by its author to be unsympathetic to the Austrian School (and indeed was criticized by Hutchinson for lack of commitment to evolving positivist ideas).

Nevertheless, it is this shift of emphasis away from *competition as a market process* that Kirzner sees as explaining the evolution of neo-classical economics into its present state of sophisticated mathematical models, econometric techniques and massive empiricism. This, aided by the (intellectually less fundamental but practically significant) Keynesian Revolution, submerged the earlier Austrian tradition, whose current revival is to be explained essentially by growing disillusion. But criticism of the relevance of mathematical and econometric sophistication and excessive technical baggage, while justified, should not be misunderstood. These are the consequence of a deeper failure to appreciate fundamental insights which are crucially important for 'economic understanding' of the real world. The 'serious flaws' that result are identified as an excessive preoccupation with the state of equilibrium; an unfortunate perspective on the role of competition; insufficient attention to the role and subjective character of knowledge, expectations and learning in market processes; and a normative approach heavily dependent on aggregation concepts, to the neglect of market coordination.

While my brief is an evaluation of general equilibrium and market process, all four of these identified 'flaws' bear on the problem, which is the less surprising when it is recalled that Hahn identifies the need to deal with a 'sequence economy' (that is, with what Kirzner would call 'processes') as an important outstanding problem of general equilibrium theory (see also Hahn, 1973). Consequently, I shall summarize Kirzner's comments under all four heads:

Equilibrium theory is a central concern of neo-classical economics, attention being directed to the specification of the mathematical conditions that must be satisfied. Much of the theory starts from the assumption that the data are consistent with markets being *already* in equilibrium. This approach is responsible for the mathematization of the subject and for the disappearance of the innovatory or decision-making entrepreneur.

The Austrian approach does not deny the usefulness of the equilibrium concept as a tool of analysis. But the neo-classical formulation fails to recognize the crucial importance of market processes. Effectively, these are taken for granted, and assumed to operate in so rapid and 'equilibrating' a fashion, that the analysis can properly assume the instantaneous achievement of equilibrium. This is unrealistic, and leads to a totally false perception of the social usefulness of the market. Contemporary theorists are not unaware of the problem, but are unable to deal with it within the neo-classical framework: 'it is widespread awareness of this crippling handicap which contributes to the crisis-like atmosphere surrounding . . . economic theory' (Kirzner, *loc. cit.*, p.116).

Competition The neo-classical conception of competition is static rather than dynamic, which is a perversion of meaning and a distraction of attention from the all-important market process. A neo-classical 'perfect market' is already in 'full equilibrium', buyers and sellers have no discretion in respect of price, no one can or need 'compete' in the sense of 'outdo', as real people do in real markets. The attempts to replace this 'bizarre, unrealistic and unhelpful' notion (such as theories of monopolistic competition) have failed through their own inadequacies or been largely ignored by mainstream theorists. The standard, static conception still dominates and makes it impossible to study the real dynamics of competition, which necessarily violate the conditions of static perfect competition.

This situation, Kirzner argues, reinforces dissatisfaction with contemporary theory among specialists who find themselves handicapped by it (he cites industrial-organization theorists as an example).

Knowledge, expectations and learning The failure to recognize the role of knowledge in the face of radical uncertainty, and of learning processes in dynamically competitive markets, Kirzner sees as the 'deeper flaw' responsible for the general equilibrium and perfect competition constructs which he regards as fundamentally misconceived. Decisions are seen as somehow determined by 'objective data'. Until quite recently, the neo-classical theorists were 'entirely comfortable' with the assumption of perfect knowledge. In consequence, argues Kirzner, two questions received no attention: the extent to which buying and selling decisions must express expectations about other people's buying and selling decisions, and the fact, demonstrated by Hayek (Hayek, 1948), that market equilibrium must imply mutually sustaining expectations with respect to each other's actions among market participants.

The consequence is a neglect of the role of *entrepreneurial discovery* in an uncertain world. The nature of competitive market processes is misunderstood, and the fundamental importance of learning sequences to an understanding of market processes and equilibrating tendencies is ignored.

Allocation, aggregation and social welfare The neo-classical misperception of the nature of market capitalism encourages aggregate notions of 'social allocational efficiency' and the un-critical use of aggregate measures such as GNP. But aggregate concepts of choice and the welfare of 'society as a whole' can have only a metaphorical meaning. Welfare is concerned with individuals, and Kirzner cites Hayek's observation that no single mind 'knows' what resources are available in a 'society', or what the ranking of 'social goals' 'should' be.

In contrast, the Austrian approaches normative judgement by way of methodological individualism and subjectivism. There is no *objective* entity called 'output', no way of measuring 'aggregate' welfare, e.g. by 'adding up' observed prices (which are disequilibrium prices anyway). The social relevance of the market lies in its mobilization of scattered information, and the interesting normative issues concern such matters as individual plan-coordination, the modification of expectations by market experience, and the contribution of disequilibrium prices to improved anticipation by way of entrepreneurial discovery.

The way forward
Kirzner is aware of the efforts being made to remove the limitations of neo-classical theory, but argues that the need is for fundamental reconstruction rather than the development of ever more sophisticated equilibrium models. The theory must be extended in ways that escape the mechanical character of the neo-classical equilibrium construct,

and permit the study of market interaction processes with spontaneous learning and imperfect knowledge.

There must be a place, in Kirzner's phrase, for the role of the *filter of the human mind*. We need a theory that permits study of how individual decisions are likely to be modified by the discovery of error; an awareness of radical uncertainty (one inescapable source of which is that external changes are not *mechanically* linked with economic consequences, the two being related by the perceptions and expectations of those who observe or discover them); and a recognition of the *futurity* of the time-dimension within which economic decisions must be made.

Kirzner does not believe that such a reconstruction is impossible. 'Neoclassical mainstream economics possesses great virtues', which by implication he wishes to retain. But he is aware that the means to incorporate his 'fundamental insights' will need to be explored 'with a humility that sophisticated model-building is somehow unsuited to generate'.

In sum, Kirzner sees a meeting of minds as both possible and desirable. But there is no burning conviction that it is likely to happen.

A comparative appraisal

This section is the first of a two-stage 'evaluation'. The procedure may seem cumbersome. But as I hinted earlier, I find myself fully satisfied by the position of neither school. Nevertheless, a confrontation of the two 'orthodoxies' undoubtedly provides valuable insights, and I suspect (though I would be delighted to be proved wrong) that there will be many who may accept these without also being convinced by my own views of their further implications.

It is useful to begin by observing how much the two schools claim to hold in common. Both (at least as represented by Hahn and Kirzner) see cause for dissatisfaction with the state of our discipline. But both see neo-classical economics as 'fundamentally sound', and equilibrium as a fundamental concept. Hahn sees the need for ways to supersede general equilibrium theory: but these will be intellectual descendants rather than rejections. Kirzner asks rather for the rehabilitation of fundamental insights which earlier neo-classicists understood. But the emphasis on process to which this leads him is mirrored in Hahn's identification of the central importance of the problems of the 'sequence economy'. In relation to equilibrium, the divergence concerns interpretation. The idea has normative significance for both: Hahn shows this sufficiently by the terminology he adopts, Kirzner by such things as his interest in how consistency would emerge when the 'mechanical character' of neo-classical equilibrium theory is abandoned. Finally both identify the problems of decision-making through time (uncertainty, knowledge, ignorance, expectations, learning) as of crucial importance.

The sincerity of the Austrian belief in the 'great virtues' of neo-classical economics is exemplified by the great freedom with which writers of Austrian persuasion, while castigating the 'excesses' of neo-classical sophistication, continue to make use of the fundamental analytical apparatus (such as supply and demand curves) without subjecting these devices to the kind of scrutiny that the 'fundamental insights' would seem to invite.

What then is the fuss about? As an eminent positivist once asked me: am I not being asked to pay attention to the fact that I have been speaking prose all these years? More directly: the Austrians make some telling points, but is there anything in their arguments that cannot ultimately be absorbed into mainstream economics, following the kind of developments that Hahn and others have identified?

There is much more at issue than that, and the fact that this is not more widely and practically recognized must be accounted as much a failure of conviction among Austrians themselves as an unreasonable intellectual intransigence on the part of others.

Note that Kirzner speaks with two voices. The gulf between his view of the 'necessary reconstruction' and that of Hahn is much greater than his claimed acceptance of the corpus of neo-classical economics would lead one to expect. Hahn perceives formidable problems emerging for general equilibrium theory. But nothing insoluble: rational expectations and new 'non-Walrasian' constructs will get us there in the end. Kirzner, directly and by implication, sees this route as hopeless. The need is to *escape* from neo-classical equilibrium constructs, and to replace them by something capable of embracing the role of the filter of the human mind, market interaction with spontaneous learning and imperfect knowledge, and the lack of any mechanical link between present and future in a world in which futurity implies radical uncertainty and the occurrence and perception of error. What Kirzner does *not* explore is which of the 'great virtues' of neo-classical economics can be retained, and what must necessarily be discarded, in a reconstruction that would meet these requirements. It is clear that he regards 'sophisticated model-building', mathematization, technical complexity and so on as obstacles to progress. But we are clearly concerned with something more fundamental than a need for simplification: and the first step in reconstruction must be to tease out what it is.

Economics is concerned with aspects of human behaviour in an environment specified in physical terms and in time. So much is common ground: both schools recognize the importance of the treatment of time and its implications (knowledge, expectations, information, belief, learning). The essential difference (the subject-matter of the 'insights' that concern Kirzner) concerns the specification of the essential (inescapable) characteristics of that behaviour and that environment in the context of time. It is here that the difference lies, and once its nature is recognized, the possibility of 'reconstruction through compromise' begins to seem more remote.

Neo-classical general equilibrium theorists acknowledge the problems created by time: Hahn writes of the model 'collapsing the future into the present'. The means to deal with these problems is by way (e.g.) of 'more sophisticated theories of expectations'. Hahn recognizes that there is not at present a 'psychologically plausible account', much less the axiomatic foundations of a satisfactory theory. But there is no clear recognition that this situation might imply the need for a new specification of the relevant problem rather than the development of better ('non-Walrasian') models which would not materially damage the neo-classical conceptual framework. The central components of that framework (some of them explicitly stated in the sources I have relied on, others implicit because too much the common currency of neo-classical theory to need iteration) are:

1.   The future is in some (not entirely clear) sense assumed already to exist, in that, at least in part, it is 'known'. In Hahn's definition, e.g. the firm-as-agent is 'assumed to know a set of blue prints or *production set* which gives the menu of activities from which it must choose'.
2.   Even if the future is not assumed to be fully 'known', it is treated as 'knowable' in the sense that we can explain it by such devices as known 'objective' probabilities, the treatment of information as a marketable 'good' (rather than as a transaction in 'opinions'), and (potentially) by means such as 'rational expectations' models, in which rational agents can learn 'what is the case' (though *how* this is to be learned remains to be demonstrated).
3.   The role of *subjectivity* is recognized only in the existence of tastes and preferences as the determinants of agent behaviour (and hence of 'outcomes'). If the problem is otherwise recognized (as in Hahn's identification of the problems of 'belief'), it is seen as evidence of the need for better models, but not as a reason to question the fundamentals of the general theory.
4.   A further manifestation of the neglect of subjectivity is observable in the treatment of cost. Agents are described as choosing between

alternatives that incorporate future contingencies. But the subjective character of the opportunity-cost concept implied by this is ignored or misunderstood. Indeed, much of the concern about the practical possibility of exhaustive markets in future contingencies appears to stem from confusion about the nature of cost. Hahn sees the fact that certain markets will not open because it 'does not pay to do so' as an obstacle to the achievement of Pareto efficiency. But 'does not pay' can only mean that individual agents, appraising their own situation, predict that transacting in such a market would not be in their best interest. That is, the opportunity-costs of creating such a market are perceived by the potential participants as not worth incurring. If this is the case, how can the absence of such markets possibly be regarded as 'sub-optimal' or 'inefficient', if the criterion of efficiency is the satisfaction of individual preferences?

5. Consistently with this, but in a fashion that I find obscure, ignorance of the future appears to be seen as leading to 'inefficient' behaviour by agents rather than as an inescapable characteristic of the human condition (and hence a permanent and fundamental feature of the problem to be studied). What appears to be implied is that there is some stock of knowledge about the future which agents 'ought' to have, and some consequent set of decisions that they therefore 'ought' to take, and that it is these that identify an 'efficient outcome'.

The same general line of reasoning is exemplified by the treatment of 'mistakes'. In so far as 'mistakes' (unforeseen outcomes of plans) are admitted to consideration at all, it is in fashion that permits their correction by learning. That is, the original 'mistake' ('disequilibrium') results in 'adaptations' towards a new situation that satisfies the 'consistency conditions' (equilibrium). It might be argued that this is simply a useful way of identifying the conditions that are necessary for a 'Pareto-efficient' outcome to exist. This is of interest if learning in fact makes the future more 'knowable' in the sense that, through learning, we are approaching a universe in which the future will already be known: uncertainty will have been abolished. This in turn would appear to require a belief that there is an ongoing (and discoverable?) nexus linking past, present and future time. But if this is not the case, and if there is thus no reason to expect that the 'consistent' outcome of the learning models will not be continuously prevented by the occurrence of new unforeseen sources of 'mistake', then the relevance of the model to the conditions of the world in which men must live becomes much more questionable, and the case for treating the 'equilibrium outcome' of such models as having either practical or normative interest becomes much weaker.

6. If 'mistakes' are simply self-correcting 'disturbances' (disequilibria), there is no adequate role in the neo-classical universe for discovery and innovation, since it is the essence of these activities that they are likely (indeed are intended) to change the outcome of other activities (that is, generate 'mistakes'). This is the underlying reason for the failure of mainstream economics to generate a plausible theory of entrepreneurship.

These six criticisms are in general consonant with Kirzner's arguments. But presented in this way, they cast doubt on the proposition that neo-classical economics, and with it general equilibrium theory, while perhaps standing in need of substantial 'restructuring', is 'fundamentally sound'. Rather, only fundamental change is worth discussing, since progress will be stifled without it.

It must be recognized that the difficulties stem from the initial specification of the problem. They are embodied in the assumptions made about the characteristics of man and his environment within which human (including economic) activity takes place.

This proposition can be explained and supported by reference to some relevant characteristics. The list is illustrative rather than exhaustive:

1. Men live in a physical environment which is less than imperfectly understood, about which they can make new discoveries, and whose future development is incompletely foreseeable.

2. Human behaviour is purposive. But men's purposes are not scientifically 'given', unchangeable, or directly 'knowable' by other men.

3. Human action takes place through time. Men pursue their goals by acting on decisions taken 'now' in the expectation of desired consequences in 'the future'. This process of human decision is characterized by the need to choose, since the implementation of some courses of action is perceived to exclude others. The choices are made in the context of the other characteristics of the human environment, which means that the future is perceived as both unknown and in significant respects unknowable. It follows that the actual outcomes of choices may be different from those expected, and indeed that men will comprehend (and may plan for) future outcomes that lie outside any of the specific expectations they hold 'now'.

The criticisms of neo-classical economics and general equilibrium theory can be condensed in the proposition that the essential implications of these characteristics are assumed away. The common defence against this proposition: that the assumptions concerned are necessary and 'legitimate' simplifications, is unconvincing. The purpose of simplification is to separate fundamental causal relationships from more specific or restricted aspects of a problem. The test of 'legitimacy' is that the additional information/characteristics can be incorporated into the general (simplified) model in order to explain more complex or 'sophisticated' situations. But if what is assumed away is of the essence of the problem, then greater complexity will generate not greater insight but more sophisticated confusion. This is the most cogent reason for the Austrian objection to neo-classical 'complexity', which is not always clearly articulated but cannot rest upon an objection to intellectual sophistication *per se*.

In respect of appropriate specification of the problem, the Austrian approach is clearly superior. Kirzner's insistence on such things as the importance of the filter of the human mind, radical uncertainty and spontaneous learning, constitutes a much more persuasive description of the real world of human decision. What then, is needed to persuade non-Austrians to accept it? In trying to answer this question, I shall rely less heavily on Kirzner, since I am inevitably concerned with a more general and 'interpretative' appraisal.

The most important general requirement is that Austrians themselves should recognize, and insist upon, the fundamental nature of the changes in underlying assumptions that are needed, rather than continue to claim that no more is needed than the (re-)recognition of some particular insights. That particular misconception has had a life of more than a century (and is to be found between particular professed members and generations of the Austrian School itself). It is time it was laid to rest. This requires that the Austrians come to terms with the radical implications of their own insights, as a necessary preliminary to the persuasion of others. To conclude this section, and as a useful introduction to the next, I make two suggestions to this end, relevant to my evaluation of the concepts of equilibrium and process.

While Austrians are critical of neo-classical general equilibrium theory, they are clearly interested in consistency, and in the role of the market process in producing 'harmony'. Although there is much ambivalence, I think it a reasonable generalization that for the Austrian School this harmony is an 'efficiency' concept: it has normative content. But the formulation is uneasy, for in a world in which disappointed plans are to be expected, whether from 'mistake' or from 'discovery', the definition of an 'efficient' market process as one in which all expectations (and outcomes) are consistent becomes subject to the same criticisms as the neo-classical formulations. It cannot plausibly be defended as a 'benchmark', since it must clearly be possible, in the Austrian world, for a decision-maker to be 'efficient', without necessarily being 'right'. The concept of 'Austrian efficiency' needs clarification, if only because, while it is valuable to be able to demonstrate that the king has no clothes, the argument becomes more convincing if one can also suggest how to dress him.

It is my personal suspicion that this problem also has its roots in history, in that the Austrians saw choice as the touchstone of freedom, and market choice as a significant aspect of that choice and hence of freedom. This naturally generates an interest in the contribution of the market to 'harmony'. It is perhaps not too fanciful, if a little unkind, to suggest that this same philosophical position perhaps accounts for the Austrian perception of entrepreneurship. True, the Austrian model finds a place for the entrepreneur, and he does cause change, and hence 'mistake' (disappointed expectations). This is clearly superior to the neo-classical position. But the Austrian entrepreneur is typically not *too* disturbing a creature: he is the specially gifted character who 'takes advantage of hitherto unforeseen opportunities', and so helps things along while producing a bit of upheaval. (The perception of 'the future' might be not too unkindly described as a set of parcels, already lying about, waiting to be discovered by the entrepreneurial eyeglass.) It is no doubt an interesting perception of one kind of entrepreneurial activity, poor at explaining Rubik's Cube, better at explaining its sale as a Christmas gift attached to a key-purse. But there seems to be some inconsistency, for example, between Kirzner's perception of the human situation (above), and the role that he ascribes to the entrepreneur (Kirzner, 1979) which is limited in the ways I have described, and invites the conclusion that Kirznerian entrepreneurship continues to exist only because of 'exogenous' changes in tastes or technology. This may make entrepreneurship easier to reconcile with efficiency-as-harmony. But it blurs the 'fundamental perceptions' upon which Kirzner insists, and damages the Austrian position in so doing. There are other perceptions of entrepreneurship, such as Schumpeter's 'creative destroyers' and Shackle's 'imaginative choosers' (of whom more later). These are no less persuasive than Kirzner's description; they are fully consistent with his perception of the universe of human decision, but they fit very uneasily with the notion of efficiency-as-harmony. The Austrian model needs to be able to incorporate them, even if the result is a greater break with neo-classical tradition and with 'harmony' concepts of efficiency than Austrians now envisage. They must accept the implications of their own insights.

My second suggestion concerns the use of evidence. This is not the place for a general critique of 'neo-classical positivism'. It is enough to say that the testing of hypotheses derived from an intellectual construct with the deficiencies I have described using historical data of uncertain status derived from the 'real world' is unlikely to produce many trustworthy new insights. The criticisms advanced by Austrians are cogent. But it does not follow that there is no place for evidence. This is a matter about which Austrians seem to differ. But it is not easy to find convincing arguments against the subjection of arguments to the test of disproof. There is ample room for debate as to the utility of different kinds of empiricism: it is my own belief that the Austrian approach lends itself more readily to experimental than to extant econometric methods. A greater interest in such matters among Austrians would not only be intellectually sensible: it would also encourage others with potentially valuable technical skills to accept that the Austrian criticism of 'high technology' is something more than a form of intellectual Luddism.

Radical subjectivism and procedural liberalism

The last section attempted an appraisal within the broad 'rules of the game' specified by the two schools. It concluded that there is less scope for intellectual accommodation than Austrians appear to believe, and that, apart from 'in-house' improvements in respect of such matters as the treatment of entrepreneurship and the use of evidence, they need also to come to terms with the fundamental changes demanded by their own intellectual insights.

In this final section (the second stage of my evaluation), I shall develop this theme by suggesting a way forward. There are two sets of arguments which in fact merge, but which are distinct in scope in that the first set can plausibly be treated as concerned with a broadening of the concepts presently thought of as 'economic', while the second requires that the logic be taken still further, to incorporate this expanded view of 'economics' into a more embracing view of the nature of choice-in-society. The particular arguments are not original, though they are inadequately recognized in the form I offer them. Indeed they demonstrate the difficulties identified at the outset in summarizing the ideas of a 'school'. Specifically, there are distinguished writers (Hayek and Lachmann in particular) who would commonly be labelled 'Austrian', but whose writings are sympathetic to either or both of the positions I shall describe.

Radical subjectivism

Littlechild (1985) provides an interesting perspective on the radical subjectivist position. For the neo-classical economist, the form the future can take is known in advance, and the study of process is relevant only in so far as it contributes to a better understanding of equilibrium, or of the identification of the processes (or properties of processes) which will or will not lead to an equilibrium. For the Austrian, 'tomorrow' is a vector of which the agent knows some components but not others (Littlechild, 1985, p.29). He knows there will be others, but not what they will be, so cannot form a probability judgement as to their occurrence. Equilibrium for the Austrian determines the *direction* of process. It is approached by the elimination of the unsuccessful (the 'losers'). The Austrian formulation is a closer approximation to the realities of decision-making in the world we live in. But it is less than convincing in explaining *why* process should take any particular direction through time: 'mistakes' may produce 'gains' rather than 'losses', and it is arguable that if 'process' eliminates the 'inefficient', then the future will be becoming more 'knowable' in the absence of 'exogenous' disturbances. This seems to me to be compatible with, e.g., Kirzner's view of entrepreneurship, but it sits uncomfortably with the Austrian general view of the nature of the world.

The 'radical subjectivist' position is a rejection of both these interpretations, though it is clearly closer to the Austrian than to the neo-classical. Littlechild uses the term to describe a 'distinctive approach' (it could hardly be called a school), which he exemplifies by the writings of Shackle (1969, 1979), Lachmann (1976, 1977) and Wiseman (1983). The essence of the radical subjectivist position is that the future is not simply 'unknown', but is 'non-existent' or 'indeterminate at the point of decision'. The alternatives between which decisions (choices) are made are the product of the individual imagination. This is what engenders uncertainty. Agents are concerned not just with estimation or discovery, but with the *creation* of choice. Agents are aware of their vulnerability to the independent imagination-induced acts of others, and hence of the flimsiness of their conjectures about the future. In such a world, the decision environment is *qualitatively* as well as *quantitatively* uncertain: there is what Langlois calls 'structural' as well as 'parametric' uncertainty (Langlois, 1984).

If, as the radical subjectivists argue, the world is characterized by structural as well as parametric uncertainty, then 'mistakes' are not aberrations from 'efficiency', but an inescapable fact of life. We live in Shackle's 'kaleidic' world, in which the economy is:

subject to sudden landslides of re-adjustment to a new, precarious and ephemeral, pseudo-equilibrium, in which variables based on expectation, speculative hope and conjecture are delicately stacked in a card-house of momentary immobility, waiting for 'the news' to upset everything again and start a new disequilibrium phase. (Shackle, 1972, p.433).

As Littlechild (1985) points out, it is not inconceivable that such a situation could be incorporated into the Austrian or even the neo-classical constructs. But it would require some remarkable intellectual contortions. More important, what would be the point? If 'equilibrium' changes each time any one agent changes his mind about the intentions (future actions) of others, and if the relation between these changes and the 'actual' intention of these others is by its nature incapable of direct observation, what possible use is the concept either as an explanatory tool or as a normative ('efficiency') concept?

Worse, it is a further implication of the radical-subjectivist position that the very *formulation* of the economic problem is called into question. Both neo-classical and Austrian schools specify the *objects* of choice independently of the *agents* of choice. That is, the *knowledge and beliefs* of the agent are distinct from his *preferences*, save only that search and discovery may be directed by preferences. The radical subjectivist finds this distinction unreal: agents devise schemes of action that appeal to them, reflect their fears or hopes: they choose between their own 'imaginative visions' by reference to criteria known only to themselves. This phenomenon of 'cognitive dissonance' is becoming more widely recognized by economists (it is supported by evidence from psychology): and not only by those who would consider themselves 'radical subjectivists' (e.g. Arrow, 1982). It clearly has far-reaching implications for the study of economics: so far-reaching that they are best dealt with in the broader context which follows.

Choice as social process
Once the complex nature of the act of choice in a world with the characteristics earlier elucidated has been recognized, the relevance of neo-classical equilibrium concepts to any useful notion of social efficiency disappears. While Austrian process fares somewhat better, there remains a need to develop the analysis in ways that question the value of any related concepts of efficiency-as-consistency.

More fundamentally, the argument must cast doubt upon the very idea that there can be a notion of 'market efficiency' that is somehow separable from 'social efficiency', much less that 'social efficiency' must always be furthered by measures (such as changes in social institutions) which improve 'market efficiency' whether defined in neo-classical or in Austrian terms. That choice is a pervasive phenomenon, occurring whenever individuals believe themselves to be faced with mutually-excluding alternative courses of action, and that there is no distinct act of choice that can be labelled 'economic', is not a new discovery: it is quite clearly postulated by Austrian economists in particular. Yet it is not unfair to argue that not only do they thereafter concentrate upon the study of *market* choice (because 'that is what economists study'), but treat 'efficiency' in the implementation of market choice as the touchstone of *social* efficiency. I have nowhere found a satisfactory justification for this.

If our concern is with the values that I identified in the Introduction: 'the political realization of a social order of freedom', and 'the concept of a free society', and we place these objectives (efficiency concepts) in the context of the argument of this paper, does it now follow that the choice-environment appropriate to any notion of 'social efficiency' (and within that any useful notion of 'equilibrium') must be wide enough to embrace *all* individual acts of choice-within-society?

I cannot adequately develop this theme here: but the direction in which it points seems to me clear. In so far as acts of choice are based upon imagination in uncertainty, an individual is 'free' when he conceives those acts of choice not to be improperly coerced by the environment within which his choices must be made. All social institutions, and the processes by which they can be changed, are relevant to this. Briefly, it demands a Wicksellian rather than a Paretian interpretation of 'free choice', a contractarian approach to social change, and *a continuing recognition of the characteristics of the human environment that we have identified as fundamental* in this new and broader construct. If it has room for ideas like 'equilibrium', they will need to embrace (e.g.) such notions as the propensity to emigrate.

This is not to argue that the phenomena that economists study must become irrelevant: freedom from 'market coercion' is clearly an important aspect of freedom in general. But it is in the better embodiment of these ideas into a broader choice-context, rather than in the 'scientific' refinement of narrower models, that progress needs to be sought. Austrian 'process' is a step on the way: but there is a long way to go.

References

Arrow, K. J. (1982) 'Risk Perception in Psychology and Economics', *Economic Inquiry*, 20(1).

Hahn, F. H. (1973) *On the Notion of Equilibrium in Economics*, Cambridge University Press.

Hahn, F. H. (1980) 'General Equilibrium Theory', *The Public Interest*, Special Issue.

Hayek, F. A. (1948) *Individualism and Economic Order*, University of Chicago Press,

Chicago, Particularly 'Economics and Knowledge', and 'Uses of Knowledge in Society'.

Kirzner, I. M. (1979) *Perception, Opportunity and Profit*, University of Chicago Press.

Kirzner, I. M. (1980) 'The "Austrian" Perspective on the Crisis', *The Public Interest*, Special Issue.

Lachmann, L. (1976) 'From Mises to Shackle: An Essay on Austrian Economics and the Kaleidic Society', *Journal of Economic Literature*, 14(1).

Lachmann, L. (1977) *Capital, Expectations and the Market Process*, Sheed, Andrews, and McMeel.

Langlois, R. N. (1984) 'Internal Organisation in a Dynamic Context: some theoretical considerations', in *Information and Communications Economics: New Perspectives* (ed. Juswalla and Ebenfield), North-Holland.

Littlechild, S. C. (1985) 'Three Types of Market Process', *Economics as a Process* (ed. Richard N. Langlois), Ch. 2, Cambridge University Press.

Shackle, G. L. S. (1969) *Decision, Order and Time in Human Affairs*, 2nd edn Cambridge University Press.

Shackle, G. L. S. (1972) *Epistemics and Economics*, Cambridge University Press.

Shackle, G. L. S. (1979) *Imagination and the Nature of Choice*, Edinburgh University Press.

Wiseman, J. (1985) 'Lionel Robbins, The Austrian School, and the L. S. E. Tradition', *Research in The History of Economic Thought and Methodology* (ed. Warren J. Samuels), vol.3, JAI Press.

Wiseman, J. (1983) 'Beyond Positive Economics – Dream and Reality', in *Beyond Positive Economics*, (ed. J. Wiseman), Macmillan, (reprinted as Chapter 8).

13 Crusoe's Kingdom: Cost, Choice and Political Economy*
(With S. C. Littlechild)

Foreword

The origins of this paper are referred to in Chapter 2 and the Introduction to Chapter 8. When Stephen Littlechild and I decided to write a textbook of subjectivist economics, we planned to simplify the initial exposition of the decision-process by beginning with Robinson Crusoe alone on his island, confronted as we believed by the ineluctable fact of scarcity, but not by the complications introduced by the need to take account of the activities and plans of others. Many economists have their own Robinson Crusoe, endowed with the attributes suited to their pet intellectual problem. But few have thought to do what Stephen did, which was to go back to the 'real' Robinson Crusoe, as written by Defoe. It was a masterstroke. The book is written in a kind of stream-of-consciousness, which makes the reader privy not only to what Crusoe did, but also to the thought-processes from which his actions emerged. The translation of this into the language and analysis of subjective opportunity-cost, together with the fact that Crusoe did have a 'society' (indeed, he 'created' one), threatened to take over the whole enterprise.

When we decided to abandon the textbook, we were left with the Crusoe materials. In the spring of 1985, I turned them into a draft of the present article, destined for a volume in honour of George Shackle. What more appropriate venue?

The paper needs little further introduction. We hope that it will provide enjoyment as well as instruction. Simply, it traces Crusoe's decision-processes from the simple, brutal choices that faced him immediately after the shipwreck, through the increasingly complex situations that emerged during life on the island, and even more from the later presence of Friday and others. In our view, it is a story that could not satisfactorily be interpreted using a neo-classical model, but which lends itself beautifully to a subjective-choice exposition sympathetic to Shackle's own fundamental insights.

* Frowen, S. (ed.) (1989) *Unknowledge and Choice in Economics*, London, Macmillan.

We have our own favourite gems; such as the fact that Crusoe, alone on his island, committed resources to a defence programme as a result of seeing the print of a bare foot in the sand. (If it had been the print of a shoe, his consequent re-planning would have been quite different.) But you may prefer to seek your own, whether in the article or in Defoe's book – or to suggest to your students that they might do so.

Introduction

Robinson Crusoe is the economist's archetypal expository device. He is used to illustrate individual consumption and investment decisions before Friday is wheeled on to illustrate trade. But a reading of Defoe's novel reveals a somewhat different picture. Crusoe's own decision-making process is significantly richer than that envisaged in economics textbooks. Furthermore, Crusoe and Friday never engage in trade: their relationship is somewhere between that of a firm and a command economy.

The purpose of this chapter is not to establish what Crusoe was 'really' like, but rather to illustrate the subjectivist approach to individual and social decision processes, and to suggest that the incorporation of this approach into economic analysis would provide a more adequate model for describing and analysing both Crusoe's world and our own. The subjectivist approach is, of course, the one to which George Shackle has made such a unique and distinguished contribution.

Defoe's text places Crusoe in situations very different from those to be found in actual societies. Nevertheless, all essential characteristics of the individual decision process remain, together with important characteristics of social decision-making. Moreover, Defoe provides us with the information we need to understand these processes. Not only does Crusoe describe in detail the actions he takes: he also tells us *why* he takes them. Frequently, the aims he has in mind in taking particular decisions, and even the alternatives he rejects, are clearly indicated. Crusoe thus gives a remarkably clear picture, complete with subjective plans and accounts, of his own decision-making process and of his interactions with others.

The next section gives a brief account of the subjectivist model of decision-making, and contrasts it with the orthodox approach. Following this the review of Crusoe's life divides naturally into two parts: Crusoe alone; and Crusoe in society. The final section of the chapter contains some observations on the nature and scope of economic theory.

Alternative models of decision-making

Orthodox neo-classical economics examines the nature and implications of scarcity and choice. Each decision-maker is assumed to choose between a given set of feasible alternatives (goods or actions) in the light of a given preference function. Three aspects of choice are typically stressed:

1. *opportuntiy cost*: the cost of choosing the preferred alternative is the sacrifice of the next-preferred alternative:
2. *choice at the margin*: the decision-maker evaluates whether 'a little more' of one alternative is worth the necessary sacrifice.
3. *time preference*: the decision-maker has to compare benefits in the distant future against benefits now or in the near future.

Uncertainty is dealt with in various ways. In most introductory textbooks it is ignored: the set of choices and the outcomes of each are assumed given. In more advanced treatments outcomes are characterized by probability distributions over well-defined domains. In advanced research these probability distributions may be revised over time in the light of experience according to well-defined formulas (for example, Bayesian methods). There is always the explicit or implicit assumption that the set of choices and their possible outcomes (that is, the form which the future could take) are assumed to be known.

The subjectivist approach incorporates the first three aspects of choice noted above, but assumes a world in which choices have to be created and the future is always uncertain – indeed, in important respects unknowable. This requires a much richer analysis of decision-making. The act of choice has to be set in the context of a *process* of decision-making taking place over time, in which choice itself is preceded by the *preparation· of plans* and succeeded by *appraisal of the outcome*. Appraisal of one decision is a vital input in replanning for the next decision. We may further distinguish between short-term and long-term plans, where the former are 'embedded' in the latter.

To spell out the assumptions and implications of the subjectivist approach in a little more detail:

1. The alternatives available for choice are not somehow 'given'. The decision-maker needs to discover the opportunities, or create the plans, between which choices are made. This is the vital element of entrepreneurial insight or imagination.
2. For any identified opportunity or plan, the outcome is likewise not somehow 'given': the decision-maker must predict its likely

consequence(s). Sometimes previous experience will be of great assistance, at other times not.

3. The outcome of any decision may well differ from what was expected. What the decision-maker learns from this experience, and what implications are drawn for the future, will depend on the decision-maker's own knowledge, beliefs and personality, and will be modified by subsequent experience.

4. Decision-makers will often find it worthwhile to collect information before taking decisions. Note, however, that the collection of information is itself an entrepreneurially created plan, adopted because its benefits (in improved future decision-making) are thought likely to exceed its costs.

It is helpful to formalize the individual decision-process by presenting it in three stages. First, the development and consideration of (*ex ante*) *plans* – alternatives courses of action conceived by the decision-maker to be feasible and relevant. For each such plan, the decision-maker is conceived to prepare a 'budget' – a statement of the expected benefits and sacrifices that would result from implementing the plan. Second, *choice and implementation*: the decision-maker chooses the plan he thinks best, and acts upon it. Third, *(ex post) appraisal*: the decision-maker looks at the outcome of his plan (prepares an 'account'), and compares it with his *ex ante* expectation (the budget), the result being used when making new plans. The individual decision process is thus a form of 'subjective opportunity cost accounting'.

It is not of course suggested that plans, budgets or accounts, or indeed any other part of the decision process, are in fact written down. They exist in the mind of the decision-maker, who may or may not make some kind of record. (Crusoe, as it happens, kept a journal.) They are written down in what follows, because that is our means of communicating with the reader.

Crusoe alone

The first decision: the ex ante *plan*
Robinson Crusoe finds himself shipwrecked alone on a desert island. Having thanked God for his salvation, he takes stock of his situation. His immediate decision problem is characterized by an unusual degree of ignorance and inability to benefit from past learning (potentially relevant experience), by the great importance of the decision, and by the essential simplicity of the conceived alternatives. Since Crusoe explains his state of mind in considerable detail, we shall quote at

length. This has the further advantage of giving the reader the flavour of the text: we shall subsequently have to be content with more summary quotations. On looking around him, Crusoe says of his situation:

> I soon found my Comforts abate, and that in a word I had a dreadful Deliverance: For I was wet, had no Clothes to shift me, nor any thing either to eat or drink to comfort me, neither did I see any Prospect before me, but that of perishing with Hunger, or being devour'd by wild Beasts; and that which was particularly afflicting to me, was, that I had no Weapon either to hunt and kill any Creature for my Sustenance or to defend myself against any other Creature that might desire to kill me for theirs: in a Word, I had nothing about me but a Knife, a Tobacco-pipe, and a little Tobacco in a Box, this was all my Provision, and this threw me into terrible Agonies of Mind, that for a while I run about like a Mad-man; Night coming upon me, I began with a heavy Heart to consider what would be my Lot if there were any ravenous Beasts in that Country, seeing at Night they always come abroad for their Prey.
>
> All the remedy that offer'd to my Thoughts at that Time, was, to get up into a thick bushy Tree like a Firr, but thorny, which grew near me, and where I resolv'd to set all Night, and consider the next Day what Death I should dye, for as yet I saw no Prospect of Life. (p.47)[1]

Crusoe is clearly a cautious man. Having appraised his resources, he predicts a life-expectancy of at most a day, and sees point in making plans only for the short term (perhaps eight hours), and with the main objective of survival. The plan he adopts to this end is to sleep in the tree. Crusoe's deliberations the next night reveal that the only alternative he considered was to sleep on the ground. The decision was of great importance to him. It was also simple in its characteristics. It illustrates clearly the three stages of the decision process: the entrepreneurial creation of hitherto unthought-of courses of action, the choice between them, and the appraisal of the consequences. It is consequently worth formalising, as in Table 13.1, to prepare the way for the subsequent examination of more complex decisions.

Table 13.1   Analysis of Crusoe's first decision: comparison of plans

	Plan 1	Plan 2
Action:	Sleep on ground	Sleep in tree
Predicted consequences	Unsafe	Safe
Decision:	Rejected	Chosen
Profit (*ex ante*)	Value of safety	

These plans are subjective: they exist only in Crusoe's mind, and may not be very fully articulated even there. Only one plan can be implemented: it is chosen *at the sacrifice* of the (best) envisaged alternative. The cost of the chosen plan is the value attached by Crusoe to the best plan he rejects. Since Crusoe decided *not* to sleep on the ground, no one can know what would have happened had he done so. The cost of sleeping in the tree is therefore the *ex ante* value place by Crusoe on the *predicted* outcome of sleeping on the ground. Thus, cost in its entrepreneurial decision sense cannot be objective: it refers to a 'non-event'.

Crusoe's decision to sleep in the tree means that he attaches a higher value to the expected outcome of this plan than to any perceived alternative. In the present case this is not surprising, given that the one plan appears superior to the other in the only relevant respect. The difference between the valuation he places on the expected outcome of the chosen plan and the valuation he attaches to the expected outcome of the best necessarily rejected plan, is Crusoe's expected (or *ex ante*) profit from the creation and implementation of the chosen plan. A positive expected profit is a necessary condition for the plan to be chosen. (In the present instance, we can plausibly infer that Crusoe's expected profit was substantial, given his cursory treatment of the alternative possibility.) Even without money, institutions, or other people, we can identify the search for profit (in this general entrepreneurial sense) as the spring of human action.

Crusoe's first decision: the ex post *account.*
The next morning, we can think of Crusoe evaluating what actually happened, and comparing it with what he expected to happen when he chose and implemented his plan. There will of course only be an account in respect of the chosen plan (Plan 2), since the rejected plan (Plan 1) was never acted upon.

This is what Crusoe has to say:

> I fell fast asleep, and slept as comfortably, as, I believe, few could have done in my Condition, and found myself the most refresh'd with it, that I think I ever was on such an Occasion. (p.47)

It is not clear what other 'such Occasion' Crusoe has in mind, for there is no evidence that he had experience of sleeping in trees. But the implication is quite clear: the plan turned out better than expected. He survived the night and was surprisingly comfortable.

This unexpected comfort is an unanticipated or windfall gain. It is of course a purely subjective concept, being the comparison which Crusoe himself makes between his actual state of well-being in the morning, and the state which he had expected to be in. That is, it is based on a comparison of his plan and his account (Table 13.2). If, instead, Crusoe had fallen out of the tree, or been attacked by a bird or a snake, so that the outcome was worse than expected, this reduction in well-being would be an unanticipated or windfall loss.

The concepts of unanticipated gains and losses both refer to a comparison between the chosen plan and the account. They are calculated *ex post* – that is, from the point of view of the decision-maker *after* he carried out his plan. They are based on a comparison between *predicted* outcome and *actual* outcome. Associated with each chosen plan are thus an *ex ante* profit and an *ex post* gain or loss. The decision-maker deliberately searches for profit, whereas the subsequent gain or loss derive from considerations which he had failed to predict or to take into account.

Table 13.2   Analysis of Crusoe's first decision: comparison of chosen plan and account

Chosen plan (2)	Account
Safe	Safe and comfortable
Windfall gain (*ex post*):	Value of comfort

Hindsight error and replanning
Upon awakening, Crusoe is surprised to see that his ship has been cast up within a mile of the shore. This suggests to him that the previous night's decision to abandon ship was a mistaken one:

> and here I found a fresh renewing of my Grief, for I saw evidently, that if we had kept on board, we had all been safe. (p.48)

This is an example of the role of learning in the subjective planning process. But in so far as he is blaming himself Crusoe has fallen into a kind of account-appraisal error which we might call the 'hindsight error'. For if we turn back to the description of the shipwreck, we find Crusoe explaining the state of mind of himself and his crew quite clearly. He saw them as 'in mortal peril of their lives' and to abandon ship was the only plan that offered a prospect of survival: that is why it was adopted. As the time of the *account*, Crusoe rightly notes that the rejected plan (to stay on board) had earlier been valued less highly than the subsequently observed outcome justified. But it does not follow that Crusoe took the wrong action *at the time of decision*: to argue this is to assert that he should have taken account of an outcome that could not be known at that time. However, Crusoe might learn from the account to interpret the evidence for abandoning ship somewhat differently, in the unlikely event that he found himself in the future in circumstances presenting what appeared to be a similar choice. (Of course, there is no possibility of 'hindsight error' if there is no uncertainty and the 'facts' will bear only one interpretation.)

The purpose of the account is not merely to record the past. Comparison of the account with the plan provides the basis for learning, and consequently for re-planning in the future. Crusoe's experience (learning) during the first night increases his confidence that, if necessary, he can sleep reasonably comfortably in a tree the next night. But he will also want to know whether he can sleep safely on the ground, concerning which he has little experience or information as yet, beyond the fact that he has not actually seen or heard anything dangerous.

When night-time comes, Crusoe hits upon a third plan which seems preferable to either of his previous plans:

> what to do with my self at Night I knew not, nor indeed where to rest; for I was afraid to lie down on the Ground, not knowing but some wild Beast might devour me, tho', as I afterwards found, there was really no Need for those Fears.
>
> However, as well as I could, I barricado'd my self round with the Chests and Boards that I had brought on Shore, and made a Kind of a Hut for that Night's Lodging. (p.53).

This quotation describes how the *ex post* appraisal (the account) of the first night's experience is combined with the experience and changes in assets (chests and boards) of the intervening day-time (see below) to produce a preferred plan for the second night that is different from anything that was (or indeed could have been) considered when the plan for the first night was chosen

The first night's experience *contributes* to the development of this new plan, but does not *determine* its content. Crusoe cannot be sure that he has correctly interpreted the outcome of his completed plan. Indeed he subsequently learns that the value attached to safety from wild beasts was unnecessarily high, since in fact there are none. But Crusoe rightly does not evaluate his planning behaviour as inefficient or incompetent. As noted above, this would be the case only if, at the time of appraisal, he considers that there was evidence available to him *at the time of decision* that he should have taken into account.

A whole day's decision-making

Now that the ship has been sighted, new possibilities emerge:

> I wish'd myself on board, that, at least, I might save some necessary things for my use. (p.48)

How is this aim to be accomplished? Crusoe swims out to the ship and round it twice, looking for a way to get on board. Eventually he spies a small piece of rope hanging down, by which he clambers up. Luckily the ship's provisions are still dry, but how are they to be got back to the shore?

> Now I wanted nothing but a Boat to furnish my self with many things which I foresaw would be very necessary to me.
> It was in vain to sit still and wish for what was not to be had, and this Extremity rouz'd my Application. (p.49)

Crusoe hits on the idea of cutting some of the masts and tying together the pieces to form a raft. With the help of this innovation, he is able to transport a load of cargo back to the island. Before he unloads the raft, however, there is a more pressing task to be done:

> My next Work was to view the Country, and seek a proper Place for my Habitation, and where to stow my Goods to secure them from whatever might happen: where I was I yet knew not, whether on the Continent or on an Island, whether inhabited or not inhabited, whether in Danger of wild Beasts or not. (p.52)

Taking a gun and powder, Crusoe 'travell'd for Discovery' to the top of a nearby hill, and finds that he is on an island:

> I found also that the Island I was in was barren, and as I saw good Reason to believe, uninhabited, except by wild Beasts, of whom however I saw none, yet I saw Abundance of Fowls, but I knew not their Kinds, neither when I kill'd them could I tell what was fit for Food and what not; . . .
> Contented with this Discovery, I came back to my Raft, and fell to Work to bring my Cargoe on Shore, which took me up the rest of that Day. (p.53)

There are several interesting aspects of this first day's activities:

1. These two plans (to get supplies and to view the country) were not somehow 'given' to Crusoe: he created them by acts of imagination. The values he attached to them reflected his conjectures as to what results they might yield.

2.   Crusoe's plans for the day were constrained in two respects. First, only a limited number of daylight hours were available. There was not time to make *several* trips to the ship *and* explore the island *and* build a secure dwelling *and* hunt for fresh food, all in one day. It was therefore necessary to choose the most important activities and leave the rest for another time.

3.   Second, given the activities which had been chosen, it was necessary to choose in which order to carry them out: that is, to assign priorities. Crusoe evidently thought it most important to get supplies from the ship first, but spying out the land then took priority over unloading the raft.

4.   Crusoe did not find it worthwhile to spell out his plan in absolute detail. To carry out the first plan (to get supplies) in fact necessitated solving two further problems: how to get on board the ship, and how to get the supplies back to the shore. No doubt he had a general idea of what might still be on the ship, and what he needed, but the final choice was best left until he had got on board and seen what was actually available. Similarly, his plan to climb the hill embodied no prediction at all as to what he would discover there. The purpose of that activity was precisely to obtain information in order to make better plans in future.

5.   The exploitation of the boat was seen as important to *short-term* survival. As the boat's existence was likely to be of limited duration, Crusoe expected the opportunity cost of deferring its exploration to be very high. The value he associated with climbing the hill was the expected improvement in *longer-term* planning from acquiring new information (learning). The two plans are thus concerned with different time-periods, but are not independent. They are *rival*, in that they cannot be undertaken simultaneously, but they are also *complementary*, in that fulfilment of one affects the potential of the other. This 'plan embedding' is a fundamental characteristic of decision-making through time: we return to it below.

Scarcity and choice.

The notion of choice in the face of scarcity is central to all modern economics. We have already noted Crusoe's problem of which activities to carry out in the limited time available on his first day. For another illustration, consider his choice of what items to load on his makeshift raft, and what to leave behind:

> My Raft was now strong enough to bear any reasonable Weight: my next Care was what to load it with . . . having considered well what I most

wanted. I first got three of the Seamens Chests . . . the first of these I filled with Provision viz. Bread, Rice, three Dutch Cheeses, five Pieces of dry'd Goat's Flesh . . . as for Liquors, I found several Cases of Bottles belonging to our Skipper . . .

While I was doing this, I found the Tyde began to flow, tho' very calm, and I had the Mortification to see my Coat, Shirt, and Wastcoat which I had left on Shore upon the Sand, swim away . . . this put me upon rummaging for Clothes, of which I found enough, but took no more than I wanted for present use, for I had other things which my Eye was more upon, as first Tools to work with on Shore and it was after long searching that I found out the Carpenter's Chest, which was indeed a very useful prize to me. . . .

My next Care was for some Ammunition and Arms; there were two very good Fowling-pieces in the great Cabbin, and two Pistols, these I secur'd first, with some Powder-horns, and a small Bag of Shot, and two old rusty Swords. (pp.49–50).

Crusoe thus takes all the provisions he can find, but only some of the clothes, tools and ammunition, and none of the other equipment or parts of the ship.

Notice how Crusoe's choice is influenced by his current circumstances: the value to him of each commodity is determined solely by its ability to serve his present purpose of survival. Thus, the Carpenter's Chest was 'much more valuable than a ship Loading of Gold would have been at that time' (p.50).

Value at the margin

The next day, it occurs to Crusoe that 'I might yet get a great many Things out of the Ship, which would be useful to me . . . and I resolv'd to make another Voyage on Board the Vessel, if possible' (p.53).

The question now arises: how many trips to the ship should he make? The more trips he makes, the less valuable will be the cargo left on the ship. Yet each trip there and back takes the greater part of a day. At what point will it be more useful to turn to other activities such as searching for food or building a more secure lodging? That is, when will the benefits of an additional trip (the 'marginal benefit') fall below the cost of an additional trip (the 'marginal cost')? As before, marginal cost is the benefit associated with the best *alternative* activity (such as building a better lodging).

Crusoe's opinion is that anything that can be salvaged is worth more than the fruits of any other activity, since he will never again have the chance to visit the ship: 'as I knew that the first Storm that blew must necessarily break her all in Pieces. I resolv'd to set all other Things apart, 'till I got every Thing out of the Ship that I could get' (p. 54). (He continues, 'then I called a Council, that is to say, in my Thoughts, whether I should take back the Raft'. Throughout his life on the island, Crusoe is having to weigh up alternatives in his mind and take choices that are in no sense predetermined.)

Recall that on the first trip Crusoe brough provisions, one set of clothes, the carpenter's chest and some ammunition. On the second trip he brings nails, hatchets, a grindstone, several muskets, the rest of the clothes and a hammock. Next, he chooses ropes, canvas, the sails and a barrel of wet gunpowder.

Even though on each trip Crusoe methodically chooses what appears to be the most valuable remaining cargo, he does not have complete information and there are still occasional surprises:

> But that which comforted me more still was, that at last of all, after I had made five or six such Voyages as these, and thought I had nothing more to expect from the Ship that was worth my medling with, I say, after all this, I found a great Hogshead of Bread and three large Runlets of Rum or Spirits, and a Box of Sugar, and a Barrel of fine Flower: this was surprizing to me, because I had given over expecting any more Provisions, except what was spoil'd by the Water. (p.56)

On later trips all Crusoe can salvage is cables and ironwork. By the eleventh trip 'I had brought away all that one Pair of Hands mights be suppos'd capable to bring' (p.56). Nevertheless, he goes back once more, and is again surprised:

> tho' I thought I had rumag'd the Cabbin so effectually, as that nothing more could be found, yet I discover'd a Locker with Drawers in it, in one of which I found two or three Razors, and one Pair of large Sizzers; with some ten or a Dozen of good Knives and Forks; in another I found about Thirty six Pounds value in Money, some *European Coin*, some *Brasil*, some Pieces of Eight, some Gold, some Silver.
>
> I smil'd to my self at the Sight of this Money. O Drug! Said I aloud, what art thou good for, Thou are not worth to me, no not the taking off of the Ground, one of those Knives is worth all this Heap, I have no Manner of use for thee, e'en remain where thou art, and go to the Bottom as a Creature whose Life is not worth saving. However, upon Second Thoughts, I took it away. (p.57)

That night, a storm blows up and destroys the remains of the ship. Crusoe's appraisal concludes that his chosen course of action was the right one:

> In the Morning when I look'd out, behold no more Ship was to be seen: I was a little surpriz'd, but recover'd my self with this satisfactory Reflection, viz. That I had lost no time, nor abated no Dilligence to get everything out

of her that could be useful to me, and that indeed there was little left in her that I was able to bring away if I had had more time. (pp.57–8)

This episode illustrates the pervasiveness of marginal evaluation. We can think of Crusoe's choice of successive bundles of cargoes as a set of plan-comparisons: the condition for taking a particular bundle must be that its value to him exceeds the value of the best rejected bundle. Simultaneously, Crusoe is making another marginal evaluation: each 'best' bundle of cargo is compared against the use of his time in some other activity. In the event, Crusoe was able to decide repeatedly in favour of fetching cargo because of the limited period over which the ship and its cargo were expected to be available. Deferring the fetching of cargo would be much more costly than deferring any other activity. This again illustrates the importance of time (and the relation of marginal valuation to time) in the planning process. This is our next topic.

Plans for different periods of time
When Crusoe was first cast up on the island, his only goal was to survive the night, for he expected to die the next day. His planning horizon went no further. But in the morning, feeling refreshed, he constructed a plan for that day: namely, to get supplies from the ship and to explore. Although this plan did not itself go beyond the end of the first day, it could only be understood in the context of a longer-term plan – a 'survival plan' for the next few weeks, months or even years. That is, Crusoe implicitly had both a short-term plan and a longer-term plan, where the former was designed partly as a means of achieving the aims of the latter. Short-term and long-term plans are thus not independent, but are chosen by the decision-maker to be consistent with each other.

There is, however, a trade-off between benefits which are expected to occur immediately and those which are expected to take longer to emerge. Consider Crusoe's problem of how fast to consume the provisions he brought out from the ship. After an earthquake strikes, he feels in need of a drink:

> and now to support my Spirits, which indeed wanted it very much, I went to my little Store and took a small Sup of Rum: which however I did then and always very sparingly, knowing I could have no more when that was gone.(p.81)

Crusoe is consciously refraining from consuming the rum, saving it and maintaining a store of it. In effect, he is having to answer two questions: How much satisfaction will a glass of rum give me at some time in the future, compared to a glass now? Even if I expect greater satisfaction in the future, is it worth waiting for? Crusoe will only take a drink if the value he attaches to the satisfaction of a glass of rum now is greater than the value he attaches to the anticipated satisfaction from drinking that glass of rum in the future. His short-term consumption plan is thereby co-ordinated with his long-term 'provisioning' plan.

A new possibility arises when Crusoe discovers that a dozen ears of corn have sprung up in the shade of a rock:

> I carefully sav'd the Ears of this Corn you may be sure in their Season, which was about the end of June: and laying up every Corn, I resolv'd to sow them all again, hoping in Time to have some Quantity sufficient to supply me with Bread: But it was not till the 4th year that I could allow my self the least Grain of this Corn to eat, and even then but Sparingly. (p.79)

Here, Crusoe is not merely storing the corn which he refrains from consuming: he is investing it in a form of production calculated to yield a larger quantity later in the year. His short-term plan is to forgo the consumption of a specified amount of bread (made from the corn) in one season, in order to implement a longer-term plan to enjoy a greater quantity of bread the next season.

Of course, when plans extend into the future, an allowance has to be made for the risk of unforeseen circumstances:

> I had lost one whole Crop by sowing in the dry Season: but now my Crop promis'd very well, when on a sudden I found I was in Danger of losing it all again by Enemies of several Sorts, which it was scarce possible to keep from it: at First, the Goats, and wild Creatures which I call'd Hares, who tasting the Sweetness of the Blade, lay in it Night and Day, as soon as it came up, and eat is so close, that it could get no Time to shoot up into Stalk. (pp. 115–116)

Crusoe solves this problem by enclosing the ground with a hedge, and setting his dog to guard it. However, his problems are not yet over:

> But as the Beasts ruined me before, while my Corn was in the Blade; so the Birds were as likely to ruin me now, when it was in the Ear. (p.116)

The plan which he eventually adopts is to shoot three of the birds and hang them up as scarecrows to deter the others. None the less, his corn crop is much less than initially expected.

Comment
Although there is much interesting material still to come, Crusoe's behaviour has now encompassed all the essentials of the individual

decision-process. First, we have the opportunity-cost problem identified as the choice at a point in time between conceived mutually exclusive plans for the immediate future. Second, we have the opportunity-cost problem as a problem of marginal valuation. Third, we have the notion of (simultaneous) planning and decision-making for different future time-periods with the implied opportunity-cost problems created by the embedding of short-term plans within longer-term ones. This is in the dual sense that the adoption of a short-term plan creates opportunity-costs beyond the short-term plan-period, while at the same time the choice of short-term plan will itself be influenced by the content of longer-term plans.

The creation of capital
Crusoe provides a detailed explanation of how he allocates his time:

> *First*, My Duty to God, and the Reading the Scriptures, which I constantly set apart some Time for thrice every day. *Secondly*, The going Abroad with my Gun for Food, which generally took me up three Hours in every Morning, when it did not Rain. *Thirdly*, The ordering, curing preserving, and cooking what I had kill'd or catch'd for my Supply; these took up great Part of the Day: also it is to be considered that the middle of the Day when the Sun was in the Zenith, the Violence of the Heat was too great to stire out; so that about four Hours in the Evening was all the Time I could be suppos'd to work in. (p.114)

The distinction between hunting and 'work' is essentially between activities directed to the satisfaction of current consumption demands (current supply) and activities ('work') that do not increase available consumption immediately but are expected to enhance the future flow of consumption.

Crusoe is conscious of using his limited work-time ineffectively.

> the many Hours which for want of Tools, want of Help, and want of Skill, every Thing I did, took up out of my Time: For Example, I was full two and forty Days making me a Board for a long Shelf, which I wanted in my Cave; whereas two Sawyers with their Tools, and a Saw-Pit, would have cut six of them out of the same Tree in half a Day. (pp.114–15)

'Want of Help' is discussed below (but note here the similarity to Adam Smith's pin factory). In respect of skill, Crusoe describes what is nowadays called 'learning by doing':

> The working Part of this Day and of the next were wholly employ'd in making my Table, for I was yet but a very sorry Workman, tho' Time and

Necessity made me a compleat natural Mechanick soon after, as I believe it would do any one else. (p.72)

Of more general interest is the discussion of Tools. These are capital goods which are valuable not because they themselves can be consumed, but because they can be used to produce more effectively or quickly other goods which can be consumed. Crusoe decides to allocate work-time to the making of tools – 'A Pick-Axe, a Shovel, and a Wheelbarrow or Basket', for the purpose of digging into the rock for my farther Conveniency' (p. 73) – that is, to enhance his future consumption possibilities (standard of living). He finds the tools very difficult to make.

Previous experience (learning) provides him with insights: he is *aware* of the nature and utility of the items he decides to make. However, he lacks not only access to other people's skills (division of labour), but also the co-operating devices and materials that he would have used in his previous societies. Consequently, work-time must be spent in *search* (for example, discovering suitably hard wood and other materials) and in *innovation* (inventing ways to transform these materials into usable instruments). He spends four days in fashioning a usable shovel, attempting in vain to make a basket (no bendable material) and a wheelbarrow (no wheel), but developing instead a kind of hod for carrying purposes.

These activities are uncertain of outcome, both as to their success (Crusoe could not be certain of finding materials and methods that would meet his objectives), and as to the time they would take. Thus, his 'capital planning' (tool-making) involves essentially the same opportunity-cost concepts as the other activities we have examined, and can be formalised in the same kind of plans and accounts. Also, Crusoe's capital plan is again to be seen as one aspect of his total decision process, though it is described independently for convenience.

Crusoe's capital plan is characterized by its end-purpose, which is to produce outcomes that are valued not of themselves, but because they are expected to make possible the implementation of other plans with more highly valued outcomes than would otherwise be possible. For example, the shovel (an outcome of the capital plan) is wanted because it makes possible plans for a flow of consumption (for example, accommodation) that could not otherwise be envisaged. Crusoe's valuation of the outcome of the capital plan is thus determined by his valuation of the changes in the outcomes of the (capital-using) plans that he believes the capital plan makes feasible. Further, his decision to implement a capital plan must be the outcome of an opportunity-cost appraisal which compares the final added value expected to result from the availability of the tools (which are the expected physical outcome of the capital plan) with the value resulting from spending time on other plans (notably, the construction of a fence around his cave).

This may seem a somewhat circuitous way of stating what is fairly obvious. But its implication is not trivial. The illustration demonstrates all the characteristics of indirect production and derived demand (save for division of labour, for obvious reasons), in a situation without money or interpersonal exchange. It does so in a way that aids understanding of a range of economic phenomena, including economic stability and growth. It is clear from Crusoe's description that the time available for work is what is left over after short-term subsistence needs have been met. No expected outcome from the capital plan could have a value sufficiently high to compensate for falling below subsistence level. Thus Crusoe establishes a rule for allocating resources between current consumption and capital plans: plan-failure in the former (production of less than a subsistence outcome within the time initially allocated) will always result in the reduction of the time allocated to the capital plan by as much as is needed to ensure subsistence. This rule (the treatment of capital investment as a residual activity) will persist until such time as the available capital makes possible levels of consumption sufficiently above subsistence for the risk of trading off incremental consumption against capital creation to merit Crusoe's consideration. It is clear that we have here the elements of an explanation of economic growth. It is also worth pointing out that rules of the kind described are to be found operating in actual and more sophisticated social enviroments.

Does it matter who Crusoe is?

Does it matter (to an economist) who Crusoe is? In some respects, it does not. Both introspection and observation suggest that all people have certain things in common. Whoever Crusoe is, we can be fairly certain that when shipwrecked on the island, he will try to survive (though we cannot be *completely* sure; if the rest of the Crusoe family were destroyed in the wreck, the effect on Crusoe's desire to live would depend on who Crusoe was). We can assume something about his knowledge and beliefs; for example that he will expect the sun to rise tomorrow (it is only in respect of such matters that we can think of him acting on the basis of 'objective probability'), that he will have general knowledge of his need for food, water, and protection from the elements, and that he will have some understanding of the physical attributes of his observed environment.

But from these very general concepts there is a progression of physical and other attributes, experience, desires, beliefs, and knowledge, about which men must be expected to differ more or less substantially. These differences concern matters of crucial importance for Crusoe's behaviour, and hence for the economist's understanding of that behaviour. The particular attributes of Defoe's Crusoe are amply described: we have drawn attention to some of them. Clearly, these attributes help to determine what Crusoe does, since they determine both what plans he can envisage as possible of fulfilment, and what values he attaches to the outcome of those plans. As we shall shortly see, the 'native cannibal' Friday has very different knowledge, abilities and values; his plans and decisions would have differed from Crusoe's in many important respects.

An amusing example is provided by the following episode. After a couple of months on the island, Crusoe decides to rear a flock of tame goats in order to have a convenient supply of food, but it is six years before he gets around to building an enclosure for them. Only then does he discover what any stock farmer (and presumably Friday) would have realized from the start:

> now I not only had Goats Flesh to feed on when I pleas'd, but Milk too, a thing which indeed in my beginning I did not so much as think of, and which, when it came into my Thoughts, was really an agreeable Surprize. (p.147)

Other examples abound. Crusoe's timorousness causes him to live for years in fear of wild beasts (and to plan and act accordingly), even though he never sees one. A different Crusoe might have given greater weight in re-planning to his (negative) experience. Others would not necessarily have made the same inference (and decisions) from experience of earthquake:

> I began to think of what I had best do, concluding that if the Island was subject to these Earthquakes, there would be no living for me in a Cave, but I must consider of building some little Hut in an Open Place which I might surround with a Wall as I had done here (pp.81–2)

nor have been so risk-averse as to adopt the following plan:

> as I was sowing, it casually occur'd to my Thoughts, That I would not sow it all at first, because I did not know when was the proper Time for it; so I sow'd about two Thirds of the Seed, leaving about a Handful of each. (p.104)

Crusoe in society

The initial awareness of others

Before being shipwrecked, Crusoe lived in societies in which he had rights, and in which he was expected to respect the rights of others. He understood the nature of property as a characteristic of these rights: the ability to do particular things, or to deny others such an ability. On his island, there were no others whose rights needed to be respected. After four years, he is seeing himself as an absolute monarch of his island:

> I was Lord of the whole Mannor; or if I pleas'd, I might call my self King, or Emperor over the whole Country which I had Possession of. There were no Rivals. I had no Competitor, none to dispute Sovereignty or Command with me. (p.128)

For another eleven years or so, Crusoe accepts this state of affairs. In our formal language, no entry concerning other people appears in his plans or accounts. All this changes on the day that:

> I was exceedingly supriz'd with the Print of a Man's naked Foot on the Shore, which was very plain to be seen in the Sand. (p.153)

Crusoe does not find it easy to interpret this. He decides that it must mean that boats occasionally visit this island; this possibility creates 'a new scene of my life' – a need for plan-revision. It is in keeping with Crusoe's cautious character that the re-planning is essentially defensive: he devotes considerable time and resources to the creation of a fortification with placements for his muskets, and spends a month finding and developing a remote piece of land on which to keep part of his stock of tame goats as a precaution against the main flock being lost. These fortifications could be created only by the sacrifice of other plans: there is an opportunity-cost involved. But this cost is less high than the cost that Crusoe attaches to failing to protect himself.

Notice that this plan-revision occurs *before* Crusoe has had any actual contact with other persons. The *possibility* of their arrival is enough to induce him to change his present plans to take account of the predicted consequences of such contact. Initially, at least, the possible arrival of others is viewed entirely negatively: the value of the plans currently favoured by Crusoe is reduced by the newly envisaged possibility that these others may change the outcome adversely by their own behaviour. The text makes clear that Crusoe expected this to happen for either of two reasons: the newcomers would threaten his life or his personal freedom, and/or they would 'dispute Sovereignty' over the island – that is, invade the property rights that Crusoe had heretofore been able to take for granted.

Summarily, the *potential* appearance of other people, in unknown (unknowable) numbers and with unknown plans and attitudes, is enough to cause Crusoe to behave as though he is society, in the sense that a prediction of the behaviour of others becomes an entry in his own plans. The nature of that entry is influenced by what he learns from the footprint, which in turn is affected by his own earlier experience. His reactions and his re-planning would have been quite different had he seen the print of a shoe rather than a naked foot. From the fact of the latter, he infers that his potential social transactions will be with what he calls 'savages', whose relevant characteristics are likely to be aggression (indeed, they are likely to be cannibals) and lack of concern for the social rules with which Crusoe himself is familiar. This, together with lack of a common language, diminishes the likelihood that Crusoe will be able to transact with the newcomers without recourse to force. To protect himself, and the property he regards himself as having established in the island, he must divert resources to defending himself. (In his role as Sovereign, he decides he needs a 'defence budget'!)

Planning for social life
Subsequent events further modify Crusoe's evaluation of his situation. His initial inferences about the likely intruders are strengthened by the discovery of the remains of fire and human bones from a cannibalistic feast. Later he actually observes some savages in canoes.

A year later, a Spanish vessel is shipwrecked on rocks near the island. There are no survivors, but the event reminds Crusoe of his earlier life, and the loss of companionship:

> O that there had been but one or two; nay, or but one Soul sav'd out of this Ship, to have escap'd to me, that I might but have had one Companion, one Fellow-Creature to have spoken to me, and to have convers'd with! In all the Time of my solitary Life, I never felt so earnest, so strong a Desire after the Society of my Fellow-Creatures, or so deep a Regret at the want of it. (p.188)

Crusoe resumes life 'after my old fashion' (p.194). But his value-system has changed, and hence so have the content of his plans and his evaluation of their outcome. The text provides a fascinating illustration of the role of imagination in decision. Driven by the need for companionship, he describes how 'my unlucky Head . . . was all this two years fill'd with Projects and Designs, how, if it were possible, I might get away from this island' (p.194).

He can conceive no immediately practicable plan. But from dreams and speculation he conceives an ingenious *contingent* plan: a plan which is not at present feasible, but which he prepares himself to implement should the necessary preconditions eventuate. Essentially, he conceives a plan to escape from the island by using a savage who has become his servant and who will act as his pilot and provide information and skills not available to him alone. The plan will become feasible only if he can acquire such a servant, and Crusoe imagines how that could happen.

> I made this Conclusion, that my only Way to go about an Attempt for an Escape, was, if possible, to get a Savage into my Possession: and if possible, it should be one of their Prisoners, who they had condemn'd to be eaten, and should bring thither to kill. (p.199)

This is of interest in several ways. First, the plan differs from the other types of plan so far considered in that it is not capable of immediate implementation: it will become practically relevant only if triggered by future events that Crusoe believes to be possible but which may never occur. It is thus not a plan that can be currently selected for implementation, and so lies outside the current opportunity-cost framework, save in so far as Crusoe has sufficient belief in the possibility, and/or sufficient interest in seizing the opportunity should it arise, to divert resources away from currently valuable uses. This kind of contingency planning is a natural feature of decision-making through time in conditions of uncertainty. (A real-world counterpart of Crusoe's contingency plan would be the 'scenario planning' by which some large corporations attempt to safeguard themselves against extreme outcomes that might occur were the beliefs underlying their plans and decisions to prove drastically mistaken.) The withdrawal of resources from other valued uses to ensure their availability for a contingency plan is also a special example of the concept of idle resources – the resources are 'doing nothing', but the value attached to having them available is greater than the value to be had from committing them to another use.

Within the contingency plan, it is also noteworthy that Crusoe envisages capturing a savage who is running away. Already, that is, he is thinking in terms of the co-ordination of his own plans with those of other people. A savage wishing to escape being eaten is likely to behave in ways that are potentially consistent with Crusoe's actions designed to separate him from his captors. Without knowledge of who he will be, or indeed of anything about him save his status as a prisoner,

Crusoe can nevertheless write into his plan a prediction that the savage will implement a plan of his own conducive to fulfilment of Crusoe's plan-objectives.

In contrast, Crusoe expects that the captors will have plans competitive with his own. Not only will the successful implementation of the plans of Crusoe and the escaper rob them of their dinner, but there is no reason to believe that the captors' objectives and plans and those of Crusoe might be co-ordinated by negotiation. Crusoe certainly sees the resolution of this problem not in an attempt at plan-reconciliation, but in the removal of the inconsistency by the removal of the disruptive planners: his own plan provides for the captors to be killed or driven off. This having been done, his contingent plan for the longer term involves negotiation and co-ordination in the development of his relationship with the rescued savage.

The creation of society
A year and a half later, the necessary preconditions are met, and Crusoe is ready to implement his contingency plan. Five canoes arrive on shore, containing at least thirty savages. They kindle a fire and begin to dance around it:

> While I was thus looking on them, I perceived by my Perspective, two miserable Wretches dragg'd from the Boats, where it seems they were laid by, and were now brought out for the Slaughter. I perceived one of them immediately fell, being knock'd down, I suppose with a Club or Wooden Sword, for that was their way, and two or three others were at work immediately cutting him open for their Cookery, while the other Victim was left standing by himself, till they should be ready for him. In that very Moment this poor Wretch seeing himself a little at Liberty, Nature inspir'd him with Hopes of Life, and he started away from them, and ran with incredibble Swiftness along the Sands directly towards me, I mean towards that part of the Coast, where my Habitation was. (p.201)

Luckily, only two savages pursue the prisoner;

> It came now very warmly upon my Thoughts, and indeed irresistibly, that now was my Time to get me a Servant, and perhaps a Companion, or Assistant; and that I was call'd plainly by Providence to save this poor Creature's Life. (p.202)

At this point, Crusoe intervenes: he knocks out one pursuer with his gun, shoots the other, and rescues the prisoner.

The contingent plan has been triggered, implemented, and has had the predicted outcome. At this point, Crusoe's account would show the achieved profit as equal to the *ex ante* profit envisaged in the plan: there is no windfall gain or loss. Although we are not given the same access to the thoughts of the prisoner as to those of Crusoe, it is plausible that the prisoner experienced a windfall gain, and there is supporting evidence for this in the gratitude he shows to Crusoe. Since he was not aware of Crusoe's presence on the island, Crusoe's actions must have produced an outcome from his plan that was significantly better than predicted.

But when Crusoe has rescued his prisoner, much still remains to be settled. How will they arrange their affairs, with each now concerned with the relation between his own actions and those of the other?

In so far as Crusoe's narrative can be relied upon, they quickly devised satisfactory rules of conduct – in effect a constitution:

> I beckon'd him again to come to me, and gave him all the Signs of Encouragement that I could think of, and he came nearer and nearer, kneeling down every Ten or Twelve steps in token of acknowledgement for my saving his Life: I smiled at him, and look'd pleasantly, and beckon'd to him to come still nearer; at length he came close to me, and then he kneel'd down again, kiss'd the Ground and laid his Head upon the Ground, and taking me by the Foot, set my Foot upon his Head; this it seems was in token of swearing to be my Slave for ever; I took him up, and made much of him, and encourag'd him all I could. (p.204)

> In a little Time I began to speak to him and teach him to speak to me; and first, I made him know his Name should be Friday, which was the Day I sav'd his Life; I call'd him so for the Memory of the Time, I likewise taught him to say Master, and then let him know, that was to be my Name. (p.206)

This quick agreement arose because each saw the contract being offered by the other as consistent with his own requirements for a workable constitution, and both expected the implied commitments of the other to be honoured (Crusoe because he believed himself able to *require* obedience, Friday because he trusted the indication of continuing goodwill from the man who saved his life). Crusoe offers Friday security in return for obedience, and Friday values freedom less highly than the benefits he anticipates from Crusoe's friendship and goodwill. Although they are from quite disparate earlier societies, neither sees the inequality implied by Friday's commitment of himself to 'bondage' as destructive of agreement. It is clear that they both expect to gain from the arrangement; but it is also clear that the property in himself that Friday offers and Crusoe accepts is not identical with (for example) the property that Crusoe believed himself to have in his goats or his island.

In terms of our earlier construct of plans and accounts, a constitutional solution emerged because there was consistency between the plans the two citizens decided to implement. If, instead, Friday had chosen to try to run away, or to kill Crusoe, there would have followed further plan-revisions, and there is no reason to suppose that the same constitutional outcome would have emerged. There was no *automatic* tendency towards this outcome; harmony emerged because each person's expectation of the behaviour of the other was confirmed by events.

The agreement reached does not give the two parties equal rights. It is an agreement about *process* (how decisions are to be taken), not about *outcomes* (what is to be achieved). Essentially, Crusoe will take all the decisions and Friday will obey orders: they are establishing a command economy. Yet it is always apparent that there will be flexibility in the interpretation of this division. Crusoe's first order to Friday is to bury the two prisoners: but Friday is left to decide how and where this is to be done. Moreover, it does not follow from the agreement that Friday will lose all ability to recognize opportunities for action that would improve his own expected situation, or to develop and propose plans to this end. The change is that Friday's plans cannot now be implemented without Crusoe's approval, and Crusoe may value the proposals differently. Thus:

> As we went by the Place where had bury'd the two Men, he pointed exactly to the Place, and shew'd me the Marks that he had made to find them again, making Signs to me, that we should dig them up again, and eat them; at this I appear'd very angry, express'd my Abhorrence of it, made as if I would vomit at the Thoughts of it, and beckon'd with my Hand to him to come away, which he did immediately, with great Submission. (pp.206–7)

Friday has used imagination and alertness to conceive and propose a plan of action. He cannot implement it because Crusoe attaches a different value to its expected outcome, and uses the constitutional rules to forbid it.

Production specialization and the division of labour

We have noted that one aspect of Crusoe's contingency plan was to acquire a servant. This master – servant (or principal – agent) relationship can be thought of as the corporate enterprise aspect of Crusoe society. The activities of Crusoe and Friday, so regarded, are concerned with the direct satisfaction of their own wants rather than with a market. Nevertheless, their relationship exhibits the characteristics of group behaviour that we associate with a firm, in which Crusoe is the manager (major decision-taker) and the two of them provide labour services. So regarded, we find their activities characterized by technological constraints, by indirect learning, and by division of labour and specialization.

An immediate problem facing the enterprise is specified as follows:

> I begun now to consider, that having two Mouths to feed, instead of one, I must provide more Ground for my Harvest, and plant a larger Quantity of Corn, than I us'd to do; so I mark'd out a larger Piece of Land, and began the Fence in the same Manner as before. (p.213)

Crusoe is here coping with a technological problem. If the available land is equally productive, then the amount of additional fencing needed to double the output of corn will be less than twice that needed for Crusoe alone: resources are economised when the area planted is enlarged. But more labour may be needed if the additional land is harder to clear, or less corn will be grown per acre if it is less fertile.

The role of indirect learning is exemplified in a number of ways:

> The next Day I set him to work to beating some Corn out, and sifting it in the manner I us'd to do, as I observe before, and he soon understood how to do it as well as I, especially after he had seen what the Meaning of it was, and that it was to make Bread of; for after that I let him see me make my Bread, and bake it too, and in a little Time *Friday* was able to do all the Work for me, as well as I could do it my self. (p.213)

Earlier, we observed Crusoe learning from his own evolving experience: by the *ex post* evaluation of the outcome of his plans (interpreting the account). Now, we observe indirect learning (education and training and what might be called 'learning-by-watching'). Friday learns (acquires skills) not from his own experience but from the transmitted experience of others.

The process is not unilateral. Crusoe seeks new knowledge from Friday about their geographical environment, ocean currents, and other matters relevant to his plan to escape from the island. Friday's skill with bow and arrows opens up possibilities of specialization and indirect production (since they are a substitute for non-replaceable ammunition). When the enterprise turns from bread-making to boat-building, Friday is the teacher as well as the pupil: he can tell Crusoe which trees will be most suitable, and has greater dexterity in handling a simple boat, though he does not have Crusoe's knowledge of the use of masts and sails.

Changing tastes; learning-in-society

We earlier observed Crusoe learning-by-doing, and the last section exemplified indirect learning in the context of production. As the story of Friday's cannibalism illustrates, learning influences what people want as well as what they can do get it. When Crusoe and Friday return to the feasting place whence the latter escaped:

> I caus'd *Friday* to gather all the Skulls, Bones, Flesh, and whatever remain'd and lay them together on a Heap, and make a great Fire upon it and burn them all to Ashes: I found Friday had still a hankering Stomach after some of the Flesh, and was still a Cannibal in his Nature: but I discover'd so much Abhorrence at the very Thoughts of it, and at the least Appearance of it, that he durst not discover it; for I had by some Means let him know, that I would kill him if he offer'd it. (pp.207–8)

But the simple exercise of authority does not satisfy Crusoe:

> I thought that, in order to bring *Friday* off from his horrid way of feeding, and from the Relish of a Cannibal's Stomach, I ought to let his taste other Flesh. (p.210)

Accordingly, Crusoe shoots a kid and stews some of the meat; Friday 'seem'd very glad of it, and lik'd it very well' (p.212). Crusoe then 'resolv'd to feast him the next Day with roasting a Piece of the Kid' (p.212). Friday is finally convinced:

> when he came to taste the Flesh, he took so many ways to tell me how well he lik'd it, that I could not understand him; and at last he told me he would never eat Man's Flesh any more, which I was very glad to hear. (pp.212–13)

Notwithstanding his position of power, Crusoe adopts a relatively complex strategy combining regulation and persuasion, clearly in the expectation that this is more likely to produce the desired change in Friday's consumption behaviour. The decision framework within which this situation can be comprehended is correspondingly subtle. It can be conceived as a problem in public choice, with Crusoe as the head of a command economy able to stop Friday indulging in cannibalism by order (by 'passing a law' backed up by force). But it is possible that Friday may resent such a law, and indeed may, because of it, question the social order that he earlier accepted (by his symbolic submission to Crusoe). Thus, although able to enforce his will, Crusoe may yet think the cost of doing so too high, relative to an alternative plan that recognizes that Friday has rights and that seeks his co-operation. Crusoe may also think such a second plan better because he has concern for

Friday's welfare, and thinks a change in his desire for human flesh preferable to an embargo upon his eating it. Crusoe's plan succeeded. But there was no *certainty* that it would do so: there is no objectively 'right' solution to such choice-problems. (The primitive situation has its counterpart in actual societies: for cannibalism, we might read any current issue of public policy involving choice-constraints, such as smoking bans, compulsory use of seat-belts, drug control, etc.)

The extended Crusoe society

Three years after Friday's arrival, Crusoe has completed all his preparations for leaving. Suddenly another boat of savages arrives, with three prisoners for their usual feast. Crusoe and Friday succeed in rescuing two of the prisoners, one of whom is a Spaniard, while the other turns out to be Friday's father.

The society on the island has now doubled in size, but, as Crusoe observes, the members continue to act as a group under his own leadership: it is still a command economy:

> My island was now peopled, and I thought my self very rich in Subjects; and it was a merry Reflection which I frequently made, How like a King I look'd. First of all, the whole Country was my own meer Property; so that I had an undoubted Right of Domination. *2dly*, My People were perfectly subjected: I was absolute Lord and Law-giver; they all owed their Lives to me, and were ready to lay down their Lives, *if there had been Occasion of it*, for me. It was remarkable too, we had but three Subjects, and they were of three different Religions. My Man Friday was a Protestant, his Father was a *Pagan* and a *Cannibal*, and the *Spaniard* was a Papist: However, I allow'd Liberty of Conscience throughout my Dominions. (p.241)

Once more, each member brings new knowledge and abilities to both the making and carrying-out of plans. Friday's father assures Crusoe 'that I might depend upon good Usage from their Nation on his Account' if he makes a voyage to the mainland. The Spaniard informs him that there are sixteen more of his countrymen on the mainland who would be glad to join in making a boat in which to escape.

Crusoe is inspired to take advantage of these possibilities, and begins to implement a plan to do so:

> But when we had gotten all things in a Readiness to go, the Spaniard himself started an Objection, which had so much Prudence in it on one hand, and so much Sincerity on the other hand, that I could not but be very well satisfy'd in it; and by his Advice, put off the Deliverance of his Comrades, for at least half a Year. (pp.245–6)

The Spaniard's objection, which causes Crusoe to revise his plans, is that, if all his countrymen arrived shortly, there would be insuffîcent provisions to feed everyone. (It is not unfamiliar today as an argument for restrictions on immigration to prevent dilution of the capital stock of the community.) The argument convinces Crusoe, and he restricts himself to despatching the Spaniard and Friday's father to the mainland in a canoe. So we see Crusoe, the 'absolute Lord', changing his plans as a result of the insight provided by one of his subjects (thus providing further support for the proposition that few interesting social situations can be understood wtihin a context restricted to the giving and receiving of orders).

Shortly afterwards, an English ship reaches the island, enabling Crusoe to return to civilization, taking Friday with him.

Subjectivism and mainstream economic theory
In this final section we briefly note some implications of the Crusoe story for economic theory.

1. The decision process illustrated in the foregoing pages is complex but not conceptually difficult. It provides a stylized exposition of Crusoe's behaviour as he himself describes it. In this regard, it stands in clear contrast with orthodox neo-classical formulations of the economic problem. Any attempt to explain Crusoe's behaviour in purely probabilistic terms (implying 'given' alternatives and ranges of future outcomes) would fit uneasily, if at all, with Crusoe's perception of his own situation and decisions.

2. The subjectivist approach describes Crusoe's decisions and actions in terms of plans: the creation, choice between, implementation and retrospective appraisal of plans conceived by Crusoe himself in the light of his available knowledge, desires, and evolving experience. It is characteristic of this description (a) that only Crusoe himself knows what plans he conceives and how he chooses between them (the readers know only what Crusoe wishes to tell them); (b) that the outcome of plans often differs from prior expectations (and hence that the planning process through time embodies a learning process); and (c) that the decision process is not a process of choice between known alternatives, but a selection between alternative futures subjectively conceived by Crusoe to be attainable. In the subjectivist approach, it may be noted, innovation is not a particular kind of economic activity. The very act of choice is necessarily an act of innovation.

3. We noted that it did matter who Crusoe was. The implications are far-reaching. A world in which it does not matter who takes

decisions (which is a not unfair description of at least some orthodox neo-classical formulations of the economic problem) is not
an approximation or simplification of the world we live in, but a
perversion of it. There is no objectively determined 'right' choice
of plan in a world in which the future is unknowable and people
have different experience and beliefs. Hence there is no unique
'optimum allocation of resources between uses'. Further, since it
matters who takes decisions, it matters how control over resources
is acquired.

4. Crusoe and Friday needed to develop rules (constitutional arrangements) that would govern their conduct towards one another. These
issues lie outside what is usually considered to be the realm of the
economist. Economic theory assumes these questions to have been
settled. They concern questions of political philosophy and conflict
resolution. The intellectual framework linking these broad questions with the usual subject-matter of economics is that of public
choice. Crusoe in society illustrates strikingly that the present formulation of the subjective decision-process can be applied to all
situations in which individuals conceive the need to choose between
plans which are mutually exclusive; whether to join a social group
or stay outside it, whether to negotiate with others or try to kill
them, whether to accept social rules (for example, concerning property rights) or reject them, as well as whether to rest or try to make
a hod.

5. Deriving from this, an intellectual construct that will permit evaluation of alternative social arrangements must itself embrace all
kinds of choice-situations; a concept of 'economic efficiency' that
is narrower than this is of limited usefulness. A full understanding
of social decision processes thus requires a public choice model that
embraces market transactions but is not confined to these. The
importance of this proposition is reinforced in the case of the
Crusoe story by the virtual absence of the exchange relationship,
which is so dominant a feature of orthodox economic analysis.

6. One reason why constitutional agreement between Crusoe and
Friday was not difficult to reach is that both the negotiators saw
the other as a *potential collaborator* rather than as a rival. We
observed Crusoe's pleasure in the absence of rivals, and Friday
wished to subject himself to Crusoe rather than to compete with
him. Cooperation of this kind can be explained only within a model
that comprehends *group behaviour*. Individuals join groups rather
than act alone because they value the expected benefits from cooperation higher than the expected costs of accepting the constraints

on behaviour implied by group membership. This is a straightforward opportunity-cost proposition whose importance tends to be obscured by undue concentration on individual exchange. It is important not only in the Crusoe story, but also to an explanation of the diverse (but intellectually unified) forms of group-participation (firms, trade unions, churches) to be found in actual societies.

7. Even in the primitive conditions of Crusoe's Society – a closed command economy with no exchange and no outside contact – we find the standard problems of economics emerging, but in forms that mainstream economics does not explore. A significant illustration is the neglect of learning, which we find playing a key role in the Crusoe economy. Learning-by-doing is important to an understanding of the behaviour of Crusoe alone. When Crusoe's behaviour has to be coordinated with that of others, the concept becomes more sophisticated, but clearly no less important. Indirect learning (including 'learning-by-watching') affects both the creation of goods and services and the values that individuals place upon them. This is recognized in the specialist study of the economics of human resources, including education, but it is not yet seen as a central component in economic theory generally. The economic problem is so specified by economists that the possible role of learning is emasculated. A decision-process that does not allow mistakes cannot easily evolve an explanation of learning from them.

8. The final illustration of the change induced by Crusoe in Friday's tastes lies quite outside the scope of orthodox economics in its present form, requiring a planning context that incorporates both 'political' and 'economic' decision-processes. The orthodox neoclassical model treats tastes and preferences as exogenous. The economist's concern is restricted to the consequences of specified changes in them, without concern for the reasons for the change. In reality, of course, individuals may change their tastes, and are not indifferent to the tastes and preferences of others. They may try to change the tastes of others (a partial recognition of this is to be found in the economics of advertising), or even to constrain or encourage their behaviour, for example by subsidizing particular products or by inhibiting access to them. In a command economy, the ruler is in a position to change the consumption patterns of his subjects by *diktat*; he orders the subjects to abstain from particular forms of consumption. But familiarity with the concepts of public choice would suggest that this is too narrow a view: the success of such a policy will depend upon continued acceptance by the subjects of the constitutional arrangements from which such a policy

emerged. The commander may therefore see other forms of persuasion as preferable to the use of power.

The final illustration emphasizes the need for a formulation of the economic problem that is subjectivist in nature, but catholic enough to embrace all the planning contexts that the problem identifies as relevant – from making constitutions to inter-individual persuasion and/or learning. Such a formulation will need to start from the more embracing concepts of public choice rather than the narrow ones of interpersonal direct exchange. But there is a long road to travel.

Notes

The material for this article was first collected in the summer of 1980, in the course of writing a subjectivist textbook on economics. The authors were Visiting Fellows at the Center for the Study of Public Choice, then at Virginia Polytechnic and Institute, Blacksburg, Va. We are grateful to the General Director, Professor James Buchanan, for providing facilities; to colleagues and guests of the Center, particularly Professors Buchanan, Kirzner, Vaughn and Yeager, for helpful comments; and to George Pearson for arranging financial assistance.

In the event, Crusoe threatened to take over the whole textbook, and it was deemed politic to give him an article of his own. The present version was drafted by Wiseman in the Spring of 1985, while a Visiting Scholar at the Center, who had by then moved to George Mason University.

1. Page references are to Daniel Defoe, *The Life and Strange Surprizing Adventures of Robinson Crusoe of York*, ed. J. Donald Crowley (London and Oxford: Oxford University Press, 1976).

14 The Way Ahead: A New Political Economy

Foreword

The writings here collected together show an evolving pattern of thought, beginning with a set of doubts about the nature of costs, and developing from this fairly specific concern into an overview of the rationale of choice-in-society. This embraces a critique of orthodox economic theory that I believe to be fundamental and compelling. But more important, it provides the philosophical underpinning for a more fruitful formulation of the problem.

It is inherent in my arguments that this new departure should take the form of a 'political economy' rather than a simple reconstruction of economic theory. I have argued that such a reconstruction is indeed required: but it needs to evolve within an expanded logic of choice which treats the market as one social institution among many others, albeit an institution with unique and valuable characteristics for the achievement of the goals of individuals-in-society. Effectively, the model I shall develop is the elaboration of a particular perspective of the logic of public choice, within which market choice is to be comprehended. In this brief chapter, I can do no more than provide a skeleton; a set of 'programme notes' for the book upon which I am about to embark. Particularly, there will not be space for detailed examination of the implied reforms of orthodox economic theory, in addition to explanation of the intellectual environment within which such reform needs to be undertaken. But I would hope that the earlier contributions have indicated what is needed, at least in general terms. Normatively, the model needs to conform to a Wicksellian rather than a Paretian notion of 'efficient choice': there is no role for orthodox welfare economics. Factually, the world to be described and explained is that of the radical subjectivists, characterized by the unknowability of the future and the inevitability of human error. In such a world, 'social equilibrium' can have only the most tenuous general meaning, and neo-classical 'market equilibrium' no useful meaning at all.

It does not follow, and I am far from suggesting, that the whole of 'orthodox' economic theory needs to be discarded. The goods do get on the supermarket shelves, and the development of economic theory has been instrumental in explaining how it happens. But they are not

265

always the right goods, and we are less successful in explaining how things go wrong. In this regard, the very techniques which have contributed so much to the improvement of our understanding are becoming obstacles to future progress, and the increasing sophistication of technique is now contributing more to intellectual complexity than to improved understanding. There are large and intellectually challenging problems to be tackled in creating a new analytics which assumes no more knowledge of the future than men can plausibly be expected to possess, yet retains the powerful insights of present theory where these do not prove to be suspect. That is why we came to see the task of writing a textbook of subjective economic analysis too daunting. Such a book presently requires too much of an intellectual quantum leap to be generally acceptable to teachers, and a textbook that is not reasonably widely adopted must be deemed a failure. But the time for that will come. Meanwhile, we must make a beginning. Ideally, the task should be that of specialists in public choice, for it is in the development of their ideas that the future should lie. But they first need to recognize the fundamental incompatibility of their evolving (public choice) ideas about society, and the kind of logic of choice that they still allow orthodox economics to impose upon them.

The purpose of this essay is to suggest, in inadequate outline, an alternative and superior intellectual construct, whose potential advantages I believe to outweigh the obsolescence of intellectual capital its adoption would imply. The nature of this construct, and its academic antecedents, are foreshadowed in the earlier material, and particularly in the text and references of Chapters 5, 9, 10 and 11. It brings together the broader normative implications of Wicksellian public choice, and the factual propositions of radical subjectivism concerning the decision environment.

The characteristics of the social universe
Human behaviour derives from men's purposes, and from their perception of the environment in which they live and act. Important characteristics of these are:

1. *Men have goals*. That is, their behaviour is in fact purposive, in the sense that they can rank the expected outcome of the plans of action they consider in terms of their desirability. But neither the goals nor their expected outcome and ranking can be 'known' save by the individuals concerned. Others can know only what the individual chooses to tell them, or the outcomes that resulted from actual decisions (implemented plans).

2. *Scarcity is endemic.* Not all desirable goals can be achieved. For this to be true requires only the existence of time. If not all individual goals are capable of simultaneous achievement, then goals have to be perceived as *rival*. That is, the implication of scarcity is that men must choose.

3. Time has three phases, bearing different relationships to acts of individual choice:

   The continuous present is the moving point in time at which current decisions are being taken. Concerning it, an individual can 'know' the events directly observed to be happening 'now', and may also observe 'reports' of other events which are said to be happening (e.g. the individual may observe actual transactions taking place in a market, and also reports of other transactions (such as the prices at which securities are reported to be trading)).

   It is characteristic of the continuous present that observation of it by any individual can only be partial and incomplete, however sophisticated the 'information aids' at his disposal. Also, observations in the continuous present can of themselves tell individuals nothing about change. Each observation is like a single frame in a cine film. If such a frame showed an automobile, there would be no way to tell whether the vehicle was stationary or about to crash into a wall.

   The past has already happened and cannot be changed. It ends at the continuous present. About the past, we have the 'historical record'. This consists in the 'facts' and materials that men recorded in earlier continuous-present time. The characteristic of the historical record is that it comprises the things that men then chose to record. It will thus be incomplete, both because not everything can be recorded, and because men decided what to keep 'now' in the light of their current goals and perceptions, and these will not be the same as the goals and perceptions of those who later use the record when making their own continuous-present plans. Also, the accuracy of the historical record will be affected by the fact that it must pass through 'the filter of the human mind'. (To illustrate. The social accounting conventions currently used to record the 'facts' about the economy of most countries are the intellectual by-product of Keynesian ideas. The records of earlier periods were not in this form, and countries have been able to 'reconstruct' earlier records only to the extent that data collected for other reasons has proved to be relevant.) In consonance with the cine-film analogy, the historical record consists of facts concerning physical events and the observed outcomes of earlier plans (but not the reasons for those outcomes); and of received 'opinions'.

The future has not yet happened. About it, men can have only *opinions*, related to past experience (learning). Since men can (must) choose how to act, their chosen acts, together with the evolution of the physical world, are continuously creating the emerging future. If this is so (as it must be), then the future cannot be known 'now' (that is, in the continuous present). The future is unknowable, and is so perceived by individual decison-makers. This, essentially, is why assumptions implying that the future is known, or in some sense 'knowable', in the continuous present, is not a useful simplification of the study of human decision-processes, but a gross perversion of it. It inhibits study of fundamental characteristics of the decision-process.

It does not follow, and is not being argued, that men will behave at random. In the light of past experience and observation, they will have greater belief in the occurrence of some future events than of others, and they will use learning (below) to try to improve their ability to adapt to the emerging future. But the future cannot be made 'knowable' by any of the kinds of information we have described in relation to the different phases of time. Many of the problems that economists have always seen as their subject-matter, and still others that are relevant to the wider decision-enviroment I myself think appropriate, are importantly characterized by unknowability, and this must continue to be so failing the establishment of some ongoing reliable nexus between past, continuous present and future. There is no reason to believe that such a nexus exists, much less that we shall ever identify it.

4. *Man is a learning animal.* Learning-from-experience will change decision-behaviour (the content of the plans and predictions men conceive and consider, and the way they choose between them). But learning cannot make the future 'knowable' in the continuous present. The future being planned for can never be 'known' to be a replication of, or simple progression from past futures. Indeed, in important respects there is no unambiguous evidence that learning is making the future more 'knowable'. Scientific progress, for example, has increased our understanding of physical relationships, and through this our ability to control and predict certain kinds of physical event. But the same developments have also increased the possibility that we may be killed by men of whose existence we are unaware.

It follows that the only permanent 'laws' we can hope to establish must be grounded in unchanging characteristics of human nature (if there are any). All other so-called 'economic laws' must be capable of being conditioned by learning. For the most part, all we can hope to identify are 'tendencies' or 'conditional regularities', which may change as a result of our learning about them and changing our behaviour accordingly. (An earlier paper suggested that there is here at least a partial explanation of the changed outcome of 'Keynesian' policies over the period since they were first used. Learning has changed the behaviour responses of those affected by the policies.)

5. *Men are gregarious.* That is, they have a biological/emotional preference for living in family and extended-family groups. But their participation in groups is itself an act of individual choice, conditioned upon a continuing belief that the constraints imposed by group participation are made acceptable by the anticipated ongoing gains from membership. The participation of men in societies and other groups does not eliminate scarcity (since time still makes individual ends rival). But it does change the ways individuals can and do adapt to its existence.

The act of choice
In a world with the characteristics I have described:

1. The (unavoidable) acts of individual choice concern *the future*. They are a selection by individuals between courses of action ('plans') conceived by them to be possible 'now', by reference to their expected results ('value') in the future.
2. Since the future is unknowable, the outcome of individual plans must also be unknowable. The plans men conceive, and their choice of the plan to implement from the set of conceived plans, are *acts of imagination*.
3. An individual will choose to implement that conceived plan which he expects to have the best outcome (highest 'value'). Given scarcity, this must imply the rejection of other conceived-as-desirable plans. We can call the necessarily sacrificed plan to which the individual attaches the highest expected 'value' the opportunity-cost of the plan chosen for implementation. Notice that:

    • Cost is incurred when the chosen plan is implemented (since this is the point at which the alternative conceived plans become unattainable).
    • Since the cost is a *forgone alternative course of action* which is

never implemented, and 'known' only to the individual decision-maker. All that others can observe are the resultant *actions* and *outcomes* – the *consequences* of individual choice.

4. Acts of choice are a continuum in time. The time-sequence of the individual decision-process can be described as follows:

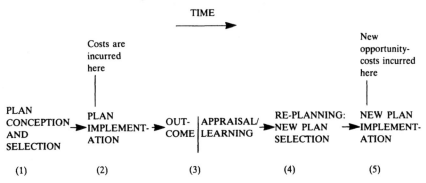

1. The individual imagines alternative believed-to-be-achievable plans, based on his past 'learning', experience, judgement, beliefs about the world, and selects the 'best' plan for implementation.

2. Implementation of the chosen plan necessarily implies the rejection of the best of the alternative conceived plans. It is the sacrifice of this never-to-be implemented plan that constitutes the cost of implementing the chosen plan. (Note that both the chosen and the opportunity-cost plan may contain entries for 'outlays' which are expected to be incurred when the plan is implemented. They are simply components of conceived plans. The indiscriminate use of the term 'cost' to embrace both this kind of projection and the historic record of actual outlays is a fertile source of confusion, which, as earlier papers have pointed out, is encouraged by the assumptions about knowledge of the future made by neo-classical theory.)

3. These 'forward-looking' stages generate an 'outcome' – the consequences of the implemented plan. This is when appraisal and learning occur. These are 'backward-looking' activities concerned to evaluate the actual outcome of the plan against its expected outcome.

This is a complex process: appraisal and learning are individual and judgmental rather than simple 'scientific' activities. They involve:

(a) a comparison of the outcome of the implemented plan with the predicted outcome. The purpose is to make judgements about *cause*. This could be forecasting error, imputable to reasons from which the decision-maker might 'learn', in the sense of becoming aware of new possibilities which can influence future behaviour. Or the reasons for difference may be more remote from the content of the plan, in the sense that, although the decision-maker believes he can identify them with reasonable confidence, he is less sure that he can use the new knowledge when re-planning (since e.g. he has no reason to expect similar events to recur).

In fact, the application of 'learning' to re-planning is rendered continuously hazardous by the permanent unknowability of the future, which means that 'new learning' is always being applied to a future whose characteristics cannot be assumed to replicate the past.

(b)   The same exercise needs also to be carried out in respect of the rejected plan (or plans), in order to appraise whether the choice of plan could itself have been improved. This is even more an exercise in conjecture, since it requires the use of imagination to evaluate the outcome of a plan that was never in fact implemented.

4.   The 'new knowledge' from appraisal and learning becomes an 'input' to the use of the individual imagination to conceive and choose between a new set of plans, following which:

5.   A new plan is implemented and new opportunity-costs are incurred.

The process has been described as a succession of events. Practically, individuals may have plans which are overlapping in time, and wholly or partly contained one within another. There will be as many points of decision (re-planning) as the individual believes to be useful (this is itself an opportunity-cost problem: plans will be revised only as and when the time and effort spent in doing so is expected to generate an adequate 'yield' in terms of plan outcome). It may be noted in passing that this description accommodates the notion of period analysis much more easily than the neo-classical long- and short-period, fixed-factor type model. At any time, an individual will have plans for as many future time-periods ahead of the continuous present as he thinks useful. These plans (acts of imagination) exist co-terminously, and embody elements of each other to whatever extent the individual believes them to be mutually dependent.

The nature of 'social efficiency'
What characterizes an efficient social situation in the kind of world I have described? Efficiency can have meaning only in relation to the achievement of goals. For an individual, the goals are personal ones. But for the individual-in-society, the pursuit of individual goals must be expected to affect others, whether because these others make a necessary input to the implementation of individual plans, or because they are affected, positively or negatively, by the pursuit by individuals of their own plans. Consequently, in a social (group) environment, the notion of efficiency must embody some procedure for weighting the respective goals of the individual members.

For reasons set out in earlier chapters, I take the *libertarian* weighting as my starting point. The goals of all individuals carry equal weight, and all individuals have equal access to the society's decision-making structures. This is a value judgement. Citizens who did not accept it might find other social situations preferable to the ones it identifies as 'efficient'. (Practically, only a minority of the world's population lives in societies in which the libertarian postulate would appear to be dominant.) But the postulate is ethically appealing. Beyond this, I adopt it because, first, it is the most convenient reference point even for the study of societies that depart from its requirements. Second, any other value judgement must give special rights to some citizens. The onus would appear to be upon those who favour this to provide a justification for such discrimination. I have never encountered a convincing justification, save that the special rights have been voluntarily conceded by other citizens, and are capable of withdrawal by those same citizens through procedures that also have their voluntary agreement. But this is not really an exception, since such conditional delegated special rights are fully compatible with the libertarian position. The problem lies not with the possibility of the delegation of rights through consent, but with the claiming of special rights by some that do not require the agreement of others.

It is characteristic of the universe I have described that 'inefficiency' can not be identified in any simple way with 'plan failure', in the sense that plans have outcomes different from those predicted. Indeed, 'plan failure' in this sense is something that individuals will learn to expect; they will not be surprised by it and will try to take it into account when devising and choosing between plans. (Though not by assuming that the future is pre-ordained in some 'objectively-probable' way. All they know, from past experience ('learning'), is that events frequently develop in ways different from those expected when plans are implemented.) It follows that a useful notion of 'efficiency' must be more concerned with the social processes through which individuals pursue their personal goals/values, than with the actual outcome of implemented plans.

Efficiency, then, must be concerned with the extent to which the institutions of a society are responsive to the values and choices of individual citizens. The orthodox Paretian interpretation of this requirement is less satisfactory than a Wicksellian one. The Paretian welfare optimum, deriving from the neo-classical logic of choice-through-markets, identifies an efficient situation as one in which no citizen can be made better off without some other citizen becoming worse off. Practically, the welfare optimum has come to be associated with *claims over resources*. The Wicksellian criterion is much broader: it requires that no policy be implemented to which any citizen objects. The two might be treated as formally compatible if it is assumed that citizens would object to proposals which they expected to make them worse off. But the Wicksellian formulation is preferable because it is free of any implicit or explicit assumption of the superiority of choice-through-markets. The language of objection is explicitly concerned to emphasize the assertion of the paramountcy of individual values, whatever those values might be, through the totality of social institutions which facilitate the translation of individual preferences into actual policies. Further, a naive interpretation of the Wicksellian rule, requiring that citizens reject all proposals not expected to benefit them directly, would be unduly and unnecessarily restrictive. The more sophisticated version, relating the notions of better-off and worse-off to the totality of expected consequences of acceptance or refusal of specific proposals emerging in time-as-a-continuum, is more remote from the orthodox interpretation of Pareto-optimality. But it also more appropriate both to a realistic interpretation of subjective opportunity-cost, and to the notion of efficiency as 'process', in the specified context of time and unknowability.

At present, the Wicksellian interpretation is used particularly by writers in the political economy/constitutional public choice school. The burden of my present argument is that this development cannot continue to coexist intellectually with a neo-classical economics that either ignores non-market choice, or treats other choice-related institutions as 'inputs' to Pareto-efficiency as measured by 'market choice'. The 'new' public choice needs to absorb 'market economics', within a unified intellectual framework with the characteristics here being summarized.

Efficient social arrangements in time-as-a-continuum
For the citizen, an efficient social situation will be one in which individual values are perceived to be adequately recognized by institutional arrangements and emergent policies. The citizen can be conceived to evaluate any proposal for policy or institutional change in terms of its direct consequences, including any predicted consequence for the situation of others, in so far as their welfare enters the citizen's own value-system. To the extent that the citizen attaches value to continued participation in his society, the response to any proposal will also be conditioned by this. That is, the opportunity-cost calculus will incorporate some estimate of the consequences of rejection for the reciprocal (voting) behaviour of others. The appraisal thus contains three distinct elements ('values'); the predicted direct benefit or loss to the citizen, the value attached by the citizen to the consequences of the policy for the situation of others, and the value inputed to the consequences for the citizen concerned of the changes in the behaviour of others predicted to be induced by his own decision to support or reject the present proposal. In making and revising plans in time-as-a-continuum, the citizen is engaged in the continuous reappraisal of these three elements.

It follows that citizens will accept as efficient social arrangements incorporating some policies and/or institutions by which they believe themselves to be disadvantaged. There will be arrangements by which citizens consider themselves to be coerced: coercion would appear to be a normal characteristic of social existence if individual value-systems differ. All that is necessary for efficiency as defined is that individuals, given their personal value-systems, do not believe themselves to be *improperly* coerced. The concern of the political economy/constitutional development of the theory of public choice is to identify the kinds of social arrangements that will contribute to the achievement of efficiency in this sense. This is not simply a new way of looking at 'traditional' economic problems; though it is that. It is also a way of using the insights of an expanded logic of choice to illuminate a broader set of policy issues than orthodox economic analysis can encompass. It is in this sense that the outcome has to be seen as a 'new political economy'. (Chapter 10 develops this theme at greater length, in the specific context of policy related to inhibition of choice.)

The efficient institutions of a libertarian society
The argument so far indicates one rule that must be a necessary part of any efficient (libertarian) system of social arrangements. *That is the rule that there can be no rule that does not incorporate an acceptable procedure (rule) for its own change.*

This follows from the identification of coercion as the criterion of efficiency, together with the existence of unknowability as a necessary characteristic of the human decision-environment. *Unknowability* implies that citizens will decide whether to agree to proposals concerning social rules, procedures and policies by reference to their own predictions about the consequences of agreement. But there is an ongoing likelihood that their predictions will be falsified, and that (e.g.) instead of the predicted acceptable consequences of an agreed policy, there may emerge unforeseen outcomes that citizens regard as unacceptable. Unless there are revision procedures which are themselves acceptable for adjusting such 'mistakes', citizens will regard themselves as improperly coerced (and their society as inefficient), notwithstanding their previous agreement.

Given this first rule, we need to consider what other characteristics of a society bear upon the question of the efficiency of its institutions. How do we *identify* the absence (or presence) of unacceptable coercion? What kind of questions do we ask? The essential philosophical concept is that of contractarian liberalism, given operational content by use of the notions of opportunity-cost and voice-and-exit. (The strands of the argument are to be found in the chapters already referred to. Particular intellectual forbears cited there are Buchanan (1975), Brennan and Buchanan (1985) and Vanberg (1986).)

It follows from the Wicksellian formulation that the final arbiter of efficiency is the individual, who must himself decide whether the rules of his society leave him 'free to choose', in the sense that they impose no *unacceptable* constraints upon his liberty. This is the essence of the contractarian liberal position. Acceptance of rules which constrain individual freedom is an inescapable consequence of membership of a society; efficiency requires only that the constraints (coercion) are not regarded as unacceptable or improper: the 'contract' (procedures, rules, institutions) between the society and the citizen must itself be acceptable. The fact that men can be observed to choose is not of itself evidence of the existence of efficiency in this sense. It is indeed difficult to imagine a society in which citizens believed themselves incapable of exercising choice at all. But when are their choices 'free'? The device which Brennan and Buchanan (1985) use to illuminate this question is that of within-period and between-period choice: an idea which will be seen to be sympathetic with the related notion of time-as-a-continuum.

Within period efficiency is concerned with the answer to the question: Within any extant set of rules, do there exist policies which are improperly coercive (that is, are there 'within-period inefficiencies')? If so, are there satisfactory means for citizens to get the relevant policies changed without the need to change the rules (for example, by using existing procedures to change the government)? If the coercion can be alleviated without need for changes in the rules, then the society can be made efficient in the within-period sense. If not, we need to look at the rules which prevent the necessary changes. This is a question of 'between-period' efficiency: concern now is with the rules which exist for changing the rules from which the within-period problems are emerging.

(To illustrate: an elected government may pass laws enabling worker organizations to limit entry to particular occupations. This conferred monopoly may be regarded as improperly coercive by citizens. But the same citizens may be satisfied that the procedural arrangements for abolishing such legislation give them adequate protection. In contrast, an absolute monarch may confer a monopoly of the provision of particular services on chosen favourites. Citizens may regard this as improperly coercive if they regard the rules/procedures which exist to change this situation as inadequate.)

There are some interesting implications. 'Social efficiency' requires that the 'absence-of-improper-coercion' criterion be applied at each 'level' of within-period and between-period scrutiny (the 'levels' being a kind of set of Chinese boxes: outside the 'within-period' level of the life of a government, there lies the 'between-period' system of rules for the election of governments, which is the 'within-period' level outside which lies the 'between-period' system of rules for constitutional change, which . . .). It follows that a citizen may simultaneously be satisfied that there is nothing seriously amiss with a given within-period situation, but that the between-period rules could yet be improved. The two beliefs can coexist at any moment in time. (Note the formal analogy with the simultaneous existence of plans for different time-periods in the subjectivist interpretation of individual decision-making generally.)

What is generally considered to be even more important is the dependence of each set of within-period efficiency evaluations upon some 'prior' set of rules. We can therefore never be sure, philosophers argue, that within-period efficiency is not occurring within the context of between-period coercion. Much thought has been given to this problem of 'infinite regress': how are we to know that the initial agreement, from which all subsequent 'levels' of agreement emerge, was not itself coercive? If we cannot know, then how can we ever be sure that a society is 'efficient' in the defined sense? The outcome of the debate has been less than satisfactory, in that the suggested 'solutions' for the most part assume the problem away. However, if the world we are dealing with has the attributes listed above, the 'problem' of infinite regress would appear to be of small significance. For such a world, we have established one ineluctable rule of social efficiency: that there should exist no rule that does not incorporate an acceptable procedure (rule) for its own change. This derives from the unknowability of the future, which in turn predicates the likelihood of mistake, as much in the context of decisions about governments and institutions as in decisions about market behaviour. Rules that seem satisfactory 'today' may turn out to be wrong (coercive) 'tomorrow'; and this is an ongoing state of affairs; efficiency is a process in time-as-a-continuum. But if provision for the change of formerly satisfactory rules is itself a permanent feature of efficiency, the fact that some distant 'initial state' may have been improperly coercive does little to change the nature of the problem.

It may be illuminating to put the point in another way. Infinite regress is important if the purpose of the exercise is seen as the specification of an 'ideal end-state' – a system of rules and procedures, which, once established, will ensure an efficient society by reference to the criteria, whatever they might be, to which a particular author subscribes. This is the standard 'millennial' formulation of the problem: efficiency lies in the end-state generated by postulated social rules and procedures. There is no such end-state in the world we are considering. There are only efficient rules for the adaptation of the system to accommodate past error and the changing values of citizens, and a need for continuing vigilance on the part of citizens to ensure that what once seemed efficient does not become an obstacle to future efficiency. If efficiency is an attribute of a system of continuous adaptation, the arguments of interest concern incremental (but not therefore necessarily trivial) change, rather than the possible existence of coercion at some remote level of between-period abstraction.

From concept to evidence
The argument so far has been primarily concerned to establish the *nature* of efficiency. But where and how can we seek *evidence* of the existence of inefficiency, in the sense of improper coercion? Since the arbiter of propriety is the individual citizen, it would appear that the evidence must lie in the behaviour of citizens. But such evidence is unlikely to be easy to interpret, as a few practical examples will illustrate.

There are to be found around the world many situations in which dissident groups seek to overthrow or escape from the rules or institutions of the society to which they 'belong', and do so by means, frequently including physical violence, which themselves break the existing rules. Situations of this kind exist, for example, in UK, Spain, Turkey and other Middle East countries. The common element in such situations is that the coercion to which the dissident group objects concerns rules of fundamental importance, not infrequently embracing the rights of other citizens outside the group. In such circumstances, there may be no change in rules or institutions that would not lead to some citizens believing that they were being improperly coerced, so that any proposal would be rejected (and if adopted would be disobeyed) by some part of the population. The apparently obvious 'solution' to such problems: that efficiency requires that the citizens leave to form a separate society, is commonly too simple. Even should it be possible to find a division of rights that would be acceptable to those who do not wish to secede, there will often remain the deeper problem that the dissidents themselves do not simply seek partition, but wish rather to change the present rules *for all citizens* in fundamental ways. But these changes, needed to satisfy the present dissidents, would be regarded as intolerably coercive by tne others affected. (This is a realistic thumbnail description, for example, of the present situation in Northern Ireland.) Our analysis perhaps helps us to understand the essential nature of such problems. But it would be foolish to suggest that it must throw up solutions. There may indeed be no solution that is not improperly coercive in our sense (which should hardly cause surprise, since it must be rare for such situations to involve conflict between groups who all accept the libertarian value judgement on which our definition of social efficiency rests).

At the other extreme, individual citizens may believe themselves to be improperly coerced, for example, by the introduction of zoning restrictions affecting the conduct of their business. But it is not to be expected that they would see armed insurrection as the appropriate remedy for such a problem. What is regarded as an appropriate response will depend upon the surrounding circumstances. If there are satisfactory local institutional arrangements, the citizen may feel that adequate protection is provided by the power to vote. Or it may be felt that this alone provides inadequate protection, but that (e.g.) between-period changes facilitating mobility (such as changes in the powers of lower- and higher-level layers of government) would be enough to provide proper safeguards. Only in the extreme situation, in which the zoning restriction is seen as symptomatic of a more generally coercive environment, would the citizen be led to consider breaking the rules – in which case it is the indirect implications of the specific policy which are decisive. What is clear from both examples is that inefficiency or efficiency cannot be inferred in any simple direct fashion from the observed 'facts'.

That the observed evidence should permit no direct conclusions about social efficiency is what our earlier exposition of the nature of the problem would lead us to expect. The 'facts' need to be appraised in their specific ongoing context. Earlier chapters used the example of emigration to illustrate this. Superficially, a high rate of exit from a society/jurisdiction might be taken as evidence of dissatisfaction, since emigration is a means of escape from coercion. But if we ranked countries simply by this criterion, USSR would emerge from the appraisal as more 'socially efficient' than the United Kingdom, although in the former country the libertarian postulate is constitutionally rejected. The problem is that the 'values' involved in a citizen's decision to emigrate involve not only an estimate of the gains from escape from a coercive society and the benefits from joining a different one, but also all the other 'values' (gains and losses) expected to be associated with the decision. These may include such things as the penalties attached to leaving or trying to leave the present jurisdiction, the expected consequences for (non-emigrating) family and friends: and so on. Emigration and immigration statistics are potentially interesting evidence, but only become policy- (efficiency-) relevant in the broader context of the arrangements of a particular society.

The interpretative problem can be most simply explained by returning to the concept of opportunity-cost in time-as-a-continuum. Effectively, citizens who perceive themselves to be improperly coerced are judging that rules or policies of their society are imposing unacceptably high (opportunity-) costs on them. The observed facts simply invite *consideration* of the kind of opportunity-costs such facts seem to imply. In the example of emigration, the small numbers emigrating from USSR are clearly associated with the high cost of attempting to emigrate as well as with the perception of the direct benefits to be obtained by doing so. A similar rate of emigration from another country might require a very different explanation. It is consequently of interest to consider the reasons for this high cost; that is, the reasons why it may be difficult to escape unwanted outcomes. It is this which invites the use of the notions of *voice* and *exit* in this extended-choice context. The citizen's protection from undue coercion must stem either from the ability to change the offending rules or policies (that is, to use 'voice' by such means as voting at elections), or from the possibility of escaping the relevant obligation ('exit') for example by moving to a different sub-jurisdiction; or from some combination of these two possibilities. Using once more the example of emigration, the factual information is given

significance by being related to the two questions: What powers does the individual citizen possess to change the rules of society concerning emigration?, and: How easily can the citizen leave a jurisdiction which is considered oppressive?

This alliance of the generalized version of opportunity-cost and the notions of voice-and-exit provides a valuable interpretative technique. It is not one that lends itself obviously to sophisticated and precise empirical development, and for that reason will be the less attractive to the dedicated empiricist. But it enables us to shed new light on important practical problems, as the concluding section will further illustrate.

Some illustrations
Earlier chapters, and the examples so far used in this one, have provided a number of illustrations of policy issues which are illuminated by the proposed system of thought. In large part, the chosen problems have been of a kind that orthodox economic analysis at best handles poorly, and at worst ignores. (Migration, prohibition, smoking and choice-inhibition generally, social disruption; as well as the broad general questions of politico-constitutional economy whose consideration presupposes a broader model of individual choice.)

There is good reason for concentration upon such topics, since the broader relevance of the proposed intellectual construct is its most important single attraction. But for an economist hoping to be read by economists, it is a matter for concern that such readers may by now be feeling that the link between my concerns and theirs is becoming a tenuous one. As I indicated at the beginning of the chapter, I regard the subject-matter of mainstream economics as of paramount and continuing importance. That I have not given it more detailed attention is attributable entirely to constraints of space and time. I have suggested the lines along which orthodox analysis demands revision; it is a major task, and for another place. But to reassure my colleagues, I can in conclusion use a couple of examples to demonstrate, though in very summary fashion, that new light can indeed be thrown on familiar problems.

The first topic is that of federalism. It is a topic in which I have a long-standing interest (see Chapter 4), and also one which provides a useful bridge between different intellectual approaches. Since the economics of federalism concerns the economic implications of a particular constitutional arrangement, it would seem obvious that the intellectual construct used to study it must incorporate an identified behavioural role for government. In fact, the early literature uses the tools of neo-classical economics, which provide no role for government save as the costless and infallible agent of the policies devised by economists. Thus, what is called fiscal federalism simply imposes the standard concepts of welfare economics upon a country with a pre-existent federal constitution. This leads to propositions (e.g.) about the division of responsibility for taxation and the distribution of public benefits, but leaves the reader puzzled as to why the federal constitution exists, or, accepting that it does, why the policies pursued in a federal country should be any different from those that would be 'optimal' for an unitary state with the same population and (neo-classical) goals. Subsequent developments see the emergence of a role for government as the provider of public goods. But the general tenor of the analysis is still to specify the problem as the identification of the 'equitable' and Pareto-optimal allocation of burdens and benefits by levels of government. That is, the problem is still specified as one of 'resource-economizing' in the provision of any given level and character of (technically-determined) benefit.

The government arrives on the scene as a behavioural entity only with the introduction of public choice concepts into the analysis. Even then, the 'new orthodoxy', in the form of the median voter model, provides no truly *independent* role for government, but treats it as the passive servant of the median voter. That is, the earlier (welfare economics) analysis allows citizens to choose, but only within the (authoritarian) imposed constraints of the principles and goals specified by the economist. The standard public choice model, in contrast, permits the citizen to choose the government, but then treats the elected government as completely constrained by the promises it had to make to capture the median voter. The government begins to be treated as something more than a passive agent only with the introduction by Brennan and Buchanan (1986) of government-as-Leviathan, pursuing its own goals subject to the powers of citizens to change or constrain it. This introduction of the government as a positive group-actor is the first building-block of the kind of analytics that my own political economy would indicate as appropriate. When we add to it the propositions concerning the nature of the human decision-environment summarized in this essay, we have a model rich in new insights. Two of these have been referred to in earlier Chapters. First, the efficient allocation of functions between levels of government (and, indeed, the allocation of any functions at all to any level of government) is not something which is capable of 'technical' determination, since citizens may have preferences in such matters which are concerned not with economy in resource-use, but with their own view of the expected consequences of decisions about such matters for (e.g.) their own exposure to undesirable coercion by the agencies of government. A citizen may prefer to deal with a local bureacracy rather than a national one, even though the latter is recognized to be 'technically' more efficient (see Chapter 11).

Second, it reveals the 'public goods' approach to the explanation and evaluation of government activity as fundamentally flawed, in so far as it treats the phenomena of externalities and public goods as being somehow objective and hence unambiguously identifiable by the technician-economist. But the decision about 'publicness' is an essentially subjective one: the goods to be treated as having relevant 'externality characteristics' are those that are so identified by the individual value-systems of citizens as translated into policy through the extant institutions of their society (see Chapter 10).

Positively, the evaluation of the federal arrangement by reference to the proposed opportunity-cost voice-and-exit appraisal procedure identifies a major potential benefit which eludes the earlier formulations. The separation of powers between levels of government increases the importance to citizens of the 'exit' option (through mobility between sub-jurisdictions), and so provides a valuable potential substitute for the need for explicit rules to curb the powers of the central government Leviathan (Brennan and Buchanan, 1986).

Finally, it is an implication of the new formulation that there can be no single economically-ideal federal system, either across countries or in one country through time. This is an observation which accords with both reason and observation. (Switzerland and USSR both fit the standard definitions of a federal country.)

My second and final topic concerns the treatment of monopoly. The criterion of efficiency for the neo-classical economist is the achievement of a Pareto-optimal outcome. Since monopoly power prevents resources from moving to their most highly-valued uses, it is an obstacle to the achievement of efficiency, and it is the duty of government to prevent or remove it. This simplistic formulation runs into serious difficulties. Observation suggests that some enterprises which appear to exercise monopoly power also seem to operate at a high level of technical efficiency. It is not easy to incorporate this possibility into the orthodox model, since the analysis assumes a 'given state of the arts', which is known to all the economic actors. But it can be encompassed in the form, for example, of a proposition that monopoly may enable achievement of 'economies of scale in production', the benefits from which can be offset against the implied loss of freedom of consumer choice, though how such a comparative evaluation is to be made, within the confines of the model, has never been adequately explained. We now have the standard conclusion, with which generations of students have bored their reluctant examiners, that monopoly is against the public interest unless it generates scale economies, in which case it may not be . . . The poor student (to say nothing of his teachers) may then be confused by introduction of the notion of second best, from which it can be inferred that, if there is one monopoly which cannot be said to be against the public interest, then we cannot be sure that any of them are. The formal constraints imposed by the neo-classical model are intolerably restrictive, as is demonstrated by the extent to which economists interested in the field seek to make progress by either tacitly ignoring or explicitly abandoning them.

The Austrian School provides more interesting insights. Since the future (and hence the state of technology) is not assumed to be known, there is no discomfort involved in finding a role for innovation and technical change. Indeed, entrepreneurial discovery provides the dynamics of the system, and its appropriate encouragement and reward are an integral part of 'process efficiency' in the Austrian sense. In this world, not only is monopoly not necessarily 'wrong' (inefficient); the creation of monopoly power (in the sense of competitive advantage) is the motivating purpose of innovative behaviour. Thus, the purpose of public policy embraces both the assurance of appropriate returns to innovators by such means as the devising and implementation of satisfactory property rights in invention, and the identification and prevention of inhibitions of competition that do not have these offsetting positive characteristics (such as the creation of price-fixing cartels with the primary objective of curtailing competitive behaviour).

The Austrian formulation would appear to provide a more realistic and productive way to interpret the role of government. It is of interest in this regard that historically, economists have identified government legislation as being itself an important source of monopoly power, and have drawn attention to the 'paradox' that governments simultaneously engage in activities intended to curb and to create monopoly power. Within the neo-classical orthodoxy, it is not easy to draw from this observation any conclusion save that the governments concerned are misguided and should change their policies. It is an uncomfortable conclusion when, as has often been the case, the economists concerned have been writing in countries whose economic policies have generated high rates of output and growth. The Austrians have less trouble with such problems, being restricted only by their adherence to a concept of choice-through-markets too narrow to allow adequate development of the study of government behaviour.

It is this last development that the extended-choice (political economy) framework provides. All monopolistic behaviour is coercive of consumers in some degree, since it denies access to alternative sources of supply. But there is no reason to expect citizens to feel equally unhappy, for example, about coercion from the existence of laws concerning patent and copyright and about the coercion implied by the restriction of the right to import to a 'ruling family'. Monopoly policy needs to be evaluated in the context earlier specified, of within- and between-period efficiency, using the tools of opportunity-cost and voice-and-exit to decide what measures are called for. These might be anything from the application of existing law to newly-emergent and potentially coercive (monopolistic) situations, through the reform of the law within the existing institutions relevant for that purpose, to changes in the institutions themselves (because – as with the family monopoly of imports – existing institutions have proved inadequate to protect citizens from what they regard as improper coercion).

It may be observed that there is nothing in these last propositions that is not well known and acceptable to practitioners not yet enlightened by the insights of the 'new political economy'. But in so far as that is true, it is so because sensible men refuse to be constrained by the intellectual inhibitions of inappropriate models. There is presently a marked intellectual gap between the policy inferences that can be derived from orthodox economic analysis, and the considerations that commonly appear to influence public policy towards monopoly. Given its prevalance, and given the growing legislative influence of people who would call themselves economists, this gap is not to be explained by the intransigence or stupidity of policy-makers. The gap exists because of the inappropriateness of the model. It would be my contention that the requirements of public policy towards monopoly can be fully comprehended only within a model of choice of the kind I propose, and that acceptance of this would close the present gap between theory and practice, and in doing so make a significant practical contribution to the generation of more efficient (in my sense) control policies. It would not produce some 'agreed' policy towards monopolies and mergers; it is inherent in my position that there is unlikely to be such a policy. But it would provide coherence in an area of policy in which that virtue is sadly lacking at present.

References

Brennan, G. and Buchanan, J. M. (1985) *The Reason of Rules – Constitutional Political Economy*, Cambridge University Press.
Buchanan, J. M. (1975) *The Limits of Liberty: Between Anarchy and Leviathan*, University of Chicago Press.

Vanberg, V. (1986) 'Individual Choice and Constitutional Constraints – the Normative Element in Classical and Contractarian Liberalism', *Analyse and Kritik*, Vol. 8.

Index